Acclaim for STANLEY CROUCH'S

THE ALL-AMERICAN SKIN GAME,

OR,

THE DECOY OF RACE

"You come away from *The All-American Skin Game* fired with new enthusiasms. . . . Crouch challenges your assumptions and arouses your curiosity. And that is what a good cultural critic is for."
—*The New York Times*

"The rewards [of reading *The All-American Skin Game*] come from the author's uncommon mind and character—his search for unexpected connections, his courage to tell the truth, his disregard for conventional wisdom."
—*Newsday*

"Devastatingly, frighteningly lucid. This book is an example of Crouch at his best. . . . One inevitably feels the constant, clear voice of a truth-teller and the full and deadly blow of a true intellectual warrior. As innovative as jazz, as complex as a fugue, little that Crouch writes can be ignored."
—*Kirkus Reviews*

Also by
STANLEY CROUCH

Notes of
a Hanging Judge

STANLEY CROUCH

THE ALL-AMERICAN
SKIN GAME,

OR,

THE DECOY OF RACE

The All-American Skin Game was nominated for a
1995 National Book Critics Circle Award. Stanley
Crouch is a contributing editor to *The New Republic*,
a Sunday columnist for *The New York Daily News*,
and a frequent panelist on "The Charlie Rose Show."
He was for years a jazz critic and staff writer for *The
Village Voice* and is Artistic Consultant to Jazz at
Lincoln Center.

STANLEY CROUCH

THE ALL-AMERICAN SKIN GAME,

OR,

THE DECOY OF RACE

VINTAGE BOOKS

A Division of Random House, Inc.

New York

FIRST VINTAGE BOOKS EDITION, FEBRUARY 1997

The following essays have been previously published, many under different titles: *Daily News*: "Black Power Redux Blues," "Blues for Jackie," "Dumb Bell Blues," "True Blue Rebels," "Unity '94 Blues, Part I," "Unity '94 Blues, Part II," and "Wee Wee Wee Blues." • *Los Angeles Times*: "Eggplant Blues: The Miscegenated Cinema of Quentin Tarantino." • *City Journal*: "Do the Afrocentric Hustle." • *The New Republic*: "Beale Street Redux: Tom Cat Blues," "Dizzy Gillespie," "The Measure of the Oklahoma Kid," and "On the Corner: The Sellout of Miles Davis." • *The New York Times Book Review*: "Beyond American Tribalism." • *Partisan Review*: "The B & J Blues" and "How Long? So Long." • *The Washington Post*: "Harlem on Our Minds" and "Menace II Society." • "Blues-Collar Clarity" appeared in *Second Thoughts About Race in America*, Peter Collier and David Horowitz, eds. (Lanham, MD: Madison Books, 1991). • "Melting Down the Iron Suits of History" appeared in *A New Moment in the Americas*, Robert S. Leiken, ed. (New Brunswick, NJ: Transaction Publishers, 1994). • "Who Are We? Where Did We Come From? Where Are We Going?" appeared in *Lure and Loathing*, Gerald Early, ed. (New York: Allen Lane, The Penguin Press, 1993). • "In This House, On This Morning" appeared as the liner notes for the recording of the same name by the Wynton Marsalis Septet (New York: Columbia, 1993).

Grateful acknowledgment is made to the following for permission to reprint previously published material: Harcourt Brace & Company: excerpts from *Smart Hearts in the City* by Barbara Probst Solomon, copyright © 1992 by Barbara Probst Solomon. Reprinted by permission of Harcourt Brace & Company. • Ann Landers and Creators Syndicate: excerpt from Ann Landers column (*The Washington Post*, February 25, 1990). Reprinted by permission of Ann Landers and Creators Syndicate. • Simon & Schuster, Inc.: excerpts from *Miles: The Autobiography* by Miles Davis with Quincy Troupe, copyright © 1989 by Miles Davis. Reprinted by permission of Simon & Schuster, Inc. • Oxford University Press: excerpts from *Duke Ellington* by James Lincoln Collier. Copyright © 1987 by James Lincoln Collier. Reprinted by permission of Oxford University Press, Inc. • Viking Penguin: excerpts from *Mr. Sammler's Planet* by Saul Bellow, copyright © 1969, 1970 by Saul Bellow. Reprinted by permission of Viking Penguin, a division of Penguin Books USA, Inc.

The Library of Congress has cataloged the Pantheon edition as follows:

Crouch, Stanley.
The all-American skin game, or, The decoy of race: the long and the short of it, 1990–1994 / Stanley Crouch.
p. cm.
Includes bibliographical references and index.
ISBN 0-679-44202-2
1. United States—Race relations. 2. Afro-Americans. 3. United States—Politics and government—1989–1993. 4. United States—Politics and government—1993–
I. Title.
E185.615.C77   1995
305.896'073'009049—dc20   95-10142
CIP

VINTAGE ISBN: 0-679-77660-5

Random House Web address: http://www.randomhouse.com/

Book design by Debbie Glasserman

Printed in the United States of America
10 9 8 7 6 5 4 3 2

TO THE ONE

This, my second book of essays, is dedicated to my mother, Emma Bea Crouch, who died a few years ago on Bloomsday, symbolizing for me the essential role she had played in my development as a writer. She taught me the alphabet and taught me to spell before my first day of school. I was told by her the basic truth of books, which is that you can travel all over the world from inside a library, page upon page. She always cut out editorials for me to read or pointed out pieces on science and history that she came across in newspapers and magazines. My mother also introduced me to jazz and told me stories about the elegant wonder of Duke Ellington, whom she and her schoolmates met at the Los Angeles train station, where they were awed by his deportment and the gleam of his alligator shoes. Her tales of the way young Negroes of her generation dressed and danced, of the cars they drove and the dreams they had, were introductions to a homemade aristocracy that she, a domestic worker quite proud of the quality of her work, embodied from hoot to toot. Perhaps her most important instruction was that I should always go in my own direction and make sure I never jumped off a cliff just because everybody else did. Had I always followed her instruction, I'm sure I would have gotten where I am now much more quickly. Thanks for your part in the victories, Mom, the losses were all mine.

CONTENTS

INTRODUCTION:
BLUES TO YOU, PART II

I see our American problems as very different from being too low on water and doomed on foot within the borders of an enormous desert—sweating, frustrated, able to do no more than shriek or croak at a sun that will never hear us. We Americans, no matter our superficial distinctions, are always in the middle of a dialogue, an eternal—and inevitable—democratic discourse. We have the chance to say what we want. We are able to find out—if we're willing to take punches as well as throw them—that our arms aren't at all too short to box with the jaggedly assembled gods of received ideas, of clichés, of folly, corruption, and mediocrity. Some think that very special freedom isn't important because those with whom they disagree have possession over the electronic judgment day of the mass media. This, according to them, diminishes the facts of democracy to a contemptible farce of eroded claims.

As this collection makes clear, I see it all another way. The ideas and assessments brought together here add up to the vision of a radical pragmatist. I affirm whatever I think has the best chance of working, of being both inspirational and unsentimental, of resonating across the categories of false division and beyond the decoy of race. That is: I don't care who conceives a better strategy for dealing with the polluting cynicism of mass market rebellion in our popular culture, with public education, with improving the quality of our competition in the world arena, with crime, and with the central issue of our time, which is maintaining democratic morale. It doesn't matter to me if the cow comes from the left, the middle, or the right side of the pasture; I'm concerned with whether or not the milk is sour.

This collection is about more than affirmation, however. I also take the time to woof, play the dozens, snap, pull the covers off. I call out those ideas that cause us to waste a lot of time. I mean those arguments provided by the counterfeit firefighters who sell us sieves when we should face our dragon blazes by designing better buckets, stronger hoses, and making sure the water from the hydrants gushes out with appropriate force. Sometimes the problem isn't a fire; it's the cleansing for which we need smaller hoses that won't knock us down but will do the job of washing off the muck we rise out of, head first.

My intellectual apprenticeship of hard knocks and illumination didn't come out of nowhere. Albert Murray and the late Ralph Ellison are the two figures who, as far as I'm concerned, brought it all back home. They pulled in all of the highest intellectual aspirations and achievements from the world over, then combined them with the democratic complexities so inherent to our nation, realizing in their separate work quite bold expressions of reflective insight and aesthetic creation. Both were born in the second decade of this century, Murray in 1916 and Ellison in 1914, Murray in Alabama, Ellison in Oklahoma, which, for me, made them the twin towers of a Southern and Southwestern one-two punch that flattened all of my former involvements with black nationalism and liberated me from the influence of LeRoi Jones, whose work I once copied as assiduously as Sonny Stitt did Charlie Parker's.

I have known Albert Murray for about twenty-five years and maintain an independent study with him that has had the largest single impact on my development. This great man is my mentor and far more my father than the fellow whose blood runs in my veins. Sorry, dad. Murray is a writer whose social essays, criticism, and aesthetic examination—*The Omni-Americans, The Hero and the Blues, South to A Very Old Place*, and *Stomping the Blues*— have cold-cocked so many of the simple-minded positions on American life, American art, and the meaning of art itself. Murray's novels—*Train Whistle Guitar* and *The Spy Glass Tree*—have given us a very fresh sense of our Southern heritage, one that makes understandable so many of the things obscured by the vision of those writers who reduced the South to a torturous geography of booby traps and murder. I remember when I first read Murray in an anthology entitled *Anger and Beyond*. Boy, did he seem like an oddball! He came out of his corner with another set of moves altogether. All these years later, my appreciation for his integrity, his technique, and his knowledge continues to increase. Round after round, he gets faster and his combinations are even more accurate, the coordination of his work a celebration of intellectual and aesthetic dance, grace, and honor.

The very same singular quality gives perpetual vitality to the work of Ralph Ellison, with whom I spoke on the telephone many, many times and from whom I got another original sense, chapter and verse, of the sweet science that is intellectual engagement at its most serious. His writing was all the more remarkable since he had no inspirational example from his background. When Ellison came into the ring, there had been no writer caught in his particular predicament and so willing to train with the ambition anyone who would become a champion labors through. More than any other American writer, Ralph Ellison made clear how far the intellectual and cultural meanings of Negro life were from what we had previously seen in our national letters. He chose to become a real contender, not some whining and counterfeit pug hiding from the fray behind a homemade mask of wax lumps and painted blood. More than forty years ago, the arrival of *Invisible Man* rang us into another round of revelations concerning the mysteries and the hidden meanings we face as Americans, a people so often sucker-punched by the decoys of race but just as often absorbing the meat, the bone, and the marrow of those styles we have been told to look out for, that are supposed to represent no more than cultural eye-thumbings and head butts. His first book of essays, *Shadow and Act*, went the furthest distance toward making it possible for us to see ourselves as Americans within the broadest and deepest context. Ellison realized and made clear how much we had missed by failing to bring the humanity of Negroes into our writing, how little was accomplished by reworking stereotypes, presenting black Americans in the chrome steel chains of addlepated entertainment and sentimentality. Ellison wasn't interested in captivity as a form of titillation, nor did he believe that wanting far more than all he had ever been offered was the highway to pretension and imprisonment in an ogling world of strangers. He knew that we all, in our failures as well as our victories, speak for each other, and that the job of the writer is to battle those many ways of speaking into the world of literature. When he rose from his stool with his second book of essays, *Going To The Territory,* he hadn't given in. His death in 1994 meant that a very special spirit was no longer here. My eulogy, "The Measure of the Oklahoma Kid," is included in this volume and extends upon this paragraph.

Just as important to my sense of what is is to be done is the clarity the years have allowed me in terms of recognizing my most inspirational historical forebears, the people I could never know personally. They came from nowhere to somewhere; they made a way where there was no way; they moved from outside the argument into the center of the dialogue and helped define its direction and determine its highest ideals. They were those who took that next step after intuition and began acquiring what were then the illegal particulars of literacy. Every last one of them was symbolized by the few fellow slaves Frederick Douglass used to take out into the fields where he secretly taught them the alphabet. There was no intrinsic possibility that their knowing that alphabet would ever mean anything beyond itself. It was an accumulation of information that had no built-in future. Those slaves were guaranteed neither escape from the plantation nor the opportunity to ever read a book or a map. At the risk of whatever stern punishment was thought appropriate, they were there learning the symbols that pulled the world down to the page, getting their lessons from that yellow devil Douglass, a handsome fusion of white and black blood, his mixed identity a perfect symbol of the country itself. Those slaves were expressing something far beyond anything racial; it was that most stubbornly human involvement in the development of an inner life. By acquiring the intellectual tools necessary, they meant to broaden their recognition of how the world was detailed and assessed. Whatever they looked like, from purely African to very nearly European, they were playing out their own variations on the arguments against taxation without representation. Those slaves were inserting themselves into a world beyond the one imposed upon them. That desire to go beyond one's muscles and glands, their will to journey into the realm of reflection, always strikes me as a pinnacle in the history of this country, a profound metaphor that sustains an indelible position in my own consciousness.

As for my identity, I need go no further back than those American slaves. African kingdoms, real or invented, make no impression on how I see myself, primarily because Africa had absolutely nothing to do with the conception of the ideas that eventually led to the end of slavery and were so essential to the recent history in which people the world over became more and more involved in breaking down the reign of South African apartheid. The international recognition and support of Nelson Mandela were born of the evangelical humanism at the center of modern democracy, which has no precedents in anything of African origin. Negro Americans, not Africans, were central to the enriching of that humanism through their role in the difficult evolution of American democracy. That humanism still eludes the African continent, where, however confusing it might seem to us, tribe is still largely as restrictive a division as race has been at the worst points of segregation in our nation. Yet if we look at European society prior to the French Revolution, we realize that class meant exactly the same thing as race because blood was supposed to determine how much one was innately prepared to do in the world. That is why there was nothing made of the social and sexual mixings of indentured white servants and black slaves in the early days of American colonial history. The slaughter in Bosnia also makes it obvious that tribalism is something we have to think of in much broader terms if we are to actually recognize how the dilemmas of xenophobia play themselves out in a good number of contexts that superficially seem to have nothing in common. All of which is to say that I don't doubt the humanity of Africans nor the humanity of any other people, but that my recognition of the universal and boundless potential for good, for evil—as well as the inevitable mixtures of both—doesn't change the fact that everything truly important to me is the result of American democracy and the European ideas that were expanded and refined in order to adjust to the intricacies of human experience, action, conflict, and ambition within these United States. That is probably the theme I return to more than any other in this collection, building upon it and looking at it from a number of positions and through a number of subjects.

This is not a popular position in our time because the idea of a Negro American proudly stepping into the ring of our national discourse and claiming a birthright so often denied in the past is seen as an expression of automatic allegiance. If one doesn't accept the position of outsider, he or she is thought to be an ethnically tinted hawk sitting blindfolded on the leather glove of some far right school of sociopolitical thinking. In order to be "authentic," Negro Americans, so goes the politics of perpetual alienation, aren't supposed to identify with the ideals of the country at large. We are supposed to enlist all of our energies in pretending that we are somehow part of another tradition. The other tradition is usually broken into two choices. One defines Afro-Americans as a long lost group uninformed by the African cultural principles that supply the best defense against an irrevocably hostile white world. The other borrows a set of propositions from Karl Marx and his children. In the "analysis" of Marx's descendants, we take our position in a sentimentalized proletariat, not just victimized by class but also racially excluded from getting a grip on the means of production.

All of that is just so much more hogwash. Race, class, and sex can never be ignored when analyzing the story and the meaning of American life, but categories that deny the imperturbable mixtures we should by now know make us all who we are, or categories that reduce everyone to mechanical players in a set of economic theories based always on exploitation but never on the mysteries of human appetite and the masks as well as the mechanics of compromise, seem quite naive to me. In the sixties, we rather boldly said that everyone was basically the same, that if you cut someone, he or she bled, that love was love, hate was hate, hurt was hurt, evil was evil, courage was courage, and so on and on. The struggle then was against automatic categories of preference or distance. People were told that nobody had the right to tell somebody else whom to love or what to try and become or where to live. The imperatives of human recognition were the most radical because they gave no quarter to stereotypes or to the superstitions and policies resulting from them. In the wake of Black Power, we are being told the exact opposite. Now each group is supposedly so different from every other one that it needs a special kind of treatment in order to "feel good about itself." Now separatist self-esteem is said to be the high road. We aren't supposed to have any standards because standards were all developed as forms of exclusion and oppression.

Well, I'm not down with the new model of segregation. I see Americans as people who play out variations on the same fundamental music. We play the blues, sometimes in different keys, sometimes in different meters, sometimes at different tempos, sometimes on different instruments. In place after place, that is what this book is about. It is always looking for the things that we have in common, the things that sustain our improvements of discourse and policy, the obstacles that make it difficult for us to recognize the many improvisations that enrich our commonality. There is a long and short of it—lengthy essays and speeches as well as pieces written at newspaper-column length. In every case, I am extending and reiterating my central concerns, my seeking to understand the meanings, so varied and residing in some many places, of American democracy.

Jazz is very important to my vision of life in our time. At its best, jazz teaches us how to convert the pulp frog into a prince with the swing of Louis Armstrong. Jazz is not only about transforming pulp frogs, it is also about slaying the dragon and making cuisine out of his corpse. When that dragon is our industrial world, we have to face its menace and slay the temptations of the cynical and the defeatist; we have to use the blasts of dragon fire to smelt the durable industrial lyricism that arrives through that perfect symbol of human being and machine: the musician putting personal and collective human meaning through the machinery of an instrument, swinging the blues to be here, swinging the blues to be there, swinging the blues to be anywhere. It is the transformative power of jazz and its possession of that industrial lyricism which cause me to come back to this music over and over. In fact, I believe that one of the central intellectual shortcomings of American life is the fact that so little has been done with the flexible profundity of the jazz metaphor.

Then there is the work of American filmmakers that takes on the dramatic and comic gradations of class, race, and sex with the fortitude and the subtlety necessary to go beyond the clichés of stationary alienation and give artistic form to our epic interactions, to the ceaseless absorptions that say, even against the will of those committed to divisive categories, "Made in America." There are also writers of cultural criticism and fiction whose work adds to my feeling of affirmation through the revelatory standards their writing brings to observations about the patterns of decay and exploitation that just as surely leave big boo boo in the national soup as a bear does in the woods. The central themes of this collection are usually focused on and developed through essay after essay, something like improvised choruses that take the tune more and more different places, like boxing attack plans that use the opponent as an unwilling but inevitable rhythm section. The first section lays down all the themes; the last, which is given over to the long, concluding set of combinations, "Melting Down The Iron Suits of History," hopes to sum up everything riffed on and fought through in the earlier choruses and rounds.

CODA

As I sit in the war room of my office, looking at the shelves of my books and my recordings, listening to the voices of the dead made eternal through technology or reading the latest addition to the pile of answers we can call upon to straighten out the twisted power of the riddles built like porcupines, poisonous as cobras, and as packed with foul odor as all skunks, I feel there has never been a better time to be alive. Yes, I'll tell you why. It seems to me that our heads, our minds, our ways of reasoning, have been pushed under a lot of muck, but that we are now rising, head first, from that debilitating ooze, singing, as always, the blues to give the bum's rush to the blues, the blues to give the boot to the blues, the blues notice of eviction to, yes, that same old protean blues. As we come up like that, head first, we match the tone of that eternal American saxophone which is much in its sound like the form of a swimmer rising from beneath the wet darkness on a full moon night, dripping away the guck and covered with the endless goose pimples that shape up behind the vibrato of ever so slight texturing, the timbral recognition of the evening chill, the moment of uncomfortable night wind that means we have come home, under the revealing moonlight, to a world far more complex and rewarding than the wonderful wet darkness that never denies our shapes or our rhythms, even as it obliterates their distinctions. This collection is my way of rising through battle and my offering of a cleansing hose, some towels and some robes for those readers rising from the wet darkness with me.

VICTORY IS ASSURED

THE ALL-AMERICAN
SKIN GAME,
OR,
THE DECOY OF RACE

Part One

FROM HERE TO THE HORIZON: HOW IT GOES

BLUES TO BE
CONSTITUTIONAL

A Long Look at the Wild Wherefores of Our Democratic Lives
*As Symbolized in the Making of Rhythm and Tune**

PART I: BLUE REBELLION BREAKDOWN

I stand here not as a scholar of the Constitution but as a student of
the human soul, which is what any writer with the ambition to capture the whys and wherefores of our lives must be. Before I have finished this talk, I hope to have examined the metaphor of the
Constitution as it applies to a number of things in our society, and I
hope also to have looked at a few of the elements that threaten not
so much the democratic institutions of this country as much as they
tend to lessen the morale necessary to work at the heroic expansion
of this democracy into the unlit back streets and thickets of our civilization. I have chosen to be that ambitious. And in the process of
expressing my ambition, I might kick off another version of a good
number of the pitched intellectual battles I have had with people
whom we continue to mistakenly describe by their color, since no
one has ever seen anyone who is actually white or black, red or yellow, however close a few here or there might be. That level of
imprecise identification in such a technologically advanced society
is one of the ironies of our time and our place in the history of
America and of the world.

As a writer, I find it ironic that I began working on these ideas in

*Delivered on April 7, 1995, at Michigan State University, for The Symposium on Science, Rea-
son, and Modern Democracy.

public at Harvard University in 1992, when I spoke on the thirty-seventh anniversary of the death of Charlie Parker, whose consciousness was swallowed by the grim reaper in Manhattan's Fifth Avenue Stanhope Hotel on March 12, 1955. It was nearly ten years after the performance of *Koko*—a harmonic skullcracker built on the chords of *Cherokee*—had announced Parker's ability to extend our expectations of jazz improvisation. Legend lays it down that the virtuoso Kansas City alto saxophonist died while laughing at an act on a television variety show, an electronic update of the minstrel and vaudeville tradition Parker had so poorly fought against throughout his career. A statistic of his own excesses, the innovative genius had been nursed round the clock by not a Jewish princess but a Jewish baroness, one who had driven North African ambulances during World War II yet survived to so scandalize her Rothschild family that, so continues the legend, she was paid off to badly drive her Bentley and enthusiastically host her Negro jam sessions out of sight and out of earshot.

Parker is a man I have come to know quite well since I began working on his biography in 1982. But Parker is most important to what I have to say today because he represents both the achievement and the myth of jazz as well as the trouble we Americans have deciding whether we will aspire to the heroic individuality symbolized by Abraham Lincoln and Martin Luther King, Jr., or sink down into the anarchic individuality represented by Billy the Kid and the various bad boys our society has had crushes on for over a century. However great his talent surely was, Parker was celebrated as much in the half light and the darkness of the night world for his antics, his irresponsible behavior, his ability to embody what Rimbaud called "the love of sacrilege." He was a giant of a bluesman and a jazz improviser of astounding gifts, but his position in the world and in the overview this address seeks has much to do with praise he received for being an outlaw, a sort of praise that speaks directly to a number of our dilemmas.

Since our actual preparation for becoming a democratic society was outside the law, dumping tea in Boston Harbor while disguised as Indians and fomenting rebellion, since our moral assaults on the limitations of our democracy were expressed in the illegal actions of the abolitionists who worked the Underground Railroad and predicted the sorts of activities that people of conscience would later replicate when spiriting Jews beyond the death camp clutches of the

Nazis, it is not hard to understand why we have such a high position in our pantheon for the bad boy. We love riotous outsiders as much as we once loved the sort of eloquence we no longer hear from our politicians. And in our straining against the constraints of modern civilization, we, like Baudelaire and Rimbaud, have a love of symbolic violence.

That symbolic violence has two sides, one rooted in a democratic assertion, an expression of the culture's vitality, a breaking away from European convention in pursuit of a social vision that eventually allowed for recognition and success beyond the limitations of family line and class. The other is a set of appetites focused on the exotic, bedeviled by a nostalgia for the mud, given to a love of sensationalism that completely hollows out a pretentious vulgarity. From the moment Americans joyously dumped that tea into Boston Harbor, we were in the process of rebelling against what was then a traditional denial of the colonized underdog's access to dialogue. But that Indian disguise also exhibited perhaps the first burst of what would evolve into the love of the ethnic mask as witnessed in burnt cork stage presentations and the cinematic symbol of Al Jolson's jazz singer moving from Eastern European provincialism into the Negro rhythmic bustle of American popular art.

Since the rise of American nationalism that took off at an express tempo following the War of 1812, our art has as frequently reflected disdain as celebration. We love to make fun of the rules and prick those who think themselves superior for all the wrong reasons, especially since our democracy tells us that the little David of the common man can knock down the Goliath of wealth, unfairness, privilege. We believe the smart money can always be wrong. In the first third of the nineteenth century, the Yankee Brother Jonathan and the backwoodsman Davey Crockett often outwitted the stuffed shirt, as would the burnt cork minstrel show figures who stood in for the rural whites endangered by the con men of the big city. Our art tends to pull for the underestimated and the outsider, perhaps because so many of us originate in groups and classes that were once outside the grand shindig of American civilization, noses pressed against the ballroom's huge windows. We have great faith in the possibility of the upset. There is no American who doesn't understand well the statement "They said it couldn't be done, but we did it."

That dictum is basic to our national character and underlies the virtues of our society as much as it does the vulgar volleys against convention we presently find so worrisome in popular art. What we are now witnessing is a distorted version of our own understanding of the battle between the old and the new that is basic to an improvisational society such as ours, where policy is invented to redress previous shortcomings or to express attitudinal shifts. It is central to being an American that one doesn't necessarily believe that limitations will last very long, primarily because we have seen so many changes take place in everything from technology to the ongoing adjustments of policy. It is part of our history, from Eli Whitney, Thomas Edison, Henry Ford, and the Wright brothers in the machinery of modern life to Abraham Lincoln, Martin Luther King, and Sandra Day O'Connor in political influence and high national office.

But what we see as tendencies in our contemporary popular art is what has happened to the extension of identification with the outsider to a love of the scandalizing bad boy. This is a love that has evolved in our century from the silver screen gangster to MTV gangster rap, introducing a few other kinds of bad boys along the way. We have moved swiftly from the cardboard goody-goody to Cagney, to Bogart, to Edgar G. Robinson, motorcyled forward to Brando and James Dean, hopped the racial fence to play out sadomasochistic rituals with Miles Davis, Malcolm X, and now Spike Lee, not leaving out all of the adolescent rock-and-roll intoxication our society guzzles to the point of hangovers left now by Prince or Madonna or Public Enemy. As Gregory Peck says, "The audience loves the bad guy because he will come up with a surprise."

Those surprises were first seen in our century in slapstick, with the many variations on the pie in the face of the society man and matron. That harmless disdain for smugness and pretension made us laugh when the superficially bad boy and comic figure, from Chaplin's Afro-balletic tramp to Eddie Murphy's *Beverly Hills Cop*, unleashed chaos at the pompous gathering. But Peck's observation says much about the dark glamour that surrounds the worst of rock and the lowest of rap, where the canonization of antisocial posturing and the obnoxious appropriation of the racial stereotype has been basic to rock criticism at least since the elevation of the Rolling Stones and Jimi Hendrix. As rock critic Gregory Sandow says, "It's all about the love of the outlaw. The outlaw is going against everything you want to fight in the society, he's doing all the things you would like to do and being the way you would like to be. He's beyond the pale of convention, and if he's black, it's even better."

Sandow's observation is corroborated when one reads the bulk of rock writers on the subject of rap, they who were so quick to shout down racists or fume about Jesse Helms and the 2 Live Crew obscenity trial, but are almost always willing to indulge their own appetites for contemporary coon shows, for the brute glamour of this racial replay—and affirmation—of "the love of sacrilege," of the extensions of Jolson's statement, "You ain't heard nothing yet." For these writers, and perhaps for the bulk of white rap fans, the surliest rap recordings and videos function as experiences somewhere between viewing the natives boiling the middle class in a pot of profanity and the thrill of gawking at a killer shark in an audio aquarium. For Negro rap fans we see another version of the love of the noble savage, the woolly-headed person from the street who can't be assimilated, who is safe from our American version of the temptation of the West.

All of those tendencies clearly express our young people's dissatisfaction with the shortcomings of our culture but a dissatisfaction had on the cheap. In the world of the prematurely cynical, the bad boy reigns, for he represents retreat into pouting anarchy. Of course, our kind of capitalism doggedly allows for almost any kind of successful career, even one that earns millions or television time or tenure selling defeatist visions, playing on or cultivating appetites for ersatz savagery, trumpeting segregation and substandard levels of scholarship on the campuses of our best universities. At the lowest and highest levels, say from Louis Farrakhan or from some professor of "victim studies," we hear all of the carping about the meaninglessness of American democracy, of the tainted moral character of the men who attended the Constitutional Convention and whipped the tragically optimistic fundamentals of our social contract into championship form.

Behind that carping, when what we discover is not merely opportunistic, we learn something quite distinct about the maudlin as it relates to the cynical. We come to understand that unearned cynicism, much more frequently than not, is no more than a brittle version of sentimentality. It is a failure of morale, a cowardly flight from the engagement that comes of understanding the elemental shortcomings of human existence as well as the founding fathers of this country did. Those given to no more than carping are unprepared to address the tragic optimism at the center of the metaphor that is the Constitution. They know nothing of heroic engagement, the engagement that would not allow one to misunderstand the singing of "We Shall Overcome" in the town square of Prague as Dubček stood on a balcony looking into the faces he had been exiled from seeing in the flesh by the Communist party. It is an engagement that would not allow one to miss the meaning of the Red Chinese troops having to destroy a crudely built Statue of Liberty with even cruder means when the night was filled with the familiar violence of totalitarianism in Tiananmen Square. That engagement would recognize that the very success of our struggle to extend democracy has inspired the world, and much of that extending has been the result of the efforts of people at war with the social limitations that were so severely imposed upon Negro Americans.

One cannot speak of Negro culture in this country without speaking of the blues. The blues, which I shall soon talk about in detail, have much to do with the vision of the Constitution, primarily because you play the blues to rid yourself of the blues, just as the nature of our democracy allows us to remove the blues of government by using the government. The blues is a music about human will and human frailty, just as the brilliance of the Constitution is that it recognizes grand human possibility with the same clarity that it does human frailty, which is why I say it has a tragic base. Just as the blues assumes that any man or any woman can be unfaithful, the Constitution assumes that nothing is innately good, that nothing is lasting—nothing, that is, other than the perpetual danger of abused power. One might even say that the document looks upon power as essentially a dangerous thing that must never be allowed to go the way it would were it handled by the worst among us, many of whom remain unrecognized until given the chance to push their ideas on the world. The very idea of the amendment brings into government the process of social redemption through policy. By redemption I mean that the Constitution recognizes that there may be times in the future when what we now think of as hard fact might be no more than a nationally accepted prejudice, one strong enough to influence and infect policy. So you use the government to rid yourself of the blues of government.

The Constitution is also a blues document because it takes a hard swinging position against the sentimentality residing in the idea of a divine right of kings. Sentimentality is excess and so is any conception of an inheritance connected to a sense of the chosen people. The Constitution moves against that overstatement with the same sort of definition Jesus had when his striking down the idea of a chosen people prefigured what we now think of as democracy, an open forum for entry that has nothing to do with any aspect of one's identity other than his or her humanity. I must make clear that I am not talking so much about religion here as I am about the idea that the availability of universal salvation is a precursor of the idea of universal access to fairness that underlies our democratic contract. Universal salvation means that no one's identity is static, that one need only repent and be born anew. That is what I meant earlier about social redemption: every policy structured to correct previous shortcomings in the national sensibility that have led to prejudicial doctrines or unfair treatment is a form of governmental repentance. Once again, using the government to rid the blues of government.

Yet the Constitution, like the blues singer willing to publicly take apart his own shortcomings, perceives human beings as neither demons nor angels but some mysterious combination of both. That is why the revelations of scandal and abuse that rise and fall throughout our history, including our deeply human susceptibility to hypocrisy and corruption, prove out the accuracy of the Constitution. Every time we learn of something unfair that has happened to a so-called minority group, or even a majority group like American women, we perceive anew how well the framers prepared us to face the tar and feathers our ideals are periodically dipped in—even if those framers might have been willing to tar brush some ideals themselves! Every time there is any sort of scandal or we learn another terrible thing about some president or some hanky-panky in governmental contracts, we see more clearly how important freedom of the press is and how important it is for public figures to have to account for their actions. Ask Boss Tweed, ask Richard Nixon;

both were felled by the press. The framers of this blues document could see it all and they knew that for a society to sustain any kind of vitality it had to be able to arrive at decisions through discourse that could stand up to the present or lighten the burdens wrought by the lowest aspects of the past.

In essence, then, the Constitution is a document that functions like the blues-based music of jazz: it values improvisation, the freedom to constantly reinterpret the meanings of our documents. It casts a cold eye on human beings and on the laws they make; it assumes that evil will not forever be allowed to pass by. And the fact that a good number of young Negro musicians are leading the movement that is revitalizing jazz suggests a strong future for this country. I find this true because of what it takes for young Negroes to break free of all the trends that overtake them perhaps even more comprehensively than they do the rest of American youth. I find this true because Afro-American culture is essentially oral, and any oral culture is in danger of being dictated to by whoever has command of the microphone.

There is a large dream in the world of jazz and that dream is much richer than anything one will encounter in the ethnic sentimentality of Afrocentric propaganda. What those young jazz musicians symbolize is a freedom from the taste-making of mass media and an embracing of a vision that has much more to do with aesthetic satisfaction than the gold rush culture of popular entertainment, where one takes the clichés of adolescent narcissism into the side of the mountain rather than a pickaxe, some pans, and a burro. These are young Americans who have not been suckers for the identity achieved through unearned cynical rebellion; they seek individuality through affirmation, which puts them at war with the silly attire and hairdos that descend directly from the rebel-without-a-cause vision of youth that Hollywood began selling adolescent Americans nearly forty years ago, when the anti-hero started to emerge. Less in awe of youth than of quality, those who would be jazz musicians would also *be* adults, not just shriek for adult privileges, then cry foul when the responsibilities are passed out. They have a healthy rspect for the men and women who laid an astonishing tradition down. In their wit, their good grooming, their disdain for drugs, and their command of the down home and the ambitious, they suggest that though America may presently be down on one knee, the champ is about to rise and begin taking names.

But in order to get you to truly appreciate the direction these young musicians are taking, I should conclude this talk with a longish discussion of what the blues and jazz traditions offer us in the way of democratic metaphors, aesthetic actions closely related to the way in which our very society is organized.

PART II: BLUES TO BE THERE

Transition Riff on the Big Feeling

I am quite sure that jazz is the highest American musical form because it is the most comprehensive, possessing an epic frame of emotional and intellectual reference, sensual clarity, and spiritual radiance. But if it wasn't for the blues, there would be no jazz as we know it, for blues first broke most clearly with the light and maudlin nature of popular music. Blues came up from this land around the turn of the century. We all know that blues seeped out of the Negro, but we should be aware of the fact that it also called backward into the central units of the national experience with such accuracy that it came to form the emotional basis of the most indelible secular American music. That is why it had such importance — not because it took wing on the breath, voice, and fingers of an embattled ethnic group, but because the feelings of the form came to magnetize everything from slavery to war to exploration to Indian fighting to natural disaster, from the woes of the soul lost in unhappy love to the mysteries, terrors, and celebrations of the life that stretched north from the backwoods to the steel and concrete monuments of the big city. It became, therefore, the aesthetic hymn of the culture, the twentieth-century music that spoke of and to modern experience in a way that no music of European or Third World origin ever has.

In a number of ways, the blues singer became the sound and the repository of the nation's myth and the nation's sense of tragic recognition. It was probably the sense of tragic recognition, given its pulsation by the dance rhythms of the music, that provided blues with the charisma that influenced so many other styles, from jazz to Tin Pan Alley to rock. In the music of the blues the listener was rescued from the sentimentality that so often threatens the soul of this culture, either overdoing the trivial or coating the significant with a hardening and disfiguring syrup. Surely, the Negroes who first came to hear the blues weren't at all looking for anything sentimental, since the heritage of the work song and the spiritual had already brought them cheek to jowl with the burdens of experience, expectation, and fantasy. In the sweat- and ache-laden work song, the demanding duties of hard labor were met with rhythm, and that rhythm, which never failed to flex its pulse in the church, was the underlying factor that brought together the listeners, that allowed for physical responses in the dance halls and the juke joints where blues emerged as the music of folk professionals. Blues all night in guitar keys, the development of a common source of images, a midnight-hour atmosphere of everyday people out to rhythmically scatch their own—and somebody else's—itching, sensual essences.

Yet there was always, as with any art given to the lyrical, a spiritual essence that referred as much to the desire for transcendence as it did to any particular tale of love and loss or love and celebration. In both cases, what was sometimes rightfully considered lewd could also constitute a sense of romantic completeness that was expressed with equal authority by men and women, that fact itself a motion toward women's liberation and the recognition of libidinous lore that transcended gender conventions. In fact, the first popular blues singers who rose to professional status were women such as Bessie Smith. And with the evolution of the blues singer into the jazz musician, an art came forward that was based in the rocky ground and the swamp mud of elemental experience while rising toward the stars with the intellectual determination of a sequoia. It was also symbolic, as had been the erotic wholeness basic to blues, of American democracy.

PART III: THE DEMOCRATIC SWING OF AMERICAN LIFE

In 1938, the great German novelist Thomas Mann, who had fled Nazism in his homeland, delivered a lecture from one end of America to another that was published as a small volume under the title

The Coming Victory of Democracy. It is only sixty-five pages in length, and there are a few aspects of it that are now outdated, but the overall sense of the world and the observations Mann provides about democracy connect very strongly to the processes and the implications of jazz, which brings a fresh confluence of directness and nuance not only to the making of music but to the body of critical thought its very existence has challenged in vital ways that are peculiarly American.

The vision of jazz performance and the most fundamental aspects of its aesthetic are quite close to Mann's description of democratic thought. "We must define democracy as that form of government and of society which is inspired above every other with the feeling and consciousness of the dignity of man." The demands on and the respect for the individual in the jazz band put democracy into aesthetic action. Each performer must bring technical skill, imagination, and the ability to create coherent statements through improvised interplay with the rest of the musicians. That interplay takes its direction from the melodic, harmonic, rhythmic, and timbral elements of the piece being performed, and each player must have a remarkably strong sense of what constitutes the *making* of music as opposed to the *rendering* of music, which is what performers of European concert music do. The improvising jazz musician must work right in the heat and the pressure of the moment, giving form and order in a mobile environment, where choices must be constantly assessed and reacted to in one way or another. The success of jazz is a victory for democracy, and a symbol of the aesthetic dignity, which is finally spiritual, that performers can achieve and express as they go about inventing music and meeting the challenge of the moment.

Those challenges are so substantial that their literal and symbolic meanings are many, saying extraordinary things about our collective past as well as the dangers and the potential of the present. In fact, improvisational skill is such an imposing gift that the marvelously original Albert Murray has written in *The Hero and the Blues*, "Improvisation is the ultimate human (i.e., heroic) endowment." The very history of America's development bears this out, as does much of the history that preceded it. But perhaps no society so significant has emerged over the last five centuries that has made improvisation so basic to its sensibility. Even the conflict between

Cortés and the Aztecs, for all its horrific dimensions, pivoted on the element of improvisation. As the French writer and critic Tzvetan Todorov observes in his startling *The Conquest of America*, "It is remarkable to see Cortés not only constantly practicing the art of adaption and improvisation, but also being aware of it and claiming it as the very principle of conduct: 'I shall always take care to add whatever seems to me most fitting, for the great size and diversity of the lands which are being discovered each day and the many new secrets which we have learned from the discoveries make it necessary that for new circumstances there be new considerations and decisions; should it appear in anything I now say or might say to your Majesty that I contradict what I have said in the past, Your Highness may be assured that it is because a new fact elicits a new opinion.' "

That quote sounds more than a little like an attitude foreshadowing the constitutional vision of amendments spoken of earlier, and it is also similar in tone and content to the way jazz musicians have explained how different nights, different moods, and different fellow musicians can bring about drastically dissimilar versions of the same songs. Part of the emotion of jazz results from the excitement and the satisfaction of making the most of the present, or what the technocrats now call "real time." Todorov follows that quote with an idea that is basic to the conception of improvising jazz: "Concern for coherence has yielded to concern for the truth of each particular action."

In jazz, however, *comprehension* of each particular action, the artistic truth of it, will bring from the better and more inspired players reactions resulting in overall coherence. And it is the achievement of coherence in the present that is the great performing contribution jazz has made to the art of this century.

1.

Just as American democracy, however periodically flawed in intent and realization, is a political, cultural, economic, and social rejection of the automated limitations of class and caste, jazz is an art in which improvisation declares an aesthetic rejection of the preconceptions that stifle individual and collective invention. But the very history of Afro-Americans has always been dominated by a symbolic war against the social and artistic assembly line, especially since stereotypes are actually forms of intellectual and emotional automation. In fact, slavery was a forerunner of the nation's social compartmentalization, especially the sort upheld by the pieties of stereotypes. Those stereotypes maintained that certain people came off an assembly line in nature and one needn't assume them capable of the endless possibilities of human revelation. They had a natural place, which was inferior, and they were sometimes to be pitied and guided, sometimes feared and controlled, but were never to be considered more than predictable primitives who functioned best in subservient positions.

The aesthetic revelation in the present that is so central to jazz improvisation repudiated such attitudes and rejected what Charlie Parker called "stereotyped changes." But long before the emergence of Parker, the level of virtuoso craftsmanship that evolved in the improvising world of jazz redefined both instrumental sound and technique in an ensemble where this idiomatic American music met all the criteria demanded of musical artistry. Even virtuosity took on a new meaning, a meaning steeped in unprecedented liberation. And it was no coincidence that this frontier of artistry came from Afro-Americans and eventually spoke to and for all. As this writer pointed out in an essay called "Body and Soul," "Given the attempts to depersonalize human beings on the plantation, or reduce them to the simplicity of animals, it is understandable that a belief in the dignity of the Negro and the joyous importance of the individual resulted in what is probably the century's most radical assault on Western musical convention. Jazzmen supplied a new perspective on time, a sense of how freedom and discipline could coexist within the demands of ensemble improvisation, where the moment was bulldogged, tied, and given shape. As with the Italian artists of the Renaissance, their art was collective and focused by a common body of themes, but for jazzmen, the human imagination in motion was the measure of all things."

The degree of freedom introduced into Western music by black Americans has touched some of the few truly good jazz writers deeply and has inspired in them ideas of substantial significance in twentieth-century aesthetics. Getting beyond the noble savage school that shapes the thinking of too many jazz critics of whatever hue or background, Martin Williams points out in his largely superb *The Jazz Tradition* that there has never been a music in the Western world that allowed for so much improvisation on the parts of so many, which raises telling issues. Williams articulates the depth and meaning of this improvisational freedom quite clearly when he writes, "In all its styles, jazz involves some degree of collective ensemble improvisation, and in this it differs from Western music even at those times in its history when improvisation was required. The high degree of individuality, together with the mutual respect and co-operation required in a jazz ensemble carry with them philosophical implications that are so exciting and far-reaching that one almost hesitates to contemplate them. It is as if jazz were saying to us that not only is far greater individuality possible to man than he has so far allowed himself, but that such individuality, far from being a threat to a co-operative social structure, can actually enhance society."

Williams also makes an observation that helps clarify the human *wholeness* jazz proposes through its bold performance conventions: "The Greeks, as José Ortega y Gasset has pointed out, made the mistake of assuming that since man is the unique thinking animal (or so they concluded him to be), his thinking function is his superior function. Man is at his best when he thinks. And traditionally, Western man has accepted this view of himself. But to a jazz musician, thought and feeling, reflection and emotion, come together uniquely, and resolve in the act of doing." This artistically extends Mann's phrase "a new and modern relationship between mind and life" from *The Coming Victory of Democracy*. That new relationship in this context demands a cooperation between the brain and the body that is perhaps fresh to Western art, since the levels of perception, conception, and execution take place at such express velocities that they go far beyond what even the most sophisticated information about the consciousness is presently capable of assessing. These musicians hear what is played by their fellow performers, are inspired to inventions of their own, hold their places in the forms of the songs, and send tasks to their muscles that must be executed so swiftly that all functions of mind and body come together with intimidating speed. In the process, a bold and unprecedented radiance is brought to the performing ensemble. The music of jazz uniquely proves out Mann's dictum that "to come close to art means to come close to life, and if an appreciation of the dignity of man is the moral definition of democracy, then its psychological definition arises out of its determination to reconcile and combine knowledge and art, mind and life, thought and deed."

2.

Though the skills that make for jazz are the result of a musical evolution that probably began the moment African slaves started reordering music they heard from and were taught by the slave masters, this writer would again say that it is a dangerous simplification to hear jazz primarily as a music protesting the social conditions of Afro-Americans, even if its seminal inventors were often subjected to social limitations based on race. That reduces the monumental human achievement of a sustained artistic vision that allows for the expression of every passion, from delicate affection to snarling rage at the very demons of life at large, those tragic elements that no amount of money, power, or social inclusion will hold at bay. If social problems in and of themselves were the only things that provoke the creation of great art, a century as bloody as ours would have inspired far more original and profound aesthetic achievement than it has. No, the miracle of this improvisational art is the fact that the techniques Africans arrived with evolved into *aesthetic conceptions* that reinvented every kind of American music they came in contact with, from folk to religious music to dance tunes, and finally achieved the order that is jazz, where all those aspects of American musical expression were brought together for a fresh synthesis.

That fresh synthesis was the product of a down-home aristocracy of men and women whose origins cut across class and caste, who might or might not be able to read music, might or might not have used conventional technique, but who all had in common the ability *to make musical sense* during the act of playing. In no way did their rising to artistic prominence from the bottom, middle, or top of the social strata on the steam of their own individual talents and wills conflict with the collective concerns of the music. By doing so, they actually enhanced our understanding of the music's democratic richness, proving through their work what Mann meant when he said, "Real democracy, as we understand it, can never dispense with aristocratic attributes—if the word 'aristocratic' is used, not in the sense of birth or any sort of privilege, but in a spiritual sense." A jazz musician would probably say *soul*, knowing that those who possess the deepest spiritual connection to the music can come from anywhere and *have* often enough to affirm the merit system of aesthetic expression. It is actually the whole point of democracy itself: a society is best off and most in touch with the vital when it eliminates all irrational restrictions on talent, dedication, and skill.

No matter what class or sex or religion or race or shape or height, if you can cut the mustard, you should be up there playing or singing or having your compositions performed. You should, in fact, after all the practice and the discipline necessary to push your art into the air as a professional, be taking on the ultimate democratic challenge, which means bringing into the aesthetic arena the fundamentals of Constitutional discourse, checks and balances, policy, and the amendments in which you symbolically use government to rid yourself of the blues of government. When that challenge is met, children, we hear the lucidity rising into the air that is the bittersweet truth of the blues to be there—what Hernando Cortés predicted, what the framers put together, and what we, and our descendants, as all-American children of the Constitution, will continue to reinterpret until the end of our time in the quicksand of history.

BLUES-COLLAR CLARITY

This essay was delivered as a talk at a conference held in Washington, D.C., in the spring of 1990, which was entitled "Second Thoughts on Race in America." It allowed me to work out my sense of how supposedly new directions in Afro-American consciousness were actually old-time stuff that missed, or denied, or repudiated a sturdy set of principles that underlay Negro-American morale and achievement.

Following my mentors, Albert Murray and Ralph Ellison, I have long maintained that the influence of Afro-Americans on our cultural and political life is indelible and ongoing. Just as it is quite easy to see how Negro style has affected our music, our language, our humor, our dance, and even our ways of walking and performing sports, we cannot deny the impact Afro-Americans have had on this country's movement toward the realization of the ideals that cluster in the heart of our democratic conception. In a long and tragic series of confrontations, black Americans have had to scale, bore through, or detonate the prejudicial walls that blocked access to the banquet of relatively unlimited social advancement that we acknowledge as the grand inspirational myth of American life.

This epic confrontation with bigoted policies reached its high heroic moment during the Civil Rights Movement, bringing together troops that crossed all racial lines, classes, religions, and political parties. At that point, our struggle for greater democratic purity entered an arena of political engagement that demanded dousing redneck dragon fire, transforming segregationists like Lyndon Johnson, battling the paranoid illnesses of men like J. Edgar

Hoover, and holding at bay all of the hysterically cynical tendencies toward self-pity and defeatist sulking or name calling within our ranks. The result was both a monumental shift in the national perception of racial matters and an unprecedented entree into the processes of democratic life. What we learned during those years is that the role of American democracy has come to be one of constant expansion, of inclusive motion beyond one group or one sex to all groups in both sexes. And at this point in our history, the democratic idea has grown even to include the idea that both the animate and inanimate environment should have the rights that preclude callous exploitation.

But for all the expansions of our conception of democracy and for all the victories against discriminatory attitudes and policies over the last twenty-five years, we still find ourselves facing the job of improvising the best way of going about making the democratic imperatives at the center of our society function with the sort of vitality that inspires comprehensive engagement. From my position on the battlefield, I have come to believe that a large part of what must be addressed is the nature of the enemy within, the influential dimensions of what must finally be recognized as a vision of American society that leads not toward democratic vibrance but the limitations of Balkanization. In fact, I now believe the discussion of race is far too influenced by a body of ideas reflecting the amount of decay that has taken place in the Afro-American intellectual, political, and lower-class communities.

The battle with so-called "white middle-class standards" that we still hear discussed when the subjects ranging from school performance to rap records are addressed is itself a distortion of the goals of the Civil Rights Movement. This battle would lead us to believe that there are differences so great in this society that we should actually accept a separatist vision in which the elemental necessity of human identification across racial, sexual, and class lines would be replaced by the idea that people from various backgrounds can identify only with those from their own groups. Such a conception avoids King's idea that people should be judged by the content of their character and not by the color of their skin or, if we extend that to include sex, by gender.

The nature of ethnic nationalism and of gender antagonism that has polluted so much contemporary discussion misses the point of the March on Washington in symbolic terms—that this culture is usually bettered when we have as many people as possible intelligently interacting, when quality takes precedence over point of social origin, class, race, sex, nationality, and religion. Those who came forward in the late sixties and began to trumpet the idea that there were two Americas—one black, one white—not only ignored all of the regional complexities of North, South, Midwest, Southwest, and West, but of Catholic and Protestant, Christian and Jew, as well as all of the variations that break down inside such large categories as white, black, Hispanic, Jew, and American Indian. Now those benumbing simplifications have pulled feminism into the task of making the white male the same thing that he is inside the cosmology of the Nation of Islam: the source of all evil.

This simplification is at odds with the realities of human interaction within our society, and it suggests that those removed from the proverbial seats of power are invariably limited in their freedom to be inspired. We can see that quite easily if we look at something like the controversy at Harvard, where the demand has been raised that a tenured black female be hired by the Law School. No one can be disturbed by a first-class black female professor's being hired by the department, but the argument that has begun to vibrate with hysteria about such matters implies a fundamental inferiority on the part of black female students. If we were to listen to the activists, we would conclude that black females are so incapable of identifying across racial lines that they cannot look at Sandra Day O'Connor on the Supreme Court and feel that there is a place for them in the American legal profession, perhaps one of extraordinary import someday.

Nothing in my own experience or in the experience of Afro-Americans I have met or read about corroborates the idea that, to any significant extent, people of color are capable of being inspired only by their own race or sex. To suggest that is to distort the heroic engagement that defines Negro history, a good measure of which has always been about struggling with any exclusive conception of human possibility or human identification. Yet we are now supposed to wolf down the idea that if a black child is looking at Kenneth Branagh's remarkable film of Shakespeare's *Henry V*, he or she will not be intrigued by the insights into the problems of power and struggle, of class and cultural clash, but will only be bored or feel left out because the work is something written by "a dead white man about dead white people." In its very provincialism and its racist conception of culture, such an idea opposes the richness of the best of Afro-American culture, regardless of class.

It is due to the distortions of people such as James Baldwin that we have come to believe in far too many instances that black people are such victims of racism that they are as limited as they are purported to be in the most provincial superstitions, those irrational undergirdings of discrimination. Having been born December 14, 1945, in Los Angeles, California, I can say that the people in my community, which was not so much blue-collar as *blues-collar*, were forever encouraging all of us to aspire to the very best that we could achieve and were always at war with any idea that would result in our accepting the ethnic limits encouraged by the traditions of segregated thought. Though my mother was a domestic worker who earned sometimes no more than $11 a day and often worked six days a week, she was always cutting out editorials for me to read, bringing home books that her employers either gave her or loaned, and wasn't above forcing me against my will to watch Laurence Olivier's *Richard III* when it came on, or doing the same thing when Orson Welles's *Macbeth* was shown nightly on *The Million Dollar Movie*, which I had to keep looking at until I came to understand what they were saying.

My blues-collar mother wasn't being pretentious or exhibiting the effects of having been brainwashed by a Eurocentric conception of cultural values. I was never given the impression that I was looking at some great white people strutting some great white stuff. That wasn't the idea at all. My mother knew that Olivier was a great actor and that Shakespeare was a great dramatist. She wanted me to know and experience those facts. She also told me about Marian Anderson, Duke Ellington, Jackie Robinson, and anybody else who represented exemplary achievement. The same was true in public school, where we read *Julius Caesar* aloud in class, saw films about Marian Anderson and Jackie Robinson, read Dickens, and so on. We were constantly taught that great significance was not the franchise of any single group and that we were supposed to identify with the best from whomever and wherever in the world it happened to come. We were not allowed to give any excuses for poor performance either. If we had come up with some so-called cultural difference excuse, we would have been laughed at, if not whacked on the boody, for disrespecting the intelligence of the teacher. Our teachers were tough and supportive. They knew well that the best way to respect so-called minority students was to demand the most of them.

It is not that the adults of my childhood were naive about racial matters. They knew that excellence and bulldog tenacity were the best weapons against the dragons of this society. That was the point of telling us about the struggles of the Andersons and the Robinsons. But the worst thing that you could be within that community at that time was a racist, no matter how obvious the social limitations were. Adults would say to you, "Boy, the lowest thing you can be is a man who spends all his time hating somebody he doesn't even know. You know, if you want to hold a man down in a hole full of mud, you got to get down there in that mud with him, which will make you just as dirty as the man you say you don't like because he's so damn filthy." Those Negroes I grew up under were always quick to tell you that there were just two kinds of people in the world: those who tried their best to be good and those who didn't care about being bad. They were true democrats, perhaps because they had learned the hard way what it meant when you submitted to the superstitions of discrimination. Those adults were just as proud of Branch Rickey as they were of Jackie Robinson, for each symbolized the will and the discipline necessary to expand the idea of democracy into the arena of practice.

The Afro-American tradition of which I speak is a continuation of what we learn from the life of Frederick Douglass, whose career makes it possible to see that all Americans, regardless of point of social origin, are capable of producing those who will do remarkable things. As Albert Murray points out in *The Omni-Americans*, a book all should read who really wish to know something about this country, the embodiment of the nineteenth-century self-made man is Douglass. Lincoln, the self-made Midwesterner, easily saw that. After Lincoln met with Douglass, the Great Emancipator told his secretary that, given Douglass's beginnings as a slave and his present achievements, he was probably "the most meritorious man in the

United States." Murray also observes that Harriet Tubman is surely the best example of the pioneer woman, what my grandmother meant when she complimented someone on having "shit, grit, and mother wit." Yet neither of them can be reduced to mere racial heroes. They are symbols of great American achievement against extraordinary odds.

When we address the richness of our heritage, we will understand our national heritage in the context of Western civilization to the degree that we will acknowledge it for what it is—an astonishing gathering of information from the entire world, a gathering that had its impact at least partially because of the fight against provincialism that fresh information from other cultures demanded. The experiment that is American democracy is an extension of the ideas of the Magna Carta and the Enlightenment and is also a social development of the New Testament's motion away from the idea of a chosen people. That is why a reduction of the meaning of Western civilization to "the story of dead white men" and racist exploitation distorts the realities of the ongoing debate that has lifted our social vision beyond the provincial, whether that lifting meant the debate over slavery or women's suffrage or anything else that has hobbled this country's freedom to benefit from its human resources.

The kind of defeatism, paranoia, and alienation that is fomented by the "dead white men" version of Western and national history is dangerous because it is so far from the facts of what those who made so many of the achievements thought of themselves. I have a feeling that Isaac Newton and Galileo didn't spend too much time thinking about their skin color. It is hard for me to believe that Newton got up in the morning saying, "Well, here I am, white Isaac Newton in England and, as white Isaac Newton, I think I'll go over here and try and figure out something white about gravity." I also doubt that Galileo said to himself, "Well, as white Galileo, let me look out here as a white man and see how far I can see with my white eyes. I can't see far enough, so I guess I'll have to work on a white tool so I can have a white view of the cosmos." Or can one imagine Beethoven battling to get those string quartets right and thinking, "My job as a white man who will some day be dead is to write some white notes and provide the future with the work of a great white dead man." The work of those men was too hard to be limited by such concerns.

The exploits of Negro and women aviators in the history of flying between the invention of the airplane and World War II prove that there were always those who could see past color and gender to the quality of the contribution and what that contribution might offer them in their own lives. And it is that sort of history that we must perpetually reiterate if we have any serious intention of combating Balkanization.

It is also easy to see that those who have promoted a reductive vision of Afro-American identity by posturing an antagonistic attitude toward "white middle-class standards" would do well to think about the differences between those students who come out of the business school at Florida A & M University and those students whom anthropologists Signithia Fordham of Rutgers University and John U. Ogbu of Berkeley studied at Capital High School in Washington, D.C. At the predominantly black Florida A & M, Sybil C. Mobley, dean and creator of the business school, has developed a program over the last sixteen years that is recognized by Hewlett-Packard recruiters as one of the top five in the country, one that can be counted on to produce first-level students of finance.

In the April 18, 1990, *New York Times* article about the program, it is observed that Mobley forged a curriculum that places as much emphasis on deportment, verbal skills, dress, grooming, and writing abilities as on the details of business. According to the article, Mobley's two-tiered curriculum is "one that some major American companies say the top business schools would do well to emulate." Given the high degree of interest in its business students, Florida A & M has shown that the best thing for so-called minority students is to demand that they engage the specifics of the world in which they live, not allow them to retreat into visions of victimization that diminish the will and thwart the discipline necessary to make one's own way in our society. As one of the female students says of what Mobley has built, "I know who I am. If you know who you are, you don't have to run around in a dashiki. There's a time to do that and a time to wear a suit." Eurocentric? Hardly. That is actually a reiteration of the Afro-American tradition of seeking to be the best within the terms of one's chosen arena.

Just one week later in the *Times*, the disturbing observations of the study of those high school students in Washington, D.C., were reported. The fundamental findings of Fordham and Ogbu give us important insights into some of the elements that explain what has become a noticeable performance gap between white and black students on Scholastic Aptitude Tests and in college work. Though neither the SAT scores nor college performances are discussed in the article, the idea that black students have about what constitutes ethnic authenticity says much about substandard academic achievement by Negroes. Such a circumscribed conception of "blackness" now so influences young black people that, according to the study of those high school students, "They chose to avoid adopting attitudes and putting in enough time and effort in their schoolwork because their peers (and they themselves) would interpret their behavior as 'white.' " It went on to say that there were more than a "dozen other types of behavior that the students considered 'acting white' — including "speaking standard English, listening to so-called white music, going to the opera or ballet, studying in the library, going to the Smithsonian Institution, doing volunteer work, camping or hiking, putting on airs and being on time." In other words, anything short of the most provincial way of addressing and assessing the varieties of expression and the possibilities that education exists to illuminate meant rejecting one's ethnic identity. Such self-assured provincialism is, at best, self-destructive, and is a tendency that must be fought relentlessly.

It is more than odd that we should find ourselves as Americans faced with these bizarre ideas and their effects not only on the black lower class but, as Jeff Howard and Ray Hammond pointed out in the 1985 *New Republic* article "Rumors of Inferiority," on the Negro middle class as well. What we are seeing is a retreat from community expectations and personal demands of high quality in intellectual areas. As Howard and Hammond point out, "Black leaders too often have tried to explain away these problems by blaming racism or cultural bias in the tests themselves. These factors haven't disappeared. But for many middle-class black Americans who have had access to educational and economic opportunities for nearly 20 years, the traditional protestations of cultural deprivation and educational disadvantage ring hollow." That hollowness and those clichés are surely the result of the Balkanized sense of reality that remains at odds with the best of the Afro-American tradition.

We have some very good examples, however, of what can happen when a so-called minority doesn't find itself burdened with a separatist ideology, when its people choose—as black people once knew they should—to work at more than complaining and trying to subvert the standards that promote excellence. Asian students have shown that they are capable of confounding their fellow students by rising to the challenges of higher education so consistently and so well that they seem not to understand what too many others consider the most important aspects of the college experience. They don't know that when you go to college you're supposed to pledge a fraternity or sorority, go to as many beer busts as possible, sleep through your classes, fail to do your papers, and devote large amounts of time to the incredibly significant problem of becoming popular. They obviously have a misunderstanding. They think they're supposed to study. That's why they call the campus library at Berkeley "Chinatown." When the library opens, Asian students flood in; when the library closes, Asian students are told to leave. Yet there are those who continue to wonder at the high percentage of Asian students who do so well academically! Deduction is obviously not one of their stronger suits.

The defeatist undertow that so misshapes the thinking of black youth regarding intellectual and career engagement is about more than the lack of role models, which is usually the explanation. In a letter to Ann Landers published February 25, 1990, in *The Washington Post*, a black middle-class reader complained, "Black children need role models. We read and hear too much about black pimps and drug dealers and not enough about blacks who have made it. Maybe this is what happens when the press, radio, and TV are predominantly white." Landers responded, quite rightly, that "the problems facing black youths are the same ones white youth have—no core family unit, no parental guidance, inadequate education, and joblessness." She went on to write, again, quite correctly, "You lose me when you complain of bias in the field of communications and an absence of black role models. A few who come to mind are Oprah Winfrey, Bill Cosby, Lena Horne, Sidney Poitier, Michael Jordan, Magic Johnson, Walter Payton, Mike Singletary, publishing tycoon John Johnson, Supreme Court Justice Thurgood Marshall, General Colin Powell, attorney Marian Wright Edelman,

and Dr. Louis Sullivan of Health and Human Services. I could go
on, but I'm sure you get the idea."

What we must question is the nature of the voices that black
youth choose to listen to when the difficulties facing our society are
under discussion. We must look at the problems that exist as much
in the black media as in the general media. It is incredible that neither of the two largest black papers in New York—*The Amsterdam
News* and *The City Sun*—has ever done its job in assessing the scandal of the Tawana Brawley farce and the disreputable roles played by
Al Sharpton, Vernon Mason, and Alton Maddox. Nor can we ignore
the national trend in black radio to promote paranoid conspiracy
theories and to submit to the kind of rabble-rousing that avoids the
complexity of the various levels of opposition and the necessity of
equally complex forms of combat. Nor can we fail to recognize the
way in which too many irresponsible intellectuals—black and
white—have submitted to the youth culture and the adolescent
rebellion of pop music, bootlegging liberal arts rhetoric to defend
Afro-fascist rap groups like Public Enemy on the one hand, while
paternalistically defining the "gangster rap" of doggerel chanters
such as Ice Cube as expressive of the "real" black community. The
problem with these tendencies is the same problem that existed
when racist iconography dominated media and folklore: semiliter-
ates and illiterates quite often fail to see those things as distortions;
they believe they are real. Therefore, it should come as no shock to
us when black young people, the products of an oral culture that is
ever vulnerable to the dominant voice, sink down into reductive
ideas about what they can achieve in this culture.

What must be done is rather obvious. The values of civilized
behavior must be reestablished and defined as fundamentals beyond
race. No one in this society should be encouraged to believe that
excellence, mastery of our national language, tasteful dress, reliabil-
ity, or any of the virtues that bring vitality to a society are the sole
province of the white population. Welfare laws should be changed so
that irresponsible sexual behavior is discouraged by laying the burden of support on the teenage parents, making it in their interest to
use birth control—if, in fact, they have sex at all. That is not as wild
as it immediately sounds. If, for instance, there was a cut-off point—
say, January 1, 1994—when it would become law that each teenage

parent would be responsible for 45 percent of the support of his or her child and receive only 10 percent of that from welfare agencies, and, that if either parent refused, he or she would be incarcerated in a work-study program from which the monies paid would go to the child's support, the problem would diminish quite rapidly. Those who think that absurd have no understanding of human nature.

As an example, let us look at racial attacks in the South from the end of Reconstruction in 1877 until the middle of the 1960s. They were so frequent one would have been led to believe that Southern white men were genetically predisposed to assaulting black males. Yet those attacks, what journalist Jack Germond recalls as a tradition known as "nigger knocking," fell with true deliberate speed when those who committed such crimes were punished. If something that had gone on for ninety years could be largely reined in when the society refused to allow it, even think of it as normal behavior, are we to believe the problem of teenage pregnancy would sustain itself once black kids saw it as truly opposed to their self-interest?

At the same time, it is important to note that in a black youth film like *House Party*, Warrington and Reginal Hudlin did something very important: they made it quite clear that the hoodlum element that is so often celebrated in rap recordings is a bane on the black community, something the vast majority of young black people knows already. That vision must be reinforced constantly, as it was on *Hill Street Blues*, which never failed to show the suffocating social weight extensive crime imposed on so-called minority communities. Those kinds of decisions in mass media are very important because they counter the irresponsibility of those aforementioned intellectuals who champion or attempt to be sympathetic to anything that shocks or shows contempt for the supposed "white middle-class standards" Sybil C. Mobley is so successfully passing on to the students in the Florida A & M business school.

The Mobleys of this nation should be celebrated and nationally recognized, for they are doing the real work. The public schools of this nation should follow her example and they should get whatever monies are necessary to make them the extraordinarily important aspects of democratic success that they once were. We cannot allow our public schools to remain in such bad shape and then wonder why we are having so many social problems. First-class teachers, dressing codes, and the reiteration of the importance of the inner life that comes from intellectual development are fundamental to what we must have if this society is to move in the direction of its greatest potential.

We should also think about fresh ways of recognizing Afro-American authenticity. When those who have triumphed and who represent some of the best the country has to offer are discussed, their ethnic identity is often called into question. But when they are jerks, vulgarians, opportunists, and criminals, race is somehow always important. It is time to have the term "black criminal" reversed so that the defining aspect is the criminality, not the race. After all, during the Wall Street scandal the media didn't say "crooked Jewish stockholder Ivan Boesky" or "another group of Jewish stockbrokers was accused of insider trading." Even John Gotti isn't described as "purported Italian Mafia boss." Of course, part of the problem is that manipulators of racial paranoia such as Al Sharpton, Vernon Mason, Alton Maddox, and Marion Barry will inevitably introduce color as an escape hatch. But they must not be allowed to get away with it. The recent elections in Washington, D.C., prove that those who were so willing to support Barry before the cameras didn't at all express the real feelings of the city. The people didn't go for the color con. Lincoln was right: you can't fool all of the people all of the time.

Examples such as Mobley, such as Washington, D.C.'s, Kimi Gray, such as the list of achievers that Ann Landers presented, and the country's willingness to embrace virtue and heroic engagement from every quarter of this nation on a scale that has no precedent make me quite optimistic. We must get back to the grandest vision of this society, which is that all exemplary human endeavor is the heritage of every person. It is the combination of one's ethnic and human heritage that is the issue. Every ethnic group has a heritage of its own and is also heir to symbols of inspiration as different as Michael Jordan and William Shakespeare. All people are heir to everything of wonder that anyone has produced, regardless of race, gender, and place. Anyone who would deny any person identification with the vastness of that marvelously rich offering of human achievement is not truly speaking as an American.

DO THE AFROCENTRIC
HUSTLE

Our democracy has much in common with the blues and the medical profession; it is founded in tragic optimism, an acceptance of human frailty that is not defeatist. Like that of the blues singer, our American job is to address the universal limitations of life and the foibles of human character while asserting an unsentimental highmindedness (which is the social equivalent of lyricism). Like the doctor, our democracy must face the unavoidable varieties of disease, decay, and death, yet maintain commitment to birth, to health, to the infinite possibilities of life, and to the freedoms that can result from successful research and experimentation. It is, therefore, our democratic duty to cast a cold eye on the life of our policies. We have to dismantle corruption whenever we encounter it and redeem ourselves from bad or naive policy by moving into either fresh experiments or reiterations of things that once worked but were set aside in order to try something else that promised to do the job better. No matter the pressure, we must always have the will to assess our way beyond good-sounding talk by detailing the successes and failures of periodic—and inevitable—innovations, understanding that anybody can be somebody's fool but that the condition of chump shouldn't be accepted as a constant. If we don't assert those democratic duties, we will continue to allow intellectual con artists and quacks to raise their tents and hang their shingles on our campuses, functioning as millstones around the neck of understanding.

That is why the emergence of Afrocentrism makes explicit a continuing crisis in the intellectual assessment of race, history, and culture in our nation. It is another example of how quickly we will submit to visions that are at odds with the heroic imperatives of shaping our society beyond the fragmentation of special interests. Quite obviously, when it comes to skin tone and complaint, we remain ever gullible, willing to sponsor almost any set of conceptions claiming to make fresh judgments of our society. In that sense, Afrocentrism is also a commentary on the infinite career possibilities of our time and helps us recognize that we have evolved a kind of capitalism in which anything capable of proving a constituency can become a profession. Just as almost anything can be sold as art, no matter the lack of facility, almost any kind of an idea can make its way onto our campuses and into our discussions of policy.

In the interest of serving penance and congratulating ourselves for our openness to change, we will accept a shaky system of thought if it makes use of the linguistic pressure points and pleasure centers that allow us to experience the sadomasochistic rituals we accept in place of the hard study and responsible precision that should be brought to the continuing assessment of the human elements that invariably enliven our society. Those human elements arrive either through intelligence and unsentimental invention or through error, corruption, and cowardice. Our desperate goodwill pushes us to pretend that these flagellation rituals have something to do with facing the blue steel facts of unfairness in our country and in the history of the world. The refusal to accept the tragic fundamentals of human life has led to our bending before a politics of blame in which all evil can be traced to the devil's address, which is, in some way, the address of the privileged and the successful. The politics of blame and the idea that there is some sort of potion that can right all wrong or create confidence where there is none so infest our sense of the world that we confuse the momentum of what constitutes inventive civilization with a series of techniques that have fallen upon us from the world of therapy. We don't understand—as did the geniuses who shaped the Constitution—that we must always be so cynical about the protean means of abusing power that we remain ever wary of intellectual and political pollution.

As a movement, Afrocentrism is another of the clever but essentially simple-minded hustles that have come about over the last twenty-five years, descending from what was once called "the professional Negro," a person whose "identity" and whose "struggle" constituted a commodity. James Baldwin became a master of that form, as a writer, public speaker, and television guest, but he arrived before his brand of engagement by harangue was departmentalized. Now, like most areas of specious American ideas claiming to "get the story straight," this commodity sells most as academic pancakes, buttered by the naive indignation of students and sweetened by gushes of pitying or self-pitying syrup.

At its core, though Afrocentrism has little to offer of any intellectual substance, it benefits in spades from the decline of faith so basic to how intellectuals have fumbled the heroic demands of our time. The discontinuity of ideals and actions, the blood spore that is history, and the long list of atrocities committed in the name of God and country have convinced many Western intellectuals that the only sensible postures are those of the defeatist and the cynic. As with the tenured Marxist, the Afrocentrist will use the contradiction to define the whole, asserting that Western civilization, for all its pretty ideas, is no more than the work of imperialists and racists, all seeking an invincible order of geopolitical domination inextricably connected to profit and exploitation, white over black. The ideals of Western civilization and of the democracies that have had to struggle at pushing their policies closer and closer to the universal humanism resulting from the Enlightenment are scoffed at. Where the Marxist looks forward to a sentimental paradise of workers *über alles*, the Afrocentrist speaks of a paradise lost and the possibility of a paradise regained—if only black people will rediscover the essentials of their African identity.

For all its pretensions to expanding our vision, the Afrocentric movement is not propelled by a desire to bring about any significant enrichment of our American culture. What Afrocentrists almost always want is power—the power to define, no matter how flimsy their cases might be. As with most movements built on conspiracy theories, only the sources of argument and the "proof" provided by Afrocentrists are acceptable; all else is defined as either willfully flawed or brought to debate solely in the interest of maintaining a vision of European domination throughout history and within the province of ideas. Thus, the worst insult is that critics are "Eurocentric." Further, when an Afrocentrist is charged with shoddy scholarship, the retort is that his or her purportedly revolutionary work arrives through means of research and assessment outside "European methodology." However superficial that defense might seem at first, there is an important tradition in our country's history that makes it seem at least plausible until closely examined.

One source of our willingness to accept the unorthodox is the fact that Americans have, from the sciences to the arts, as often as not had to intuit the forms that allowed for the purest expressions of the political imagination, the national sensibility, and the layered complexes of our multi-ethnic history as stylized into technological triumph and aesthetic structures. The Gettysburg Address, the Second Inaugural Address of March 1865, the electric light, the phonograph, the motion picture camera, the grammar of film, and the improvisational riches of jazz are the results of, or were inspired by, homemade geniuses such as Lincoln, Edison, Griffith, and Armstrong, all of whom made it obvious that the academy isn't the only path to grand accomplishment. As Americans, we know that the experts aren't always right and that the pieties of provincial thinking, no matter how well grounded in a long tradition, don't allow for the fluid levels of perception necessary to meet the democratic charge of our protean culture.

Jazz itself is very important to understanding this. It has both intuitive geniuses such as Louis Armstrong and Billie Holiday and unarguable intellectuals like Duke Ellington and Dizzy Gillespie. In that sense, it is a perfectly democratic music and one that arrived at its peaks outside of "European methodology." Both the intuitives and the intellectuals were rejected by the academy once upon a twentieth-century time. Those with a simple explanation will attribute all rejections to race, which can by no means be left out of the discussion, but we must remember that the work of white jazz musicians wasn't embraced *either*, no matter its popularity, and that the aesthetic expansions of this century were controversial worldwide. In short, the academic and critical resistance met by jazz musicians was in the same spirit as that met by Picasso, Joyce, and Stravinsky. This is a problem we always encounter when everything is reduced to race, to conflict between white and black—the overall context is lost. We throw out the fact that constant intellectual scrutiny and the moral imperatives of universal humanism are what enlarge the quality of our democracy, not mere ethnic allegiance. When we speak of jazz, for instance, we have to note that the overwhelming body of important aesthetic evaluation came—as it still comes—not from the black community but from the white. This is analogous to abolition, an American movement that had no parallels in Africa.

There is a clear reason why jazz musicians weren't initially accepted in academic circles. Though the intuitives could hear perfectly through harmonic structures, playing the appropriate notes for the specific chords, they didn't use theoretical terminology and would have failed harmony tests at Juilliard. Their gift was the ability to hear artistically, not randomly. The intellectuals would have fared much better, but it took both to make jazz. No matter the training, the intuitives and the intellectuals had one thing in common—the ability to achieve objective, aesthetic logic. What was important about the intuitives wasn't that they didn't study formally, but that their work made sheer musical sense. That is why they were able to so deeply influence jazz intellectuals and the music outside of jazz as well. That is also why the music grew with such speed; it drew depth and breadth from every kind of high-quality talent.

So when Afrocentrists defend low-quality work with assertions about the limitations of "European methodology," they are calling up American traditions of achievement in political thought, technology, cinema, and jazz that have homemade beginnings in common. They ignore, however, the objective quality of those achievements, bootlegging, as Gerald Early points out, the deconstructionist idea that all value comes from the outside, never from the thing itself. The question, then, is one of consensus, not reality. Dismissing objectivity as "culturally determined," Afrocentrists also ignore educated consensus, since education is seen as no more than "Eurocentric indoctrination." They achieve a unified vision not of scholarship but of polemics, maintaining that Western history is an unrelenting cultural war in which the removal of African peoples from the grand stage of history is the goal of an intellectual shadow government. That shadow government is bent on justifying and maintaining subjugation, and when literal subjugation is not the goal, then the goal is imposing upon black people a self-hating idolatry of all that is European or European-derived.

Afrocentrism, then, presents itself as ethnic liberation, a circling of the wagons within the academy, an attempt to impale Eurocentric authority on the dilemma of black intellectual rebellion. At the same time, Afrocentrism—like all of the protest versions of study that are actually extensions of soap operas in which the stars are paid to emote the effects of injustice—is about achieving the respect held for traditional disciplines while not measuring up to the standards of traditional research. Though ever scoffing at the academy, the Afrocentrists want all of the prestige and the benefits that come of being there. So Afrocentrism is also the career path of a purported radical vision that seeks tenure along with those who teach the accepted disciplines. No one should be surprised, since ours is a time in which it is not considered paradoxical to *seek* employment within a structure you claim deserves only contempt. That is because the campaign is at least partially defined as one of evangelical racial recognition, of revealing essential information that travels from the womb of Africa to the tomb of America. What better battlegrounds than the campuses of tenuring institutions?

A central component of the Afrocentric argument is that Egypt was black and that Greco-Roman civilization was the result of its influence. This means that the foundation of Western civilization is African. It is a relatively sophisticated version of Elijah Muhammad's Yacub myth, in which the white man is invented by a mad black scientist determined to destroy the world through an innately evil creature. Why this obsession with Egypt being African and black? First, monuments. There is no significant African architecture capable of rivaling the grand wonders of the world, European or not. Second, there is no written language, no body of thought comparable to that upon which Western civilization has built and developed its morality, governmental structures, technology, economic systems, and its literary, dramatic, plastic, and musical arts.

None of this, however, bespeaks an innate black inferiority, but it was seen that way when there was a need to justify the barbaric, colonial treatment of subject peoples as ruthless campaigns were waged for chattel labor and natural resources. Africans were routinely dismissed as being savages who hadn't the knowledge—or the ability—to build structures such as those that came forward from the Golden Age of Greece, that distinguished the Roman Empire, that made possible castles, great cathedrals, and marvelous bridges throughout Europe. African polytheism was a mark of arrested spiritual development in the face of the majesty of monotheism. So the Afrocentric argument is not with the Western tradition of inquiry and argument, not with the democratic vision of greatness, which is that it can come from *anywhere*, not with the moral watershed of the Enlightenment that underlay abolition; it is a debate with the colonial vision of non-Europeans that has long been under moral and intellectual attack from within Western democracies themselves. Yet none of the Afrocentric arguments—all of which are rooted in nationalism, pluralism, and cultural relativity—are original to Africa; they all have their origins in the Western tradition of critical discourse. This is something that is often missed when discussing this phenomenon. Afrocentrism is absolutely Western, no matter the name changes and costumes of its advocates.

At the same time, Afrocentrism benefits from the obsession with "authenticity" this mongrel nation of ours hides under the bed like a shoe box full of counterfeit lottery tickets bought in the hope of becoming a millionaire one day, regardless of the supposed disdain for the shallowness of the rich. As Constance Rourke observed, we are, as Americans, part Yankee, part frontiersman, part Negro, part Indian—and, I would add, part those Chinese who laid railroad steel and made such an impact on our cuisine; part also those Mexicans who invented the basic roles and skills of the cowboy and whose Southwestern food has recently become national. Yet we have long had difficulty accepting the mixtures that make us Americans, dismissing one sort of "half breed" or another—those with cosmopolitan bloodlines, those from the bottom who act like they're from the top and do it badly, those who reject a circumscribed idea of identity either out of reservations about their backgrounds or out of the ambition to go elsewhere.

More than a few of us yearn for pedigrees, wishing for access to aristocracy through the accumulated majesty of a long family line. If family won't do, then we might snatch the unwieldy crown of race for a coronation that defines the group as innately aristocratic. This has been the appeal of the Ku Klux Klan as well as the Nation of Islam—membership allows one to rise from the bottom and suddenly become part of an elite, the representative of a long historical process of superior individual and group engagement. Poor "white trash," existing at the very bottom of Southern society, becomes "real" white men at KKK gatherings, under white sheets, and when performing violent acts in defense of "white civilization." Negro criminals embrace a distorted version of Islam: they come to understand that the white man is "the devil" and that the black race is the "original" group, parent of humankind. College students swallow Afrocentrism and conclude that all of their problems result from not possessing an "African-centered" worldview, not having been prepared with the kind of education that is suitable to their history and to what their needs are in a racist society.

These are also responses to humiliation. That humiliation is the source of the hysteria that gives a terrible aspect, sort of a ruthless verve, a desire to be done with all niceties, to destroy every element of the structure that has engendered the feeling of oppressive inferiority, or the feeling of helplessly being had, from the first encounter to this very moment. It is an expression of having taken the insults of the opposition too seriously, a retreat from engagement, a dismissing of complexity in favor of the home team, a racial isolationist policy. Essential to the justification for the myopic vision that emerges is a list of atrocities—real, imagined, invented, exaggerated. The great tragedies of the white South were the loss of the Civil War and the humiliation of Reconstruction; for the black nationalist, the great tragedies were slavery, the colonial exploitation of Africa, as well as the European denial of the moral superiority of African culture and civilization, beginning with Egypt. The pinpointing of the problems might be specific to our history, but the ideas beneath their responses evolve from the conflicts between the French and the Germans following the Thirty Years War.

Reading the observations on nationalism in Isaiah Berlin's *The Crooked Timber of Humanity*, one will quickly recognize every idea that we presently hear. When Frederick the Great invited the French into Germany, France cast the longest shadow over Europe, while Germany hadn't really benefited from nor contributed much to the Renaissance. In the sophisticated world of the time, the German input was meager. In today's terminology, Germany was "underdeveloped." The French didn't let the Germans forget that fact and, eventually, a whole school of rebellious thought came into being—attacking French reason, the idea of a single, cultural vision haughty enough to assess all good, all mediocrity, all baseness. Isaiah

Berlin sums up the outraged German thinking and could be summing up Afrocentrism and all of the cultural relativism that has come out of anthropology, where arguments have been raised about conflating low levels of technology with lesser human potential:

> The sages of Paris reduce both knowledge and life to systems of contrived rules, the pursuit of external goods, for which men prostitute themselves, and sell their inner freedom, their authenticity; men, Germans, should seek to be themselves, instead of imitating—aping—strangers who have no connection with their own real natures and memories and ways of life. A man's powers of creation can only be exercised fully on his own native heath, living among men who are akin to him, physically and spiritually, those who speak his language, amongst whom he feels at home, with whom he feels that he belongs. Only so can true cultures be generated, each unique, each making its own peculiar contribution to human civilisation, each pursuing its own values its own way, not to be submerged in some general cosmopolitan ocean which robs all native cultures of their particular substance and colour, of their national spirit and genius, which can only flourish on its own soil, from its own roots, stretching back into a common past.

The success of Afrocentrism is based in the fact that it resonates forward from those arguments, all of which have become part of the process through which democracy has had to assess the very definitions of humanity in order to move beyond prejudice. But we fail ourselves if we give in to the idea that because all human communities have equal access to greatness all cultures are equal. They are not, and the ignorance, squalor, and disease of the Third World make that quite obvious, just as the rise of the Third Reich and the recent slide back into overt tribalism in Eastern Europe prove that no body of ideas or traditions—democratic, capitalist, Marxist—is forever invincible to the barbarian call of the xenophobic wild. Yet if there were not something intrinsically superior and magnetic about the way in which the West has gathered and ordered information and techniques from all over the world—North, East, South, and West—other cultures wouldn't so easily fall under the sway of what Malraux called "The Temptation of the West." The West has put together the largest and richest repository of human value, primarily because the vision of universal humanism and the tradition of scientific inquiry have led to the most impressive investigations into the varieties of human life and the laws of the natural world, slowly winning out against one kind of provincialism after another. It is Western curiosity and the conscience of democracy that have made so many inroads against barbarism within and without.

This is obvious to Afrocentrists, but it is not in their career interests to look with equal critical vision at the West and the rest of the world; it would make things less reducible to soap opera politics, the maudlin elevation of simplistic good and evil—cold, mechanized corruption dominating innocent, communal warmth. Then the real question of bringing together one's ethnic heritage and one's human heritage would come forward. It wouldn't be so easy to manipulate the emotions of administrators and insecure students. The idea of embracing a circumscribed ethnic identity wouldn't be seen as a form of therapy, a born-again order making it possible to cease being an American shackled by a feeling of inferiority and turn into a confident and wise African, albeit one connected to no specific group but bound somehow to Egypt, eschewing the fact that Negro Americans came from the west coast of Africa, whether or not some of the Egyptians were black.

The Afrocentric goal is quite similar to that of the white South in the wake of Reconstruction. Having lost the shooting war, white racists won the policy war and had victory over the Constitution, raising a flag of segregation in which racial interests took precedence over our national vision of democratic rights. The result was that nearly a century of struggle took place in which the Constitution—through blood, thunder, and jurisprudence—took its rightful place as the law of the land, with no states' rights arguments accepted. Knowingly or not, the Afrocentrist responds to the fact that sixties black nationalists and their "revolutionary" counterparts lost the struggle for the black community and failed to overthrow the government; neither the rhetoric and the costumes nor the saber-rattling and the handful of shoot-outs led to intellectual and policy ratification of a separatist's agenda. In the wake of its own submission at a later Appomatox, the Afrocentrist wishes to replicate the success of white segregationists, arguing for an inviolate way of life that precludes the national vision, one that can roll along inside of America but decide which of its laws and principles are worthy of honoring. The policy war is now one for a segregated curriculum, no matter its distance from fact as long as it preaches perpetual alienation of black and white, of the Afro-American community and the national agenda, and as long as it recognizes a "natural" condition grounded in race. This German-derived idea of fusing genetics and cultural vision declares that race transcends place, which means that black Americans are but one segment of an international black world and should shape their allegiances accordingly. All black people are essentially the same, unless their identities have been distorted by Eurocentric influences.

In essence, the Afrocentrist also follows recent precedents and wants a high-grade version of an Indian reservation, or some privileged version of the Indian nations this country now allows to ignore the national vision of human rights if that vision conflicts with tribal views of the world. That Afrocentrist variation on the reservation is then equal to the world of the Southern segregationist, who benefited from the power and prosperity of the country while holding at arm's length anything incompatible with a vision of race as a social absolute. The white Southerner was devoted first and foremost to the advantages of race and tailored the society to reinforce that devotion, grooming and affirming racism at every possible point. By attempting to win the souls of black college students and fundamentally influence what is taught to black children in public schools, the Afrocentrist seeks a large enough constituency to maintain what power now exists and extend it to what segregation once promised—"separate but equal."

Yet the central failure of Afrocentrism is that it doesn't recognize what Afro-Americans have done, which is realize, over and over and often against imposing obstacles, the truest meanings of democratic possibility. Abraham Lincoln recognized this when he told his secretary that, given his point of social origin, Frederick Douglass was probably the most meritorious man in the entire United States. Originating in tribes whose levels of sophistication were laughable compared to the best of Europe, black Americans have risen to the top of every area of our society—as scientists, educators, aviators, politicians, artists, lawyers, judges, athletes, military leaders, and so on. This was not done simply or easily. A cultural phenomenon was at the root of it. Instead of expressing their submission to white people by embracing Christianity, as black nationalists always claim, Afro-Americans actually recognized the extraordinary insights into human frailty that run throughout the Old Testament and the fact that the New Testament contains perhaps the greatest blues line of all time—"Father, why hast Thou forsaken me?" In essence, the harsh insights of the Bible were perfectly compatible with the cold-eyed affirmation of the blues, and from that spiritual and secular foundation an indelibly American sensibility evolved, one perfectly suited for the demands of this society. The result was an incredibly long line of achievement that predates institutionalizing any narrow nationalism that would segregate the world and education into Eurocentric or Afrocentric, and it is the very best argument against all forms of prejudice.

We all deny that tradition of hard-won achievement whenever our conciliatory cowardice gets the best of us and we treat black people like spoiled children who shouldn't be asked to meet the standards that the best of all Americans have met. When the records need to be set straight, set them straight. When there is new information that will enrich our understanding of human grandeur and human folly, make that information part of the ongoing dialogue that gives Western civilization its identity and that has shaped its conscience and its will. But we can never forget that our fate as Americans is, finally, collective, and that we fail our mission as a democratic nation whenever we submit to any sort of segregation that would remake the rules and distort the truth in the interest of creating or satisfying a constituency unwilling to assert the tragic optimism so intrinsic to the blues and to the Constitution.

WHO ARE WE?
WHERE DID WE COME FROM?
WHERE ARE WE GOING?

Whatever I have to say essentially results from two things, my being an American and my being a writer. As an American I am heir to a heritage far more intricate and compelling than most of what is said about it, regardless of the sayer's skin tone or class. As a writer, I am often asked to serve in an army whose purposes I consider dubious and whose leadership I look upon with great reservation. Therefore, like most of us, I am always working to avoid being pinned down between the race game and the human game. If one embraces the race game, one submits to a certain set of limitations; if one champions the human game, the charge yowled through the bullhorn of regimentation is one of naïveté. As we know, there are those who consider that charge too great a burden. I'm not one of them. No matter what I might have felt when younger and more gullible, it no longer pains me to be out here by myself when I have to be, since part of what I consider my duty is adherence to the intellectual claustrophobia any writer seeking an individual sense of life feels when invited—or commanded—into the martial cattle car of presuppositions and clichés.

So what I have to say in this essay is where I think we come from as Negro Americans, where I think we are right now, and where I think we're going. Experience and study have led me to a tragic optimism that allows no interest in idols beyond the reach of human feeling and human failing, neither building nor tearing them down. The assignment given every generation is far more complex—either sustaining or expanding civilization. That chore demands combat with sentimentality, the overwrought failure of feeling. In this eternal conflict, the writer intent on laying demons low raises weapons formed of intel-

*lect and passion against either chaos or the straitjackets tied closed
by Gordian knots of received ideas. In the following piece, my intent is
to look at some things my own way. But, as most writers secretly hope,
perhaps my perspective can rhyme with yours.*

1.

No isolated aspect of the national biography, the epic tale of the
Negro's journey from property to full participation has been at the
center of our perception of the United States for two hundred years,
and the sweep from eloquence to balderdash it has inspired is as
impressive as it is repulsive. The Negro's social evolution called for
the expansion of American democracy and quite obviously set agen-
das for other groups suffering from only partial interplay with the
ideals of the nation. But that struggle was also connected to elemental aspects of the culture's consciousness, for the moment that
the idea of a country separate from the British Empire began to form
most seriously, there was an understanding that this dream nation
of unprecedented democracy had to strain itself against the measure
of the European past and adapt to the conditions of a world part civilized and part wilderness. The debates and policies that arose in
reference to the question of who and what the Negro was in basic
and potential human terms helped let us know just how civilized
we were at any time and just how much of the American wilderness
existed in the very spirit of the country itself.

   The ongoing conflict between civilized vitality and anarchic wildness maintains a special position in the arena of ethnic identity, at
least partially because the question of being an American and a
Negro has held a perplexing and enlightening position in the long
procession of triumphs and tragedies that have given our national
life its vigor as well as the gloom we so often shroud in hysteria. As
an issue, the identity of the Negro remains king-sized because identity is such a dilemma to Americans at large and because the insecurity involved in figuring out what one actually is within the
context of this country too often allows for manipulation and shallow thinking. So many theories and misapprehensions appear, particularly ideas that are as confused as they are lacking in any real

sense of their sources, few of which are domestic and none of any significance from Africa. That may be hard for many to swallow but the cup remains before us. Our history, like the history of the world since the Enlightenment, is either one of adopting, expanding, and acting on the vision of universal humanity or rejecting it, since there can neither be thorough democracy nor a world morality based on the recognition of fundamental commonality without universal humanism.

The upshot is that, in the long process of thinking about our own Negro American identity during these roller-coaster ethnic debates and in face of national policies, we have had to either accept or reject or at least feel somewhat bemused by the cosmopolitan character of our position in this beautiful, elusive, exasperating, and violent culture. That culture includes new features and hair textures, new shades of eyes and skin tones, providing us with physical metaphors for the kaleidoscopic nature of the miscegenated national heart. Said national heart has always been as mysterious as any in history. Yet, in our own time, we should be able to easily see things that might not have been so clear to those predecessors who lived in eras when segregation, racial discrimination, and our own provincialism held in check real and imagined aspects of Negro life. Then our protracted social and psychological war against xenophobic superstition shaped political issues and determined how so many of us carried ourselves when we considered every public image and act proof or repudiation of the ideas that scandalized and beleaguered our part of the population. We might have believed ourselves more innately humble than we actually were, might have struggled against the interior devastation of the propaganda about our inferiority, perhaps even seen ourselves as captured angels socially crucified by moral cretins whose position in the world was backed up by brute force and brute force only.

In the intellectual history of these dilemmas, the idea of a "double consciousness" has been raised in an attempt to explain the nature of the Negro, and that idea has become almost an automatic reference among those who are given to less than hard thinking about what it presupposes and what it purports to explain. Examined seriously, the idea is no more than another aspect of anarchic wildness overgrowing intellectual clarity. Conceived and laid out by W. E. B. Du Bois in the first chapter of his 1903 *The Souls of Black Folk,* the condition somehow disallows consciousness of self and creates an aching split—"this sense of always looking at one's self through the eyes of others, of measuring one's soul by the tape of a world that looks on in amused contempt and pity. One ever feels this twoness—an American, a Negro; two souls, two thoughts, two unreconciled strivings; two warring ideas in one dark body, whose dogged strength alone keeps it from being torn asunder." Further, Du Bois writes, "The history of the American Negro is a history of this strife—this longing to attain self-conscious manhood, to merge his double self into a better and truer self. In this merging he wishes neither of the older selves to be lost. He would not Africanize America, for America has too much to teach the world and Africa. He would not bleach his Negro soul in a flood of white Americanism, for he knows that Negro blood has a message for the world."

Here we have a muddle of ideas that purport to explicate an alienation between national and racial identity, casting them as "warring ideals." That muddle leads us away from the facts of American life and even now puts us at odds with the tasks before the writer who would recognize experience in the rich, mysterious, and disappointing ways that it always arrives. And since all social structures must address the inevitable tragic facts of human activity—folly, corruption, and mediocrity—what is "ideal" about either being an American or being a Negro? We are never really told but are immediately drafted into a bemusing intellectual struggle if we take Du Bois at his word and attempt to explain exactly what the resolution of "double-consciousness" into a "better and truer self" would be, especially when he says of it that all the "longing" circulates around the fact that the Negro "simply wishes to make it possible for a man to be both a Negro and an American, without being cursed and spit upon by his fellows, without having the doors of Opportunity closed roughly in his face."

Even that last derailing of his own train would be fine and dandy if it weren't true that Du Bois invested more in race than a set of surfaces that innately said nothing of the individual. Du Bois, sounding yet another of the many versions of the German nationalism rooted in the thinking of Herder, apparently believed that there was some sort of innate Negro identity, an identity consisting of "Negro soul" and "Negro blood." This identity was in an ongoing struggle with America that made for "two unreconciled strivings." Such a vision includes an acceptance of the sort of dubiousness that Ralph Ellison took on in *Invisible Man* when he argued not with Du Bois but with James Joyce by saying that Stephen Dedalus had the job of creating the features of his own face, not the "uncreated conscience of his race"! Ellison knew that the problem of a race consciousness of whatever stripe negates the question of the individual and imposes some sort of "authenticity" that can trap the single human life inside a set of limited expectations. Ellison was more interested in the incredible variety possible if any nation or any group truly grasps the idea of democracy and frees itself from all ideas that negate the broad human heritage available to enriching interpretation by individuals, no matter what their ethnic origin.

This is not something Du Bois missed completely, for *The Souls of Black Folk*—as a whole—swings back and forth between ideas about racial consciousness and a sense of greater humanity, based in talent and sensibility rather than skin tone. The very confusion of the work as an entity suggests that if anyone had such double vision on the issue that an ongoing set of contradictions resulted, the culprit was Du Bois himself. Du Bois was so inaccurate that he went on in that first chapter to make claims for the effect of his double-consciousness that push aside the fact that Negroes, as Americans, are caught in the middle of the national struggle between high and low, refined and rough, industrious and lazy, articulate and ignorant, moral and criminal, sincere and hypocritical—struggles that the best writers at any point or place in history have always seen as the overriding human tale, no matter the vernacular particulars.

Du Bois, however, so strongly believed race to have the upper hand that he could explain poor workmanship in the determinist terms of his double-consciousness, asserting that "The double-aimed struggle of the black artisan—on the one hand to escape white contempt for a nation of mere hewers of wood and drawers of water, and on the other hand to plough and nail and dig for a poverty-stricken horde—could only result in making him a poor craftsman, for he had but half a heart in either cause." The long tradition of Negro excellence at everything from seamanship to rodeo skills refutes Du Bois and was the crux of Washington's argument against the free ride the skin game gave European immigrants in blue-collar arenas where Negro ability was so well documented that there could be no fair restrictions raised against it. Continuing, Du Bois asserts that because of "the poverty and the ignorance of his people, the Negro minister or doctor was tempted towards quackery and demagogy; and by the criticism of the other world, toward ideals that made him ashamed of his lowly tasks." Neither *The Confidence Man* nor *Huckleberry Finn* would allow one to perceive those problems of opportunism and lack of gumption solely in racial terms. They are central elements of the American dilemma, and the arena of color only puts its variation on them.

By claiming that the Negro who would become a man of letters "was confronted by the paradox that the knowledge his people needed was a twice-told tale to his white neighbors, while the knowledge which would teach the white world was Greek to his own flesh and blood," Du Bois both ignores America's anti-intellectual tradition and prefigures the wrongheaded James Baldwin of "Stranger in the Village," who hands over the highest literary, aesthetic, and architectural achievements of Western civilization to some Swiss ignoramuses by assuming that "the most illiterate among them is related, in a way that I am not." While implying all God's brown chillun got rhythm, Du Bois even figured out a way to choke off the inspiration of the Negro artist: "The innate love of harmony and beauty that set the ruder souls of his people a-dancing and a-singing raised but confusion and doubt in the soul of the black artist; for the beauty revealed to him was the soul-beauty of a race which his larger audience despised, and he could not articulate the message of another people."

Though we should not expect Du Bois to be a musicologist, and though he concludes his book with high praise of Negro music—albeit finally bogged down by a belief in race memory—we cannot allow him to slip by when he presents such a closed argument. Where is there *any* proof of his idea? The developments in religious and secular music, in dance and in comedy, don't support him any more than the work of Ira Aldridge or Black Patti validates his idea that the Negro artist "could not articulate the message of another people." It is also true that composers and performers such as Frank Johnson, the popular and internationally celebrated Philadelphia bandleader of the early nineteenth century, William Henry Lane, the great dancer known as "Juba," James Bland, Scott Joplin, Buddy Bolden, W. C. Handy, Eubie Blake, Ma Rainey, Bessie Smith, Jelly Roll Morton, Sidney Bechet, Will Marion Cook, James Reese Europe, and James P. Johnson had no trouble at all transforming into often innovative aesthetic design what they saw and heard in the Negro community, nor would the legions soon to follow them in show business, where the greatest Negro art appeared. None seemed overwhelmed by the opinions of any outside their own communities. Few artists anywhere in the world ever are; they are too busy interpreting and rendering the obvious and mysterious facts of humanity as they appear before them. But then the impression that Du Bois gives us, finally, is that he had little understanding of art or of the artistic process.

Perhaps as great an error as any in the double-consciousness formulation, particularly as it applies to our contemporary experience, is its missing the possibilities for varied nuance that are intrinsic to national experience. In fact, consciousness is much more complex than double. For instance, if one is Negro and a member of a long-term Boston family, or even one of two generations, that Negro most probably perceives identity in terms of the Eastern Seaboard, the city of Boston itself, of his or her neighborhood, block, class, and religion. That regionalism, which so deeply influences the way one apprehends the world, is true for every part of the country, and it is not neutralized by race. If one knows jazz musicians, for instance, pride of city and of region is basic, and it determines quite often the way in which musicians play. It also determines which musicians they celebrate apart from the figures who shape the national evolution of the musical language. And when gender is factored in, things take on yet another set of attitudes and interpretations of experience. None of these examples denies race as an element but all give a much richer sense of how varied the human dimensions of American experience are, regardless of pigmentation.

Du Bois, who was obviously the result of miscegenation, even opened the way for what would develop into abstract African racialism of the Negro kind when he wrote, "The shadow of a mighty Negro past flits through the tale of Ethiopia the Shadowy and of Egypt the Sphinx." Since American Negroes are from neither

Ethiopia nor Egypt, what we find lurking in the haze of that statement is the eventual idea of Pan-Africanism. Central to Pan-Africanism is a politics of race that assumes some sort of inevitable fairness in
a group possessed of a commonality of complaint founded in struggling against the mutual ruthlessness of colonialism in Africa and the
racial injustice of the Western Hemisphere. It purports a victimized
but essentially royal "we." The brutal totalitarian history of postcolo-
nial Africa should make clear just how naive that idea was, not to
mention the way the corrupt and irresponsible Marion Barry so cyn-
ically called for racial unity and claimed racism in an attempt to
manipulate the black majority of Washington, D. C. before his fall
from power. As one Washington wag put it, "I hate it when niggers
fuck up the motherfucking public trust, then, when they get caught,
pull out their civil rights credit card and charge racism!"

2.

Given the poorly thought-out and contradictory positions of *The
Souls of Black Folk*, why are those ideas that Du Bois presents in
such unconvincing fashion still so popular, even when he isn't
known as a source? Is it because those ideas remove Negroes from
the weights of modern life as they fall upon everyone? Is it because
those turn-of-the-century ideas allow for the avoidance of individual
responsibility and make it possible to see Negroes in something akin
to a pure state, or at least a state in which all is very simply white
and black, Western and Third World, oppressor and oppressed?
Today, given figures like Marion Barry, Uganda's Obote, Ethiopia's
Mengistu, and South Africa's Winnie Mandela, there might even
be nostalgia for those times, or at least for the simpler ideas those
times allowed.

At this point, ninety years since *The Souls of Black Folk*, it is too
late in the world for nostalgia, particularly the nostalgia that is no
more than a cover for the bitterness felt when the homespun idea
of being some sort of a chosen people is smacked by the persistent
complexities of our humanity as we actually live it—in the pitch
before dawn, or in the morning, or in public light, or in the
evening's privacy when the sun goes down and nobody else is

around. We should by now be fully aware of the fact that no ethnic group—or class—is either more or less susceptible to the richest ideas explicit in our social contract or to the steel-quilled sentimentalities of decadence. There is nothing preventing our overt involvement in the forming of either the national identity or national policy, and we also observe ourselves functioning in almost every capacity and exhibiting every inclination from the grand to the gaudy, from the idealistic to the shallow ethnic con delivered in the familiar rhythms of the church or the street, from the brave to the cowardly, from the pure to the absolutely corrupt and disgusting. Like all modern people, we see our humanity stretched across the rack of the media, where the tabloid inclinations of electronic journalism examine people not only with a microscope but also, as Richard Nixon so knowingly observed, with a proctoscope.

That brings us to a challenge demanding intellectual and emotional liberation from the clichés and political recipes that amalgamate into strange combinations of determinism, frantic fawning before fantasies of ethnic origin, and visions of paradise lost. None of those visions is sufficiently fluid or insightful in a time when the quality of our criticism should make it possible to address the riddling manifestations of the human spirit in the truest terms of our own technological moment, in the very same ways that the most uncompromising minds have always had to when struck by the demands and the revelations of the mechanistic age. But in order to do that we need to move toward a freedom that steps beyond the lightweight vision of racial solidarity that discourages the insights expected of serious writers and intellectuals.

Only the deaf, dumb, and blind wouldn't know that we have more than a little candor stuck in our craw. Yet so many of us are afraid of being called self-hating or neoconservative that we function too often like espionage operatives who cannot be expected to tell the truth publicly for fear of being castigated unto unemployment or ostracized as traitors. The serious shouldn't be daunted by any of that and should realize that were a writer like Balzac presently alive and Negro and penning material about, say, Washington, D. C., the charge of self-hatred would quiver with rage from the pages of reviewers. A Negro Balzac would look at the folly, the corruption, and the mediocrity with humor, psychological insight, and an extraordinary sense of place, class, and the particulars of occupation. He or she wouldn't get lost in the problem of public relations, because the tragedy and hilarious absurdity of human life form immutable facts no one with a grounding in the rich irony, criticism, and affirmation of the blues or of literature and true intellectual engagement could miss.

If we are to rise above the mud of racial limitation and put our experience within the largest possible context, we have to go far beyond the overstated racial paranoia and insecurity that can ensure the success that results from guilt-ridden responses. We have to assert our human heritage and understand where we truly come from in intellectual and moral terms, which means that we must be willing to let the dogs bark as our caravan moves by. We ought to know that no fundamental observations about the wonders or the horrors of human beings over the last two hundred years have originated with us, because we came into the discussion of sophisticated modern life very late, with no great African texts—none. This does not mean that the Africans from whom we are at least *partially* descended were innately inferior, which was the argument used to justify the colonizing barbarism of those willing and able to set aside ethics when abroad. Yet much of the periodic hysteria about Africa's role in the beginning of civilization is a response to the fact that our level of intellectual engagement on the grand stage of the world was quite humble throughout our tragic arrival in the Western Hemisphere. No shadowy flitting around Egypt or Ethiopia. That humble level was the result of an environment benefiting neither from great ideas nor from significant technology, an environment as far removed from the bustle of intellectual cultivation as the world of the most distant rural peasantry in Europe.

Any honest examination shows that the indigenous arenas for West African genius were much narrower than the best Europe had developed, were neither in architecture nor the sciences, in literature nor philosophy. To stand up and accept those facts within the context of our American experience is also to celebrate the extraordinary flexibility of human beings, which is the essence of the democratic ideal. After all, so many can recall those classes in which Negroes superbly taught their students math, science, history, literature, art, and so on, preparing them for careers that swept the gamut made possible by the unsurpassed clearinghouse of information that, finally, makes Western civilization the wonder that it is.

Interestingly, the Third World students who do so well at our universities rarely have any problem recognizing the wonder of Western civilization. Unlike too many glib academicians and substandard intellectuals, those foreign students aren't often overwhelmed by the ethnic versions of being parlor pinks. They aren't especially impressed by those among us who lounge like lizards in the comforts of this civilization while pretending our society is inferior to systems in which the opposition is either jailed or murdered, exiled or "reeducated." Those students have had to face the limitations of their own societies and quite frequently aim to work at bringing the poetic values of their traditional cultures in line with the endless vistas of information amassed by the Western world, information that has come from everywhere, which is the essence of the victory against provincialism that allowed for scientific inquiry to supersede the brutalities that usually accompanied exploration or quickly followed it.

But initially because they were in conflict with the moral underpinnings of Christianity, those very brutalities within our American context didn't go down as smoothly as many so given to listing them like to claim. One need not be religious to see that Christianity's access to all was perhaps the earliest vision of universal humanity, a vision that would have indelible impact on the struggle against slavery and the eventual fall of racism written into the policy of law. And however many examples one can find of Christian leaders willing to align themselves with colonial savagery, there is the equally significant fact that from the very moment African slaves were brought into America there were those who debated the issue and saw the business of bondage as antithetical to the ethics of the religion.

Conversely, it is important to face the fact that there was no great African debate over the moral meanings of slavery itself. There is no record whatsoever of an African from a tribe that wasn't being enslaved arguing against the very practice of capturing and selling other Africans. Historians in or out of Africa have found no African William Lloyd Garrisons, no African abolition movement, no African underground railroad, no African civil war in which the central moral issue was slavery. As Nathan Huggins observed in his gloriously unsentimental *Black Odyssey*, "The racial irony was lost on African merchants, who saw themselves as selling people other than their own. The distinctions of tribe were more real to them than race, a concept that was yet to be refined by nineteenth- and twentieth-century Western rationalists."

Even so, the distinctions of race are less important to this argument than the fact that the conception of universal humanity never arrived to thunder against the conventions of those African cultures in the way that it did in Europe as a result of the Enlightenment, when the most extraordinary thinkers sought to identify with others beyond the limits of nationality, language, and the styles that characterized European societies, that made them French or German or British or whatever. The degree and the rate at which this nation's democratic ideals expanded into the furthest reaches of the society were determined by the victories in the conflict between the idea of universal humanity and the prejudicial attitudes that allowed for slavery and racial discrimination. Then, moving outward from Europe and America, the conception of universal humanity has come to take such a position that no contemporary leader of a nation—regardless of his or her *real* feelings—feels free to suggest that any other people from any place in the world are somehow innately inferior. Such political conventions have no precedents in world history and are the result of ideas that have developed since the American and French revolutions, our own Civil War, and the scientific research that has proved universal humanity much more than a good idea, leading to remarkable achievements, such as blood transfusion and organ transplants.

But whenever the question of universal humanity is raised in the context of Negro American history, we must know that figures such as Frederick Douglass, Harriet Tubman, Rosa Parks, and Martin Luther King have a significance far beyond the provincial. Two examples of that significance were observed in the singing of "We Shall Overcome" in Prague and the carrying of placards that read the same words in Tiananmen Square. Seriously examined, those Negro leaders and symbols of resistance to dehumanization have a moral ancestry rooted in the ongoing Western debate that has led to the redefinitions of society and of the rights of the people in it. That Euro-American ancestry, far more than anything from Africa itself, also fuels the combination of ethnic nationalism and evangelical liberation politics domestic Negroes bring to high-pitched rhetoric over the issue of Nelson Mandela and his struggle.

Making these observations, however true, puts one at odds with the patronizing idea that Negroes are somehow so incapable of existing as adults in the contemporary world that they should always be handled like extremely fragile children who must be fed the myths that "make them feel good about themselves." But the world will be what it is no matter how much anyone attempts to pretend otherwise. And what is needed in every sector of our society is a willingness to look at issues for what they are, to recognize the complex dimensions of our identity, to embrace the tradition of the serious writer and intellectual in Western civilization and reject ideas as flimsy as the ones Du Bois puts before us in that first chapter of *The Souls of Black Folk*.

Though some might argue that Du Bois was doing well for his time, I say that we can do much better for our time and for all time. We have behind us, about us, and before us a tale as inspiring and depressing as any in the history of the modern world. It is filled with politics, intrigue, war, romance, humor, victory, loss, illumination, treachery, adventure, despair, epiphanies, and all of the components that traditionally inspire everything from epigrams to epics. If we are to do better by this tale, we must follow the examples of writers as far removed as André Malraux and Ralph Ellison, Thomas Mann and Albert Murray, Lincoln Kirstein and David Levering Lewis, F. Scott Fitzgerald and Charles Johnson, H. L. Mencken and Gerald Early. In order to do so, we have to sharpen our intellectual swords and take to the field, intent on drawing blood as the demons of anarchic wildness bear down on us again, filling the air with dust and expecting to run us over. No matter the numbers of those demons and no matter the thunder of their mounts, as the incremental delivery of work resulting from midnight oil and accurate observation always guarantees, an upset is in the making, one that will result from the unsentimental but affirmative dictates of the miscegenated national heart that has made us all that we finally are and all that we will ever be.

THE B & J BLUES

This talk is preceded by a comment I made from the audience before moving up front to deliver my talk as part of the next panel during a conference on anti-Semitism organized by The Partisan Review *and held in cooperation with the 92nd Street YMHA, New York, in the spring of 1994. There was much fear and trembling about the rising and sulfurous clouds of black anti-Semitism. I heard cap pistols where others heard a wildfire.*

PRELUDE

I just want to say that I think that the problem of black anti-Semitism is nowhere near as large as people think it is. I want to say very clearly that I don't think you can evaluate the nature of a particular community by how particular professors relate to their students in what has been called "victim studies courses," because as often as not, those professors are there on the basis of very specious ideas held by the institutions themselves. And they often maintain their positions primarily because "victim studies" on campus is about the ransoming of campus order. So what college campuses do is, they say, "Well, how much money will it cost us to keep the black students' feet off the president's desk this year? Oh, two or three hundred thousand? Give it to them. How much to keep the homosexuals' feet off? Two hundred thousand? Give it to them. How much to keep the women out? Three hundred thousand? Give it to them." That's how it actually works. Now what happens oftentimes, you'll end up with charlatans like

Leonard Jeffries, who was replaced by a black professor who discovered that for twenty years Jeffries had done no research, he had written nothing, nor had anybody else in his department. But when Jeffries went to court, he had letters from the white man saying, "Yeah, you're doing a good job, Len. Doing a good job, Len." Now as far as I'm concerned, he should have won forty million dollars from them. They should have been made homeless; the entire administration that made the decision should have been put on videotape and those videotapes should have been sent to every American university, and it should have said to administrators, "This could be you."

PART 1: THE MICKEY FINN AND THE MINSTREL FACE

The connection between Negroes and Jews is one that has been nearly exhausted in discussions, whether serious or anti-Semitic. More often than not, the talk circles around abundant clichés of mutual difficulties with societies spiritually afflicted by prejudice. This is true, but far too simple. The coming to power of Christendom led to Jews being demonized by the dark and poisonous side of the udder from which drips also the milk of Western civilization. So if someone somewhere in the world takes Horace Greeley's suggestion and goes West, culturally, the trip might lead to as much darkness as light, for our prejudices are as much of who we are as is our high-mindedness. For instance, one can be sure that when Commodore Perry arrived in Japan a hundred and fifty years ago, he didn't sit in paper houses sipping tea and listening to complaints about Jews.

Since then, however, the Mickey Finn of anti-Semitism has been squeezed into those Far Eastern cups, which is why Japanese businessmen show themselves as most unfortunately Western when they speak of Jewish conspiracies in the business world, not acknowledging that the Japanese dependency on Middle Eastern oil has nothing to do with Jews, not acknowledging that there are no meaningful numbers of Jews in Japan. They are late arrivals in a very old tradition. Neither Negro-Americans nor black Africans have had the ongoing demonic role imposed on them that Jews have. Most of the antiblack justifications for unfair play came into our American lives

long after John laid down the lousy laws about Jews in the New Testament. Slavery, of course, transformed Africans who were considered livestock into Americans. As Americans, Negroes have also
been Christians—a commonality held with both the whites who so
often made their lives so hard and the whites who saw in the same
Christianity the moral reasons to support revolt against the dictates
of slavery and against the later racist ideas put into segregated policy.

But there is a strong connection between Negroes and Jews in our
society, and it has played itself out quite profoundly in show business, for one, where exchanges took place that are rarely discussed
with any accuracy. In that arena, which has had such a large influence on our national sensibility, the most important thing about the
relationship of Negroes and Jews to American music and popular
entertainment is the fact that the Negro has long been a symbol of
pure Americana. What is never observed about, say, the early film
The Jazz Singer is that the convention of blackface served as a way of
entering big-time American show business. It was a mask that freed
the Al Jolson character in the film, Jakie Rabinowitz, of his Eastern
European identity. He became Jack Robbins. But, if you recall,
when the film's Jakie was an immigrant kid *without blackface*, he
performed in bars doing Negroid dance and song routines, shuffle-
dragging and sliding his body for the entertainment of afternoon
drinkers. In fact, if you look at a good number of successful Jewish-
American entertainers of Jolson's generation, you will discover how
the mask of the Negro, even so insultingly simplified, helped them
through the hoop of popular art. However racist, the blackface, the
rolling eyes, the physical rhythms, and the long march of expressions from comedy to pathos formed a means of instruction. This
was the most immediate way of learning how to express the rhythms
and timbres of American feeling.

I would suggest that what is most important about the parallels
between Negroes and Jews is the tragicomic sensibility, as it has
translated itself into music, dance, comedy, and drama. From the
Old Testament's tragic vision of human frailty, from the Passion of
Christ and perhaps the greatest blues line ever written, "Father, why
hast Thou forsaken me?" Negroes fashioned one side of their vision:
perhaps from the incantational percussion of Africa, and what I can
only call a heroic recognition of the vibrance at the center of exis-

tence, Negroes have transmuted pathos and tragedy into exultation through the rhythmic lyricism of swing. And if there is anything we can recognize when we speak of Jews, especially the Russians who came into American show business, it is a very definable and unusual quality: a cynical joie de vivre—in short, another kind of tragicomic sensibility.

Finally, for their part, I believe that Jews, because they were neither black nor Christian, were perhaps able to sense the connecting elements of the national soul, and to produce work that spoke with democratic accuracy to Negroes and whites. This, of course, is something that Negroes did as well. And when Negroes and Jews stared one another in the eye aesthetically, I can only say what Count Basie said of Lester Young, a single syllable that compresses the explosive vitality of this congress of form and human feeling: "Wow!"

PART 2: BLUES FOR TODAY

In the contemporary world there is much concern about the purported spreading of the Jew-baiting blues by people like Louis Farrakhan. Many think this indicative of the fact that something is going on in black America. As with most ideas about Negroes that arrive through mass media and through the short-order pulse-takings of our academies, this stuff is overrated and no more than the kind of hysteria that anti-Jewish feeling always whips up. While the Crown Heights riot burned itself into the New York night, there were all kinds of lamentations about increasing racial hostility in this town; but when a local news reporter was finishing up her television spiel with the hand-me-down phrase "Reporting from embattled Crown Heights," a number of black kids who were standing around interrupted her and observed that they didn't know who those violent people were in their streets every night. The kids said those people didn't live in the community, in the neighborhood, and were coming from somewhere else. They themselves had lived around Jews all their lives, these young people told the television reporter, and made it clear that they got along well with them. When Pete Hamill went out into the Crown Heights streets he corroborated that fact: the bottle throwers and name callers were from outside the community. In other words, it was a setup, just as the Washington Heights riot was rigged by drug dealers to make it clear to the police that when one of their fellow traders in addictive powders went down under a lawman's bullets, they would go to the streets. There *are* divisive forces out here, but they represent tips, not icebergs. For all the attention, the ranks of the Nation of Islam don't swell. They have never swelled.

One central reason for this is that Negro-Americans are not puritanical and have never been attracted to religious orders that frowned upon joy. The members of the Nation of Islam are a dour bunch—far too dour to ever appeal to more than a cult faction of the black American community. Louis Farrakhan, Khalid Muhammad, and Chicago's Steven Cokely are applauded for the way they shake an anti-Semitic Mickey Finn, but few step up to the bar. What we really have, and this is also connected to the denial of the murders of European Jews, is the desire for recognition through the outrageous. This cannot be disconnected from the fact that our society has celebrated for far too long the romantic idea of rule breaking, not the rich complexity of mediating between the spirit of the law and the letter of the law—a theme that, as Peter Stowell observes, John Ford addressed so brilliantly in his films about the challenges at the center of American democracy. Our democracy is founded on a high-minded conception of commonality and individuality, not narcissism and perpetual alienation. But if we accept alienation as a painful iron mask no one can see through and through which we cannot express our souls, we too often mistake hostility for the highest expression of honesty, and vulgarity for vitality. At least since the loss of faith that arrived with black power and followed Vietnam and Watergate, we have failed to prove, over and over and over as all civilizations must, what the burdens and wonders of civilized behavior and discourse really amount to—one of which is standing up to irrationality, not worshiping it as the deformed child of encounter-group therapy we pat on the head and call beautiful.

Those black kids who invite nutville Nation of Islam types onto their campuses are involved in a political version of rock and roll, a way of being outrageous and driving the adults up the walls. In this case, the adults are the whites and the black academicians who have faced the interwoven nature of our American identities. When the academic commodity sales of alienated futures resulted in such heavy trading on campuses, many were afraid to accept their American identities. They want to chuck the hyphen and what comes behind it. They want to be ethnic students first and foremost, their own versions of what they think Jews are. What we are talking about is the unflagging certitude we associate with the most strong-minded Jews. We are talking about the invincible proof of the power of the written word, the text that has carried Jews through century after century. This results, unfortunately, in some places, in what I call "oppression envy" on the part of those who don't have the great tales encoded with the level of insights into the human soul that beget the high understandings of our strengths and of our weaknesses; that tell us, as the Bible does, of the ominous responsibilities of power; that tell us, over and over, how even the most enlightened can fall to brutal humiliation. Even for all the inroads into our lives of the martial arts and the various schools of meditation and Buddhism and cuisine have had, adding an Eastern set of spices to the goulash of our American culture, the heaviest weight still comes from the Judeo-Christian heritage.

Oppression envy is mostly connected these days to World War II. It was the crucifixion of Jews in modern Europe that saved us from having too much confidence in civilization. It was a heavy tab, a tab paid in blood and one we must always remember, because what happened to the European Jews is humbling. We have to face how easy it is to mistake a toilet seat for a throne and slide down into the spiritual feces of xenophobia most foul. Genocide, without a doubt, is xenophobia most foul. Perhaps the history of the world is the history of how societies address xenophobia; to what degree they fear or persecute the Other, welcome the Other, learn from the Other. But the xenophobia that cuts at the flesh and souls of Jews is not one that comes of being unfamiliar. It is a protean xenophobia: if you hate books, you can hate Jews; if you hate business, you can hate Jews; if you hate the law, you can hate Jews; if you hate crime, you can hate Jews. For the anti-Semite, Jews exist in an endless department store that sells only resentment, paranoia, and irrationality. Because the Jew is both Moses and Jesus, we might be talking about a remarkable tale of the Oedipal impulse.

I want to conclude by saying that I have, from my experience in the world, absolute confidence in the fact that we will come through all of this; that these various yahoos and demagogues and rednecks of one hue or another will periodically bark at the gates; they will sometimes ring the bell; they may even be able to get past the doorman and defecate on the floor. But we'll clean the floor, believe me, we'll clean the floor. I don't think that we are doomed to sink down into a Babel of alienation between one group and another, which so many people today see as the fate of America. I think, finally, that when we look at almost any group of immigrants we see that there is a centripetal force to the American sensibility that pulls people in. I remember once I was sitting next to some people from either Iran or Iraq, and they lived in New Jersey, and they were the grandparents of two teenage girls who were sitting behind them. Now, the two grandparents were dressed in formal, traditional Muslim clothes, they had gotten a kosher meal—they didn't like that word too much, but they ate it—and while they were eating behind them were their two equally, I guess, Muslim granddaughters. Both of them had on extremely tight jeans, tight T-shirts with no brassieres, and tennis shoes. They both had Walkmans, and they were in the back moving to the music. Now, that perhaps didn't mean that they didn't pray five times a day and embrace the invincible truth of Allah, but it does show that they also had been pulled into the American sensibility, into American culture.

I think that what the Italian filmmaker Sergio Leone said about America is extremely important for all of us to understand. He said that what American film and entertainment did was to create an international language because it had to speak across such a greatly complicated democratic mass, and that was the reason why it not only spoke so well to all Americans, but spoke so well to people around the world. And I think that, as we come in contact with one another, whatever our backgrounds are, the charisma of humanity will neutralize most of the irrational stuff we are beset by at this particular time. I have often heard people say that our fates are all the result of decisions made in smoke-filled rooms, that there are unflagging prejudices that will never give in, but one of the things that always comes to me is the fact that Frederick Douglass used to give addresses at a time when there was no knowledge of blood plasma:

none of the scientific knowledge we have used to neutralize most racist ideas was available. Douglass would speak to people who were rather curious to see what this perhaps half-human person had to say, and oftentimes by the end of his address the entire room would be abolitionist. This is something that took place over a hundred and fifty years ago. I don't think that America has lost that spirit at all; I think that there are storm clouds that appear, but I think we're going to get through it. And to close out, I have to quote Louis Armstrong. He said: *Bop bi da, dop di da, dop di bop a do di di di bop bi bop bi bop bi da.* That's Louis Armstrong on George Gershwin's "It Ain't Necessarily So."

UNITY '94 BLUES,
PART I

As a panelist at Unity '94 in Atlanta, I was again struck by the hiring problems of our culture. The mission statement made clear that the Asian American Journalists Association, the National Association of Black Journalists, the National Association of Hispanic Journalists, and the Native American Journalists Association (which together represent more than six thousand journalists) consider themselves to "have formed a historic union—Unity '94—to inspire and motivate the nation's media companies to fully embrace diversity." They have "united to accelerate change within the media industry."

The central position "encourages media to hire and promote journalists of color as part of an effort to make U.S. newsrooms more reflective of the nation, including its 25 percent minority population." The organizations of Unity '94 wish "to improve media coverage of people of color, to dispel stereotypes and myths and to increase appreciation, sensitivity and understanding of other cultures—among ourselves, all of media and the community at large."

All of that is fine and dandy, at least rhetorically. The problem with percentages is that those using them to twist the arms of the executives in the business world give the impression that the answer to our dilemmas in the world of media will be statistical hiring. I have been out of my mother's womb too long to believe that. A richer variety of backgrounds will not automatically give a more insightful base to the reporting and the ongoing assessment of our local and national concerns unless all of those hired are either first class or have the potential to become so.

What statistical hiring *will* do is allow those of us trapped in racial and cultural simplemindedness the opportunities we need to discover the human variations of sensibility, intelligence, talent, and skill within every group. Having spent the early years of my life in a blue-collar black neighborhood and in a number of interracial situations, I discovered long ago that no group has dominion over virtue or the vices of spiritual pollution. We are all dogged by the hounds of folly, corruption, and mediocrity.

That is why I don't assume that hiring an Asian or an American Indian or anybody else automatically increases the quality of writing about minorities in this country. I also don't assume that leaving it all to the usual suspects of racial exclusion is the tastiest answer out of the oven. I think the problem we face comes down to an old Southern adage, "Don't worry about the color of the cow: see if the milk is sweet or sour."

One of the reasons I'm sure the question is quality, not color, not merely being "a journalist of color," is that I was riding on an airplane to Kansas City some ten or twelve years ago and was seated next to a kid from New York's Chinatown. He was being sent to work in one of his family's restaurants because the call of the street had been too much for him and his life and future were endangered by his gang activity.

As we talked, the kid told me how corny the movie *The Warriors* had been, because the makers didn't really understand the gangs in Chinatown. But he was in awe of a story New York journalist Mark Jacobson had done, because he had everything right. Jacobson found out how the Chinatown gangs worked, the way the turf was laid out, and who ran what. His was first-class investigative journalism.

That is what I think we have to shoot for in this land of riotous riddles and secret societies. When the hiring pattern is free of prejudice or is given to taking risks in order to develop talent, the real problem is getting rid of someone from a minority who fails to do the quality of work necessary to maintain the identity of the company. The risks are self-serving charges of racism or sexism, but they come with accepting the real duty of the media, which is to provide Americans with the facts and the richest insights that can be drawn from them. If that duty is ducked, the media may become more multicolored but the democratic eloquence our times demand will remain largely absent.

UNITY '94 BLUES,
PART II

There are still things on my mind about Unity '94, the conference of so-called minority journalists that was held in Atlanta recently. While complaints were rattled off about the media images of those who are neither white nor privileged, not much was made of how normal it is for local and national television news to hire anchors and reporters of many decidedly different backgrounds, races, sexes, and regions. We see them hosting talk shows and we read their bylines. They are part of the human quilt so basic to our identity and exist in positions of high visibility in the electronic hustling of opinions and products, soup to soap.

Consequently, the redoubtable documentation of endless camera crews and photographers makes clear some specific things about our recent past and our confused, manipulative, and too often self-pitying present moment. Whenever, for instance, footage from the Eisenhower or Kennedy years is shown, we are quite aware of how little those gathered under the pretentious term "people of color" had to do with the reporting and the public assessment of national and international life.

They were few and far between, doing their jobs under the sort of scrutiny laboratory animals get, part of experiments bent on finding out if the public was "ready" for them. As with all who must labor under the pressures demanding exceptional discipline, stoic resolve, and psychological resilience, some fell by the wayside, incapable of handling it. They suffered the combat fatigue of the workplace and the spotlight. Their career corpses became either flagstones or obstacles.

Now is another time. Things have changed to such a large extent that the rhetoric of those who seek greater present influence on media is far out of line with the reality of metamorphoses that is at the heart of the national matter. This is not to say that there isn't much business yet to be taken care of with the "white males" who are so regularly demonized that their race and gender now constitute the two crooked lines of a spiritual swastika. But it is time to own up to victories, which are many. There is, however, a resistance to saying, "We came, we saw, we conquered and are *still* conquering."

As I said on a panel in Atlanta, the audience of more than three thousand men and women in print and electronic journalism who were 99 percent not white males proved that dogged exclusion was a thing of the past. Their very presence proved that. So did their incomes.

There was a shocked hostility to that observation, which I am sure is the result of two things. One is the way the victim trump works in the career game. The other is the fact that there is a disease felling too many middle- and upper-middle-class members of designated minority groups. It is a discomfort with success so powerful that those suffering from the sickness must pretend that they are still victims in order to dodge the feeling of guilt for not being down there with the rest of the tribe.

While nearing or breaking into six figures, this kind of person waves the bloody shirt of racism, even questions the value of success, and dismisses personal achievement, publicly and privately wondering if it was all worth the sweat and the aggravation. Daily, they slink back to their fine homes in town or in the suburbs, suffering from the slings and arrows of white male power. In the worst cases, this evolves into an ethnic version of being a parlor pink, an Americanization of the well-to-do European Marxists who enjoyed all of the privileges of democracies while calling for their destruction.

This way of handling things has two serious catches. The white people know it's a con and laugh about it privately, but the young black and Hispanic kids who are afraid of "selling out" often do far less than their best because excellence is now color coded. One should always keep a hot poker ready for the backside of injustice, but it is important to polish the crown when you've damn well earned it.

BLACK POWER
REDUX BLUES

No matter how much one had read about the controversial "leadership summit" held by the NAACP in Baltimore recently, seeing and hearing in full all of the opening addresses on C-Span last weekend gave a much richer sense of what happened and what the troubles of our moment are.

Speaker after speaker used the cadences of the Negro church, even if representing black sororities, but the words were less glorious than the rhythms; it was easy to hear a body of impractical ideas that began arriving with the canonization of Malcolm X, who is the Elvis Presley of race politics, a pop black power icon mistaken for a serious thinker.

It was during Malcolm X's tenure with the Nation of Islam that woofing at white people, making windbag threats, and embracing racist Negroes in the interest of "unity" became tests for the gullible. With his death, racism was redefined as a form of integrity, something beyond white control. Brutal alienation from so-called white America was supposedly the ultimate fact, which meant that unrestrained hostility was the purest form of honesty. If one didn't, in some fundamental way, express heated animosity toward whites and toward America, mixed in with some abstract love of a fantasy Africa, then one was obviously hindered by a "slave mentality."

That is why NAACP executive director Ben Chavis made so much of not being influenced by "outsiders" and could embrace a political cactus by introducing him as "the eminent, his holiness, freedom fighter Louis Farrakhan." Farrakhan, who believes that white people are a race of "devils" created by a mad and bulbous-headed black scientist six thousand years ago, quickly went into his stuff.

He promised to lead boycotts against any in corporate America who ceased funding the NAACP because of its association with him and snorted that all black people who thought he should be avoided ought to be "defrocked," voted out of office, and sent to lie down with the slave masters they love. Clearly, if one thought it foolish to politically associate with such a man, one was only a puppet of the contemporary plantation.

The central problem is cowardly—or kamikaze—doublethink. Farrakhan is accepted into the fold by people who backed sanctions against South Africa because its social policy was racist, and who made much of the cynical way in which Republicans bedded down with the Christian right and the anti-abortion movement, capitalizing on their numbers for more votes.

Yet meeting with Farrakhan is justified "because he has too large a following to ignore" and "because he draws so many young people when he speaks." Why? They go to hear him for the same reason teenagers go to hear the most obnoxious rock bands—to soak themselves in self-righteous alienation and muddled outrage.

Do these large numbers join the Nation of Islam? No. Why? Because it is a puritanical cult that very, very few of those Negroes wearing their caps sideways and backward, their tennies untied, and their pants nearly sliding off could stomach for more than a few hours in an auditorium. They will never trade their decadent, all-American hedonism for a religious cult opposed to partying, alcohol, promiscuity, dancing, pork, and sports. And those successful Negro women shouting and clapping for Farrakhan in Baltimore wouldn't think a second about accepting the position females have in his cult.

What we presently need from civil rights organizations is a truly new agenda—independent monitoring of social programs and public service, favoring neither Republicans nor Democrats. We need to have accurate assessments of the specifics of success and failure in public education, law enforcement, the reduction of teenage pregnancy, and so on—yearly reports, region by region, major city by major city, of how well our taxes are being used.

Such reports, free of political cant, would identify those who are

achieving victories against the ravages of our moment, separating
the wheat of accomplishment from the chaff of political promises
and theory. Quite soon, those reports would influence elections,
allocations, and programs, and inspire innovational policies, allowing us to attack the corrupt and the ineffectual elements that under-
mine the handling of our national problems.

WEE WEE
WEE BLUES

The stuck-pig squeals of Benjamin Chavis just before and following the loss of his NAACP executive director's crown help illuminate the contemporary mudholes of naive race politics. Presenting himself as another of the black freedom fighters bent on "independence," Chavis felt that his fall was the result of "right wing Jews" and "reactionary" Afro-Americans. He could, therefore, avoid the facts of his own bad judgment, the impolitic, paranoid irrationality that grumbles backward to Malcolm X and the black power era.

The central problem is a very false idea about "independence." The apolitical and would-be radical black nationalist believes that there is a "black agenda" and that such an agenda should be followed, no matter whose toes are stepped on and what others think about it.

This is an extremely adolescent idea within the context of democratic politics. That's what I said: *democratic politics.* For all of its problems, America *is* a democracy, and policy is the result of many things—pressure groups, public sentiment, lobbying, media focus, and so on. No one or no group intent upon influencing national policy is ever "independent" or is ever free to associate with or embrace any group or individual whose vision is perceived by the general public as offensive, prejudiced, or opposed to the ideals of the country at large.

The Civil War and then the Civil Rights Movement ended any ideas about the politics of racial "independence" in this blood-stained democracy. The South tried secession first, which led to an overwhelming military defeat. Following Reconstruction, it jimmied the Constitution out of local practice under the banner of states' rights—"our Southern way of life"—and got away with a racist double standard for ninety years. The civil rights movement, essentially a policy war, marched the Constitution into Dixie and abolished the double standard.

What Chavis seems to misunderstand is that the same rules that now apply to white politicians, North or South, apply to him. No white politician taking the position that Chavis did on the kind of live wire in the swimming pool that Louis Farrakhan is would be surprised when his power and respectability were shocked to death in the water. If Bob Dole or Tom Foley decided that David Duke was doing something for the self-esteem of poor whites and said it was nobody's business if a highly visible white politician associated with the air-brushed racist, either man would find out something about white political "independence."

The political tasks of a group that constitutes less than 20 percent of the population are even more complex than those of white politicians and demand a much higher level of sophistication than we have become accustomed to in so-called black leaders. Since Chavis is guilty of financial misconduct and doesn't know the difference between a racist cult leader and someone of actual political significance, it is very good that he is gone.

But there is still the problem of getting to the bottom of the issue of race, which is making clear that elevating public schools and their students to high-quality performance, greatly reducing teenage pregnancy, and removing violent criminals from dominant positions in the streets constitute more than some favor to black victims or reparations for terrible marks on the racial report card.

Such actions are essential to the quality of national civilization and to dealing with the bottom line of our time, which is how well America will compete for the international appetites of worldwide consumer markets. All Americans are potential players in this new kind of team concern, where first-class products, sterling workmanship, and the disciplined creativity of well-trained workers will determine who gets what in the world economy that transcends the rhetorical whining of professional victims.

This is a battle far, far bigger than race, and the civil rights leadership should make that clear. To let Afro-American communities decay and remain oppressed by criminals is to sacrifice far too many troops in a war where quality is the highest form of ammunition.

DUMB BELL BLUES

In reading a recent article about Derrick Bell, I was taken by what I assume is his version of the position Edward Said discusses in his new, short book, *Representations of the Intellectual*. The book is a collection of six half-hour addresses Said delivered for the BBC, his chance at the audio spotlight established by Bertrand Russell in 1948 and called the Reith Lectures.

In his introduction, Said writes about the disputational role of the intellectual that he most favors and cites Malcolm X and James Baldwin as men who "define the kind of work that has most influenced my own representations of the intellectual's consciousness." He goes on to take the position that Derrick Bell must surely agree with: "It is a spirit in opposition, rather than in accommodation, that grips me because the romance, the interest, the challenge of intellectual life is to be found in dissent against the status quo at a time when the struggle on behalf of underrepresented and disadvantaged groups seems so unfairly weighted against them."

Bell is a law professor and legal scholar whose work is either praised in public or dismissed as mediocre in private, dependent on whether the occasion is one demanding convention or is safe enough to allow honesty to take on the invisible form of words spoken off the record. Bell's reputation has been built upon squawking about the supposed inevitability of racism. According to him, black Americans will never get a fair chance because the racist tattoo on the white sensibility is irremovable.

The grandstanding position he took a few years ago was a signal example of what he has become famous for. Bell left the Harvard Law School in a huff, refusing to teach because there was no tenured black female on the faculty. Harvard eventually fired him, which I respected in the same way that I did the producer of *Miss Saigon* for refusing to submit to racial casting—only Asians should play Asians.

I thought Bell's position ridiculous for a few reasons. Implicit is the idea that black females cannot identify with achievement across color lines, that unless they see someone who looks like them, well, they just can't believe it possible to make it out here in the snow hills of this perpetually racist winter. If that were the case, no black achievement of any sort would have ever taken place unless it was based on replicating some practice held over from Africa.

I was once on a panel with the literary giant Ralph Ellison that also included Bell and a number of the dinosaur dragons from the sixties. Bell had one thing seriously in common with the compatriots Elaine Brown and Stokely Carmichael: what once seemed like flame-throwing ideas to the naive were revealed in the hard light of historical complexity as no more than bluster and wet matches.

Bell took the position that there had never been a time when anything had happened in the interest of black Americans that wasn't the result of white people's acting in their own interest. I took the position that as a supposed scholar of American law, he should have known that the intellectual and political engagement of Afro-Americans had redefined every element of the social contract, expanding outward what had been a formerly restrictive vision of law and democracy. Bell, caught dismissing a noble tradition of difficult accomplishment, said that he never thought he would find himself on a panel agreeing with me and admitted to having overstated the case.

There it is. I accuse Bell and his ilk of being, fundamentally, defeatists, people who accept high positions of success, then tell those below them that *they* don't have a chance. Pay no attention to *me*: the white man wouldn't budge for *you*.

Edward Said is right that the intellectual has a job of high honor when deciding to go against the status quo—if, I must add, that status quo is out of line and unfair. The case of Derrick Bell is one of selling out to hysterical alienation by so overstating the case that the issue is smudged beyond recognition. But, after all, wasn't that a specialty of Malcolm X and James Baldwin?

ANOTHER LONG DRINK OF
THE BLUES: THE RACE CARD
IN THE SIMPSON CASE

This was published in the Los Angeles Times *on July 31, 1994, long before the formal murder trial began and long before sustained media involvement had made the case parallel in attention to the Vietnam War or the Watergate hearings. I include it here because this was the first piece that looked at the Simpson case in light of the many things about our society that it brought into view. The all-American reality of the context, which stretched out in so many directions, was made clear in this short essay. For perhaps the first time in my career, all of the predictions came true, regardless of the many twists that were beyond not only my imagination but everyone's.*

With the O.J. Simpson case, we are allowed another chance to recognize how fallacious is the idea that black Americans are some perpetually excluded group forced to watch the parade of the society from behind a barbed wire fence. If anything, the Simpson story is further proof of the fact that black Americans are at the center of our national tale, functioning both as flesh and blood movers and metaphors in the ongoing democratic debate that redefines our policies and our attitudes toward our political, professional, and intimate lives.

The impact of Afro-American culture and the Civil Rights Movement has touched us everywhere, from the dance floor to the senatorial debate. In professional athletics, Curt Flood was the martyr who led the way to the presently acceptable idea of free agentry, destroying his career in the process. Army sergeant Perry Watkins was the first homosexual that I became aware of who was openly willing to take on the military. Now, because of the Simpson case, the ravages of domestic violence have risen into high media view, just as deep questions of sexual harassment came with the charges Anita Hill laid on Clarence Thomas.

So it is impossible to discuss issues of freedom and fair play with any seriousness and not recognize the ways in which black Americans have indelibly influenced our attitudes and policies. It is also impossible to pretend that victimization has not become a growth industry. We make most-favored-victim laws, we hire separatist boneheads onto our university faculties, we tailor our history to self-flagellating theories, experience the national Peeping Tom craze for geeks on talk television, and slip through our problems on the snake oil of recovery experts.

That is why the Simpson case is so loaded. It is fused to a complexity that will play itself out in everything from eloquence to lunacy, high-mindedness to opportunism, as the trial progresses. The charges against him, and what we think we now know about his world, put us smack dab in the middle of our schizophrenic suspicion of privilege and our "wish for kings," as Lewis Lapham calls it. Simpson's American dream wealth was made possible by the gold rush aspect of our society that we most often see in the worlds of popular entertainment and drug dealing.

Though he had an objective talent that separated him from the stars of pop music and movies, Simpson moved from the back of the bus to the wheel by playing a boy's game, which meant that he excelled in the excessively celebrated adolescent world of sports. His generosity as an athlete was displayed when he brought the offensive line that blocked for him to his locker room interviews, clarifying the importance of the team to his achievements. He was the strong, nearly silent type, low-keyed and marvelous at his game.

With the blood-encrusted gore of the murders and the inevitable snooping into the darker sides of his intimate life, Simpson joined the long line of figures whose private lives have a dissonant relationship to their public images. Though race wasn't discussed at first, there was always a media code. The murdered ex-wife was endlessly referred to as "the beautiful, blonde Nicole," while he was never described as "the handsome, brown, woolly-headed O.J."

Some dismiss her description as typical mass media sexism of the sort reserved for blondes and redheads. They are partially correct because the blonde has had an unnaturally high position in our erotic iconography since the peroxide explosion of the thirties. But it is also true that her color was underlined in code because she was half of an interracial couple living in a world whisper-close to those deep-dipped in the decadence and melodrama of upper-class soap operas. Finally, there must be, in the wake of so many black brutes in the popular work of writers like Alice Walker and Toni Morrison, the question of whether this is what any woman should be prepared for from one of *them,* rich or poor, famous or nameless.

In a court of law, none of these things should matter. It would be pretty to think so, but once it is possible to play the race trump in a city that has the recent history of Los Angeles, one shouldn't be surprised to hear the card loudly smack the media table. Still, the ways in which race, class, sex, and ideas about racial allegiance can influence potential jurors, law enforcement, and the legal process itself are much more complicated than their surfaces would suggest.

Because of affirmative action, whites seem more bothered when executive positions are held by mediocre or incompetent black people than by their white parallels; the sustained, murderous barbarism of black street crime strains past tolerance to simmering hostility within the most exasperated; and the flippant hedonism of the worst upper-class black party animals instigates envy and resentment, even in certain police officers.

That is why the dirt on Detective Mark Fuhrman won't be taken lightly. His alleged hostility toward Mexicans and "niggers" in 1983, his supposed membership in a group presently opposed to female police officers, the whispered allegations of sexual harassment, and his imperious bending of the Fourth Amendment by scaling the wall of Simpson's estate, rerun all of the vilest stereotypes of the Los Angeles Police Department. This makes the possibility of his planting the bloody glove plausible among those most wary of white men with badges and guns.

Such elements give unfortunate weight to the racial admonishments put on District Attorney Garcetti by defense lawyer Johnnie Cochran and the Los Angeles civil rights establishment. A grand irony is that if Garcetti submits to the pressure and pushes for an integrated jury, black women could as easily be wild cards as not, given the resentment a large number feel toward successful black men who marry white women, thereby reducing the already limited pool available to them.

The television interview with Nicole Simpson's therapist in which the therapist said that the murdered woman told her that she enjoyed sparking her ex-husband's jealousy could make some men think she was cruelly toying with the green-eyed monster in her hot black man and paid the consequences. It is possible, with Johnnie Cochran now on the defense team, that intimations of what Clarence Thomas called "a high-tech lynching" will maintain the constant and incantational undertone of a mantra. That will make it the prosecution's slippery job to prove otherwise.

So we end up in a big, fat, peculiarly American mess, the kind that allows us to understand why one writer said she would choose a good case of murder if her intent was to ascertain the broadest identity of a culture. In this case of blonde on black, omnipresent media magnification, wife-beating, sudden wealth, workout partners, golf courses, the disco life, Bentleys rolling into McDonald's, rumors of drug-spiced promiscuity, and the ugly punctuation marks of two bloody victims in a high-rent district, we are forced to examine almost everything that crosses the T's of our American lives. What we will finally learn, however, is the smell and the taste of another long drink of the blues.

Part Two

FOR

RALPHUS

This section is a suite dedicated to Ralph Ellison, whom I often called during our many telephone conversations by the nickname "Ralphus," a joking reference to the familiar slave name Rastus. I consider the writing gathered in this part a suite because the themes of all of the pieces are connected either to Ellison literally or to the concerns he had about the challenges facing American fiction and American life. In very different ways, the writers discussed here besides Ellison—Saul Bellow, Gerald Early, Leon Forrest, Barbara Probst Solomon, and Martha Bayles—rise to those challenges, all of them addressing the complications of both the dance and the battle the individual American does with the mass. The last piece, "Blues for Jackie," is about a woman whose elegance and sorrow in the middle of her tragedy said so much about the transcendent nature of the national blues.

HOW LONG?
SO LONG

This eulogy was delivered at Ralph Ellison's memorial, held on May 26, 1994, at the American Academy of the Arts.

Ralph Ellison, *alone* of the world famous Afro-American novelists, never denied his American identity, his American birthright, his complex responsibilities as a participant in the analyzing of American meaning, which is the job of the intellectual, and the remaking of American life in the hopefully immortal rhythms and tunes of art, which is the job of our aesthetically creative. Ellison had no interest in the overpaid chitlin circuit of professional alienation and guilt mongering. He knew that all distant ethnic roots had been transmuted by the tragedy of American collision and the intricate — sometimes romantic — cultural blues of collusion.

That is why Ellison floated above the petty darknesses of race and opportunism that have brought so many devitalized dissonances to the orchestra of our national life. He was listening to a music more celestial and more in touch with the earth of our culture, the score written in the sky and in the mud, where the tales of heartbreak and hope, courage and cowardice, ambivalence and absolute accuracy tell us of the cosmopolitan bloodlines that make us Americans — part Yankee, part Indian, part pioneer, part Southerner, part Negro, part Christian, part Jewish, part Hispanic, part Asian.

Ellison understood what the Italian filmmaker Sergio Leone meant when he said that American cinema was an international language, because it had spoken across so many barriers within its own culture that it touched everyone in the world. That is what our brown-skinned writer from Oklahoma sought in his work. Those specific, those complex, those mongrel, those pugnacious, those empathetic, those signifying, those raucous, those delicate, those dancing, those wounded, those ribald, those elevated, and those down-home rhythms and tunes of the U.S.A. were what he always sought to bring to the page, allowing for liberation into the vast drama of human life that knows no limits beyond those inherent in the individual. Yes, he floated above the childish squabbles of the ethnic barnyard in search of the epic voice of the American experience, which speaks both to the ages and to the enjoyments and anxieties of the moment. Now truly an Invisible Man, Ralph Ellison is one we will miss until we join him, but we were damn lucky to ever have had such a great spirit, mind, and heart among us.

THE MEASURE OF
THE OKLAHOMA KID

When Ralph Ellison saddled up the pony of death and took that long, lonesome ride into eternity on Saturday morning, April 16, 1994, the quality of American civilization was markedly diminished. He had always traveled on a ridge above the most petty definitions of race and had given us a much richer image of ourselves as Americans, no matter how we arrived here, what we looked like, or how we were made. Alone of the internationally famous Afro-American writers of the last half century, Ellison had maintained his position as a citizen of this nation. His deservedly celebrated 1952 novel, *Invisible Man*; his two collections of essays, *Shadow and Act* and *Going to the Territory*; the public addresses he gave; and what he read and published from the most awaited second novel in this country's literary history spoke always of the styles, the intrigues, the ideas, the lamentations, and the desires that bewitchingly reached across race, religion, class, and sex to make us all Americans. This champion of democratic narrative wasn't taken in by any of the professional distortions of identity that have now produced not the astonishing orchestra of individuals our country always promises but a new Babel of opportunism and naïveté we must defeat with an inevitably vital counterpoint.

Ellison had been trained as a musician, intending to become a concert composer. But the books got him and he boldly took on the job of ordering the dissonance and the consonance of our culture into the orchestrated onomatopoeia that is the extended and subtle possibility of the novel at its highest level of success. Ellison was partially the result of the Wild West axis that had re-created jazz swing in the middle thirties and partially the fruition of the long and self-made blues line he lived, from his hometown of Oklahoma City to his apartment on Riverside Drive, in upper black, brown, beige, and bone Manhattan, where he died, getting up out of here at the age of eighty. He was much like the jazz musicians whom he admired, because his studies, his observations, and his experiences allowed him to fuse the essences of the countryside and the urban skyline into metaphoric tales almost too charismatic to resist.

At every point, he was definitely the Oklahoma Kid—part Negro, part white, part Indian, and full of the international lore a man of his ambition had to know. I sometimes thought of him as riding high into the expanses of the American experience, able to drink the tart water of the cactus, smooth his way through the Indian nations, drink and gamble all night long, lie before the fire with a book, distinguish the calls of the birds and the animals from the signals of the enemy, gallop wild and woolly into the big city with a new swing the way the Count Basie band had, then bring order to the pages of his work with an electrified magic pen that was also a conductor's wand.

In a time such as ours, there is a burden to straight shooting, and Ellison accepted it. Those troubles snake all the way back to the thirties, when the Marxist influence began to reduce the intricacies of American problems to a set of stock accusations and dull but romantic ideas about dictatorial paradises rising from the will of the workers. Because Ellison had come through all of that and, like Richard Wright, had rejected it, he was prepared for the political bedlam of the sixties. Democracy was recognized as a social and a policy expression of high-minded but realistic courage, one that demanded faith and vigilant engagement. His tutoring by blues musicians and the world of blues music had given him a philosophical ease in face of the perpetual dilemmas of human existence. Ellison recognized that immaturity and folly often result from failing to accept the possibilities and the frailties of our humanity. His morality wasn't based on anything puritanical; it was a product of the hard knocks and the refinements of this society at its most debilitating and its most vital. What he wrote of Afro-Americans at their best expressed his own sensibility as surely as the tar of that deceptively silent baby stuck to Brer Rabbit:

There is no point in complaining over the past or apologizing for one's fate. But for blacks, there are no hiding places down here, neither in country or city. They are an American people who are geared to what *is* and who yet are driven by a sense of what is possible for human life to be in this society. The nation could not survive being deprived of their presence because, by the irony implicit in the dynamics of American democracy, they symbolize both its most stringent testing and the possibility of its greatest human freedom.

The most stringent testing that Ellison himself had to face was the rejection of his stance and his work by the intellectual zip coons of black nationalism. The Oklahoma Kid took every emotional and psychological blow thrown at him; he didn't submit to the barbarian gate rattlers who intimidated so many into accepting a new segregation as a form of self-expression and ethnic authenticity. He knew that segregation was never less than an instrument of cowardice and rejected it. Those sufficiently misled tried to drum Ellison all the way out of the Afro-American experience and were not beyond calling him names to his face. They sneered at the Civil Rights Movement and integration, and substituted largely sterile threats for the difficult work of enriching this society by deepening the quality of the national dialogue that foreshadows all profound changes of policy. Addlepated African ancestor worship, Marxism deep-fried in snake oil, race baiting, and bloody street mud from the shoes of criminals whose anarchic behavior was misinterpreted as revolutionary—all served as food for substandard thought.

So by the end of the sixties, the Oklahoma Kid had a price on his head, and more than a few bounty hunters went out intending to bring his scalp back for entertainment. They didn't know who they were messing with. The writer had the same kind of leathery hide possessed by those dusky Western demons who broke horses, bulldozed, drove cattle, and wore the scars left by arrowheads and desperado bullets. Fanny Ellison, his wife of forty-eight years, recalled a luncheon where the embattled novelist sat next to one of the black power literary stooges so anxious to bring him down. Ellison said to him, "I'm a street boy; I'm mean, and I have a dirty mouth." It was an announcement of his essence and a declaration of war.

Ellison wasn't a street boy like the ones who sell pornographic novelties under the banner of rap, their nihilism made superficially complex by the editing and overlaying processes of the recording studio. He was from the same spiritual corner as Louis Armstrong, who knew of cutting and shooting but had danced in the gutter while doggedly staring at the stars. He was also of Duke Ellington's persuasion, an artist bent on the democratic eloquence that speaks only through the resolution of the primitive and the sophisticated. Citing the peerless bandleading composer and the great trumpeter in "Homage to Duke Ellington on His Birthday," Ellison clarified one more once his aesthetic vision of how artistic quality both added to the social promise of the nation and helped protect it against vernacular demons:

> Even though few recognized it, such artists as Ellington and Louis Armstrong were the stewards of our vaunted American optimism and guardians against the creeping irrationality which ever plagues our form of society. They created great entertainment, but for them (ironically) and for us (unconsciously) their music was a rejection of that chaos and license which characterized the so-called jazz age associated with F. Scott Fitzgerald, and which has returned once more to haunt the nation. Place Ellington with Hemingway, they are both larger than life, both masters of that which is most enduring in the human enterprise: the power of man to define himself against the ravages of time through artistic style.

Sneering at the tedious political pulp that would shrink Negro experience to no more than a social soap opera, the Oklahoma Kid, cigar in his teeth and fingers at his keyboard, strove to make his knowledge of race in conflict and confluence a wildly orchestrated metaphor for all of human life. He sought combinations of the concrete and the mythic, the excitement of intricate ideas and the boisterous flare-ups of fantasy. Ellison was too sophisticated to stumble into the dungeon of "magic realism," feeding on surreal hardtack and water. Like the Alejo Carpentier of *Reasons of State*, Ellison knew that the fusions and fissures of race and culture in the Western Hemisphere supply all that is needed for an unforced way out of convention. The miscegenated multiplications of human meaning and effort allow for shocking syncopations of fictional narrative and endless variations on hilarity, horror, and inspiration. Ellison understood their meaning absolutely: that American life, accurately captured, slides home with a polyrhythmic surrealism' as palpable as raised spikes. (One need think only of Nancy Reagan's sitting on Mr. T's lap at a White House Christmas party or Michael Jackson's standing next to George Bush at a press conference, even the armed guy who stormed a record company in Los Angeles some years ago and demanded to be recorded!)

The Oklahoma Kid told one writer that craft was an aspect of morality and that is perhaps why his unfinished novel took so long, even given the incineration of a manuscript near completion in the middle sixties. His ambition might have gotten the best of him. Ellison refused to say when he thought he would finish the book. This led those envious of his unimpeachable position in American writing to assert that he was some sort of a coward who couldn't face the possibility that the novel might not be up to snuff, that critics with sharpened teeth might gnaw at it like wild dogs, that a second novel might prove the first no more than a fluke, a game-winning home run from a batter destined to strike out for the rest of his career. Those who heard him lecture or read from the manuscript during the early and middle eighties doubted the skeptics. Until his disappearance from most public occasions, he gave off a remarkable sense of mission and filled the air of auditoriums with a vision as individual as it was rich. What Saul Bellow wrote of *Invisible Man* in 1952 was still quite true:

> I was keenly aware, as I read this book, of a very significant kind of independence in writing. For there is a "way" for Negro novelists to go at their problems, just as there are Jewish or Italian "ways." Mr. Ellison has not adopted a minority tone. If he had done so, he would have failed to establish a true middle-of-consciousness for everyone.

At Baruch College in 1983, he delivered a lecture entitled "On Becoming a Writer," stressing the freedom from the limitations of segregation that reading granted. Around 1924, books from the downtown library were jammed into a pool hall in the Negro section of Oklahoma City. As older men told tales, laughed, and gambled, the young Ellison investigated the unalphabetized books, which meant that a volume of fairy tales might be right next to a volume of Freud. While the books took him into worlds much broader than those he then knew, they also made it possible for him to better appreciate the contrasting humanity of a state in which a large number of whites and Negroes had facial features and skin tones affected to greater or lesser degrees by Indian blood.

Ellison's Oklahoma City was informed as much by those formally educated as by jazz musicians like Lester Young and Charlie Christian, who took innovative positions in the band battles and jam sessions of the era. Local aspirations were extended by the precedents of college-educated Negroes from the Eastern Seaboard who took on the missionary goal of traveling and educating their less fortunate brethren after the smoke of the Civil War cleared and the spiritual lion of freedom was roaring at the social limitations imposed by racism. The overall tone and message of the lecture was that the shaping of language and the comprehension of it amplified that roar in the soul of the young Oklahoma Kid, allowing him to do battle with the riddles of human life and affirm the victories that were evident in the verve of Negro culture.

In later readings, given at the Library of Congress, at The New School for Social Research, and at the Sixty-third Street YMCA in Manhattan, Ellison made it clear who he was and that—whether or not the novel ever reached publication—each time he gave public voice to his words the writers in attendance had an opportunity to witness just how big a lariat the old master was twirling. With *Invisible Man* he brought the resonance of genius to his variations on the Southern themes of dangerous racial misunderstandings and the disillusionment with Northern radicalism found in the full text of Richard Wright's *American Hunger*. The later work made it clear that he had advanced upon his initial ambitions and raised what was already a richly ironic style to a level of Melvillian complexity. The fiction spoke of childhood, of miscegenated romance, and of the various ways styles cross ethnic fences, here through personal contact, there through technology.

Taken by his readings, this writer looked up everything Ellison had published from the work in progress, some of it dating back to 1960. One of the themes was corruption and its charisma. A prominent character was a Southern senator named Sunraider. His tale was perfectly Ellisonian. A very light-skinned Negro or a white child who somehow found himself part of a traveling revival unit of Negroes, Sunraider, then known as Bliss, was "brought back from the dead" before various tent congregations. Leaving his background and misusing the lessons of his mentor, the Negro preacher Hickman, Bliss went into politics, changed his name, and became notorious for a version of public speaking he had learned at the knees of black people.

In "Hickman Arrives," the wounded Sunraider lies in the hospital after the assassination attempt, dreaming about his past, recalling himself nervously sucking air through a rubber tube inside the coffin as Hickman whipped up the congregation in the tent. But caught by the spirit, Hickman goes on longer than usual. Bliss is awestruck by the spontaneous eloquence as he trembles inside the wooden cigar. Chaos takes over the counterfeit Lazarus routine when a white woman claiming to be Bliss's mother bursts into the act. The hypnotic corruption at the center of the revival meeting, the fooling people for their own good and to prove the greatness of God, is a tool Bliss uses quite differently when he becomes a pro-segregation senator. Nothing is ever simple in Ellison, nor is his vision naive. In essence, Ellison was saying that Negroes, because of their charismatic relationship to American culture, have the moral responsibility to use their gifts with as much integrity as possible. Otherwise, they might unintentionally contribute to the disorder that always pushes at our culture's borders.

If the novel ever appears, good; if it doesn't, Ellison's contribution to the higher possibilities of our society won't be diminished. He outlasted two generations of attackers, the white and black writers and critics who hated *Invisible Man* and those from the black power era who found him too "white," too "European," too "middle class." With each passing year, his already published rendition of American life grew stronger and his work spoke ever more accurately of what came to pass—the fluid shifts of social position, the tragedies of corruption, the unpredictable turns that pivot on our technology and on how we interpret our heritage as improvising Americans; people whose roots stretch into Africa, Europe, Asia, and both directions in this hemisphere; people who remake sometimes perfectly and sometimes too swiftly; people who will never realize their potential unless we take on the challenge of democratic recognition, of understanding that both good and evil, folly and corruption, excellence and mediocrity can come from any place in the society. Ralph Ellison, the Oklahoma Kid, knew that we can never count on closed theories, on limiting explanations of our history—or any history. The only thing we can count on is the chaos that ever threatens our humanity and the willingness the best of us have to stand up to it. When we get lucky, as we Americans have so often, people like Ralph Ellison rear the hooves of their horses up toward the sky, then charge, taking every risk necessary to sustain the vitality of our civilization.

BARBAROUS ON EITHER SIDE:
THE NEW YORK BLUES
OF *MR. SAMMLER'S PLANET*

There are no two ways about virtue, my dear student; it either is, or it is not. Talk of doing penance for your sins! It is a nice system of business, when you pay for your crime by an act of contrition! You seduce a woman that you may set your foot on such and such a rung of the social ladder; you sow dissension among the children of a family; you descend, in short, to every base action that can be committed at home or abroad, to gain your own ends for your own pleasure or profit. . . . That man with yellow gloves and a golden tongue commits many a murder; he sheds no blood, but he drains his victims as surely; a desperado forces open a door with a crowbar, dark deeds both of them! You yourself will do every one of the things that I suggest to you today, bar the bloodshed. Do you believe there is any absolute standard in this world?

Vautrin, *Pere Goriot*

We are now mightily perplexed by the vulgarity and the brutal appetites of our culture, which Mr. Sammler sees so, so clearly, startled from page to page and in passage after passage of Saul Bellow's 1970 novel. The terrible children of our day, the worst of our politicians, and the rampant sleaze that slides up and down the classes, across the races and religions, from the cynical students to the unrepentingly jaded and old, can be traced back to the elements that are so alarming to the protagonist of *Mr. Sammler's Planet*. As a well-educated man who has smelled the molten breath and felt the bloody teeth of European fascism, Mr. Sammler is obsessed with understanding what makes or breaks a society, what causes a civilization to embrace ruthlessness as the best way to realize its ambitions and handle its fears. A veteran of World War II, he has seen killing and he has done it himself, which makes him a man for whom none of his questions exist in a speculative air unfouled by the odor of murder. His intellectual ponderings are thereby part of a drama in which he has seen the lowest the Western world has to offer. This lack of innocence makes him a hero and a thinker who is haunted by his past and startled to uneasiness by the present. Oh, yes: Artur Sammler knows firsthand how quickly the metamorphosis from the refined to the smugly savage can take place. "Like many people who had seen the world collapse once, Mr. Sammler entertained the possibility it might collapse twice."

The very conception of Mr. Sammler is expressive of Bellow's gift for bringing together the intellect, the passion, the spirit, and the flesh. The physical responses to stimulation are rendered with the same attention given to all of the many things that Mr. Sammler contemplates as he tries to get a grip on New York, America's financial capital and the pinnacle of the nation's culture. Mr. Sammler's ideas are counterpointed by feeling and sensuality to such a degree that the thoughts are themselves elements of emotion, which is something only our finest writers can bring off, the literary condition of character so complete that every aspect of consciousness takes form within the container of a body equal in the life of its senses to the spirit it carries. We get the feeling of a human being in repose, in grief, in rage, in self-protective contemplation, in unsparing self-examination, in attentive motion through Manhattan, on foot, in public transportation, in chauffeured limousine.

New York's power over the country was central to why it was chosen as the place of action. Mr. Sammler could not be in a better setting if he were to wrestle with the identity of the United States. One part of it obviously has to do with the character's Jewishness. Manhattan and Hollywood are the two places where Jews have made their deepest imprints on the country. Unlike the dream factory of Hollywood, New York is the city in which Jews took such high and influential positions across the professions—in law, medicine, education, theater, finance, fashion, music, politics, real estate, literature, science, and so on—that within fifty years the Jewish middle and upper classes became fundamental to setting the tone of the town and maintaining the Big Apple's nationally admired high culture. This was also true of the broad, popular entertainments, where Jews added the almost blues-like cynical joie de vivre of their vision to the crass vitality of the commonly understood. There were also spiritual tar pits. The theories of psychoanalysis and the rags-to-riches statistics of social history, if cleverly misinterpreted, made it possible for those mottled souls among the monied Jews to respond effectively when questioned or attacked. They used the peculiarly American tactic of the worst among the newly rich—celebration of their amoral appetites as undimmed and unpretentious vigor straight from the gutter! So, in almost endless ways, New York allowed stellar realization of the immigrant dream—access to the best one could get, given talent, discipline, luck, and moxie. The Big Apple had plenty of room for the ambitious, whether the intellectually illuminated or the crude and oily.

As a Polish Jew, Mr. Sammler feels both at home and alienated. He hears these New York Jews playing their cultural music in three keys—one bright, witty, down to earth, and high-minded; another croaking along in confused or desperate obsession with the fashionable; the last dark and daunting. He has no belief in the passing of attitudes through the blood. Mr. Sammler knows that Jews are often linked rather flimsily by some choice tales of atrocity passed down from generation to generation, and by a few religious rituals that are just as often felt no more deeply than the kind of American patriotism in which holidays inspired by the historical sacrifice and grief necessary for grand achievement are seen as yearly chances to have big, partying fun, not occasions that spark tragic recognition of the country's identity. Mr. Sammler believes that the society is threatened by a spiritual jungle rot that moves up from the depths and knows no limitations of social position or gender or power, infecting even the traditional outsiders. It is carried by those Jews who profit from pimping the chilling memory of the death camps, and it spreads all the way to the tainted grace of the suavely dressed and handsome black pickpocket Mr. Sammler observes on the bus as the novel opens.

What Bellow saw rising up from the sewers of our continental spirit has since gotten a more cavalier grip on our national passions. We aren't close to done for, but in this time of low democatic morale it is good to remember that some writers in this country aren't afraid of the big bad wolves of popular culture and refuse to slink along with the cowards of our academies, those who are all too willing to add material they despise to the reading lists of their courses—if that means their most self-serving colleagues and the oneriest students will pick some other people to harass. Bellow knew that the desire to be left alone and the willingness to make small adjustments are often at the bottom of social disorder. All of the single pieces of trash thrown out of the windows add up until the streets are filled with garbage and the stink is everywhere. Nesting inside that stink are vermin of every distinction.

When it arrived, the deeper meanings of *Mr. Sammler's Planet* were missed by those afraid that Bellow had become a racist and a fuddy-duddy who didn't recognize the importance of all the changes that were streaking—butt naked—across the American scene. Bellow had no doubt that the loud, sour, trumpeting of decay was mistaken for the spirited tune of true rebellion against all of the country's unarguable shortcomings. From the large frame to the intimate closeup, Bellow was addressing the dangers that arrive whenever the authority that comes of disciplined and responsible quality is pushed aside. As those dangers applied to the United States, the writer saw clearly the jagged quest for power from the people in the street to the talk show hosts of the mass media.

"Power," Stokely Carmichael liked to say in those days, "is the ability to define." In *Mr. Sammler's Planet*, the scuffle for power is such an important theme because the various styles of confrontational social change that came in the wake of the Civil Rights Movement were more than different techniques; they expressed completely different visions. There was unflinching rejection of King's emphasis on individuality—"the content of our character"—in favor of a false set of surface symbols, some shocking, some pretentious, some driven by adolescent dismay, but all pushing the society into a bizarre bal masque. It was important to recognize that representatives of every element of the society were in bitter struggle against what one writer called "the ordeal of civility."

The novel didn't hold back criticism of one group in order to reduce another to the pulp of the stereotype. It was made even richer by Bellow's knowledge of world history, which allowed him to nail the particulars of time and place while stepping back from the provincial concerns of American life and putting those problems within the context of the gangster politics Napoleon introduced, rejecting the Enlightenment and the democratic ideas it engendered. Bellow also reexamined the soul-slaying narcissism of impersonal sexuality and material greed. The erotic high jinks, spawned by the pop psychological battle with guilt and the freely imposed sterility of birth control pills, made a griddle of the glands upon which the spirit of romance was charred to a bitter crisp. Unapologetic greed is the perpetual nemesis all capitalist democracies must hold at bay—if they are to meet the imperatives of making money while sustaining the empathetic morality that underlies democratic policy and is equally central to the civilizing processes of modern life.

Mr. Sammler is as complex as the worlds of meaning that speed and twist into his life like fast balls, pop flies, curves, line drives, and sinkers. He doggedly tries to read the codes and numbers on each one, then respond with a well-placed smack before it moves past him and thuds into the muddy leather of incomprehension or self-deception. However differently they might arrive, and wherever in time they may have begun, the rapidly shifting human themes of order and disorder, pity and heartlessness, scientific clarity and the befogging machinery of murder are eventually ordered in Mr. Sammler's mind, each revealing aspects of its opposite. Those opposites are perfectly reflected and developed in the character of this elderly Gotham but European gentleman. There is great compassion in Mr. Sammler and there is the bitchiness of old age. He is patient and impatient. Life has brought him down a peg, however.

Before World War II, Mr. Sammler traveled in the high British air of intellectual exchange, slurping up all sorts of theories and becoming a snob in the process, one who felt that he had worked himself up out of the common worm bucket. From his superior position, he had the right to turn the miniature serpents of society with the tip of his umbrella and make note of their distinctions, either for conversation or personal entertainment. He remains an autocrat in his winter years, but, having been partially blinded by a rifle butt, stripped naked, shot, and pushed into a mass grave by the Nazis, Mr. Sammler doesn't overestimate the resources of his learning—or the values and resources of civilization itself. This Old World remnant in a progressively mannerless America isn't sure that all of the books and culture that he has absorbed guarantee his superiority to those whose ways offend him. Yet his endless cataloguing is a way of keeping himself at a remove; it also allows him to see the people who threaten or disgust him, white or black, as categories of animals—as apes, as pumas, and so on. It is only when Mr. Sammler is forced to face their human pain that he begins to achieve the kind of heroism our age demands.

Bellow lays down thematic elements early in the novel, observations that are interior monologues and stream-of-consciousness essays, sometimes the quick notes of harsh, broken phrases, sometimes sustained musings. Those who don't like that kind of thinking made expressive in novels miss what is going on. They fail to notice that those themes are realized three-dimensionally within the actions and attitudes of characters who turn up later, often using the symbols of Jewish, British, French, German, Italian, Russian, Spanish, and Asian culture in the design of their homes, the clothes they wear, the books they cite, the languages they speak, the mannerisms they appropriate, the ideas they spout. Those realizations through the characters are moral and sensitive, selfish and crude, even ignorant and compulsive. Variation is all. It allows the novel to reveal how interwoven our world is, how attitudes from across history have been mixed into the thick, rich, and befuddling gumbo of the modern age. Through reflection and realization the novelist also brings together both the wonder and mathematical indifference of scientific precision with a reverse set of phenomena—the tribal urges to crush every aspect of the opposition and the individual contempt for all others who collide with one's self-centeredness.

Mr. Sammler keeps reassessing his perspective because such contradictions seem the most consistent aspects of his reality. The sexual obsessions of older men remind him of his late friend, H.G. Wells, whom he thought shouldn't have been going gaga over girls into his seventies. But Mr. Sammler himself is the only child of a man who worked his seed into a woman when he was sixty years old! Mr. Sammler's disdain for the rich is merciless—"the rich were usually mean. Not able to separate themselves from the practices that had made the money: infighting, habitual fraud, mad agility in compound deceit, and strange conventions of legitimate swindling." Yet he and his half-mad daughter, Shula, have lived for the past twenty-three years on the generosity of Elya Gruner, a wealthy relative who came to Europe after the war and brought them from the ruins to New York.

Shula, obsessed with Mr. Sammler's finally writing a timeless memoir of his experiences and exchanges with big-time British intellectuals, steals an Asian professor's manuscript about potential space travel, *The Future of the Moon.* Though Mr. Sammler's notes were destroyed in 1939 during the German invasion of Poland, Shula—a pack rat given to desperate certainty—has no doubt that her father needs only to be goosed by some speculations surrounding the moon, that inspiration for primitive rites, science fiction, and the last frontier for human technology.

Not for nothing does the moon rise over and over in the narrative, a full disc of reflected light. It is a symbol of both the magnetic force that turns the tides and the mythical influence on the collective madness Mr. Sammler retreats from, hiding behind his interior parlor games of extremely intelligent analysis, or trying to hold at bay those referred to as "loony" or "lunatics." As an aspect of what lies in *outer* space, the moon is also part of a fugue built on the subject of space—mental space, emotional space, urban space, erotic space, and the space of the grave, where horror, equality, grief, and revenge gather.

Shula's ex-husband, Eisen, is a mad and violent Russian Jew who made it through World War II, moved to Israel, and now considers himself an artist worthy enough for fame to migrate into New York with a sack full of monstrous Stars of David and lumpy sculptures, one a childish "abstraction" of a Sherman tank. Eisen's madness and his cheerful willingness to assault or destroy give his handsomeness a charisma in the age of the diatribe that cannot maintain itself within the narrow space of words. He is a man of action, waiting for a target.

Margotte, Mr. Sammler's niece and landlady, is a German Jew who drives him mad with her analytical categories, which make her a lesser version of himself. The bulk of her family had its pulse stopped permanently by the Nazis. A bumbler who is also a fount of concern and compassion,

> Margotte swept on, enormously desirous of doing good. And really she was good (that was the point), she was boundlessly, achingly, hopelessly on the right side, the best side, of every big human question: for creativity, for the young, for the black, the poor, the oppressed, for victims, sinners, for the hungry.

However much Margotte's personality scrapes the blackboard of Mr. Sammler's sensibility, her feeling for the world and all its trouble is a microcosm of the direction that the spirit of the novel will take.

A surgeon and a successful investor, Elya Gruner is kind and sentimental as well as intelligent and shrewd, cocky and full of style, but his children, Angela and Wallace, embody the self-obsession and iciness of the time. Even so, they look upon Mr. Sammler with a certain awe, a self-entertaining respect. But the old man has few tribal stories from his position as noble patriarch: he wasn't ever very interested in his family at large; as an only child, he was—as his mother had been—spoiled and given all of the attention. Familial concerns were always immediate, from the tip of his own nose backwards. That quality, as he reflects upon it, creates an uncomfortable connection to Elya's children.

The beautiful Angela is well-dressed trash. She dutifully visits her shrink but understands nothing other than the baseness of her appetites and the consensus of what is chic, from sexual mores to political causes. The smoothly handsome Wallace is a ne'er-do-well who—straight out of the box—tries to make a fast and dirty buck by going in with some straw Mafia types from Las Vegas. He promptly flushes a bundle down the outhouse hole of their shady doings. That omnidirectional shadiness is a central theme of the novel. It even upholsters Elya's past in leopard skin: the now saintly millionaire who's brought off "many strategems of benevolence" has also done illegal abortions on the side for the rich, received large gifts of grimy cash, been repulsively chummy with Lucky Luciano, and is rumored to have hidden his boodle in his Long Island home with the help of Mafia plumbers.

These people prod the consciousness of Mr. Sammler, a man who believes in privacy, refined deportment, and protocol. Embarassed by the frankness of their concerns and how entranced they are by the gradations of filth, he measures them all as part of a belligerent era and shudders at the overall voyeurism, the obsession with the scummy and the lurid. Sure enough,

> However, Mr. Sammler had to admit that once he had seen the pickpocket at work he wanted very much to see the thing again. He didn't know why. It was a powerful event, and illicitly—that is, against his own stable principles—he craved a repetition.

Then comes another turnaround. While he is shocked when the black pickpocket sees him observing his game, corners him, and forces the old European Jew to look at his sizeable All-American johnson—a dark bat of flesh intended to smack him into submission through its mere unveiling—Mr. Sammler later remembers something quite important as he thinks about that moment:

> Sammler now even vaguely recalled hearing that a President of the United States was supposed to have shown himself in a similar way to the representatives of the press (asking the ladies to leave), and demanding to know whether a man so well hung could not be trusted to lead his country. The story was apocryphal, naturally, but it was not a flat impossibility, given the President, and what counted was that it should spring up and circulate so widely that it reached even the Sammlers in their West Side bedrooms.

The phallic exhibitionism as proof of validity and power, common to both black pickpocket and white Commander-In-Chief, is an example of how these various elements are connected for a remarkable overall effect. The black pickpocket working the bus filled with middle-class whites is given an oblique variation when Walter Bruch, a German Jew who lived beyond Buchenwald, rides subways up into Spanish Harlem, the sole white passenger among the brown and darker. Erotically magnetized to fleshy, tan arms, he goes into a drugstore where he can buy from a woman whose bouncing upper limbs stiffen his impulses. Pressing against his briefcase as the black pickpocket pressed against Mr. Sammler, Walter Bruch, who has given the girl a large bill so she has to spend time getting the change, excitedly looks upon the brown chubby arms until he loses control of the stickiness in his loins and wets his pants, humiliated and relieved by his climax.

Through Walter Bruch we are also given a look at another of Bellow's symbols—the rat. Like Camus in *The Plague*, Mr. Sammler has thought of the Nazis as rats, breeders in filth and spreaders of disease. After hearing of his problems, Mr. Sammler tells Walter Bruch that he is not as bad off as Freud's Rat Man, which is also a reference to the novel's many anal and fecal images. Elsewhere, in a long, philosophical discussion, Mr. Sammler refers to the human being as sometimes having the feeling of a rat scurrying through a cathedral. Even later, looking out the window of a limousine, Mr. Sammler remembers once coming into the meat-packing section of Manhattan and seeing a rat so large that he thought it was a greyhound.

On and on, Bellow explores his situations and his questions with writing possessed of the literary equivalent of Ted Williams, that Boston Red Sox giant of swat who could see the ball when it left the pitcher's fingers. Such clarity of context and detail give Mr. Sammler's Planet the hard sweep, contempt, pathos, and confidence of a contemporary Balzac. Balzac was the first who wanted the reader's eye and ear to travel from the flyspeck to the footstep to the ballroom to the highest—and lowest—levels of startling speculation, where all was discussed in terms of what had become socially possible and what openings there were in the human personality for all the vermin of temptation to run through. That long-seeing precision allows the novel to become epic because the fundamental issue of the epic is the meaning of civilization; it is the judgment and drama of human conduct. In the epic, all of the repercussions and benefits of action are laid out against the agreeing or warring traditions that give context to the world of the characters.

The Balzacian similarity is furthered by reexamining the way things happen in Pere Goriot, where the old man is surrounded by the dirty doings of those so much younger and so much more cynical. In fact, Vautrin, the criminal philosopher and homosexual who stirs and contemplates the rodent tar of the human soul, exposes his hairy chest to a younger man in order to intimidate him with a wound from a duel—exactly the same technique, however different the tool, used in Mr. Sammler's Planet by the pickpocket and the President. (Some say the mythic exhibitionist was a johnson-waving Johnson.) This concern with cynicism and corruption is also present in Eugénie Grandet, where the slave trade becomes the ultimate symbol of the dehumanizing process, the spiritual siphoning off that begins when the desire for profit determines all action.

Bellow, again like Balzac, gives the reader a thorough grounding in how the literate classes function in a time of corruption. The idea of a self-made American aristocracy of achievement has fallen, which means that human beings must be assessed by more than their surface trappings and their educational backgrounds. In Mr. Sammler's Planet, it would even be inaccurate to assume substance based on the obvious facts of intelligence, as with the brilliant and avaricious Wallace, who cooks up one lunatic scheme after another, proving himself, willy-nilly, a "high-IQ moron," which is how he is described by Elya, his father. All must be understood by what they will do to realize their passions.

The novel opens with a theft in order to set the stage for the recurring themes of dishonesty, intimidation, violence, and underhanded alliances. Over and over, we are shown that the scent of crime is an addictive stimulant snorted by the better-off. Mr. Sammler thinks about his experience with the pickpocket, then about the obsession with criminality that slides all the way back to Baudelaire and moves up through the Russian writers and the German thinkers. Defined as a tonic for bourgeois boredom and an alternative to the cowardliness of the privileged, this love of criminality has led so many well-to-do people to get their thrills—or increase their fortunes—by lying down, one way or another, with small- or big-time gangsters. Eventually, Mr. Sammler realizes that what has happened to him and to his family, and, finally, to Jews under the Nazi shadow of genocide, is another form of gangster politics, a variation on gang wars justified by the counterfeit science of the Reich. He also recognizes that however wonderful real science might be, its very impersonality always makes it a potential tool of murder, something he discovers again when he chooses to cover the Six-Day War for a Polish newspaper and views the charred and stinking bodies of Arabs slaughtered by the napalm the Israelis deny using. The Muslim corpses lie piled in holes just as Mr. Sammler and other Jews were when the Germans shot them down into a mass grave. The old man is not above the Israelis because his unflagging memory pulls him into the muck of his own past, as when his recurring fascination with the black criminal and with the murder committed by Raskolnikov evolves into a recollection of the way he, a half-blind Jew on the run, shot a German soldier to death for his bread and his clothes, feeling no pity, no regret, no tinge of identification when the man begged for his life as endless Jews had, hopelessly groveling in the face of their imminent murders served ice cold.

In the attempt to bring the West into dialogue with the East, to create a grand antiphony between the high intellectual probings of Mr. Sammler and those of Govinda Lal, author of the stolen manuscript, *The Future of the Moon,* Bellow overshoots and the dialogue doesn't possess the snap and the revelations of character had by almost every one of the other conversations. The rich and varied motion of the novel breaks an axle. But things are quickly repaired

and the momentum is regained as Mr. Sammler makes his way
through a plumbing disaster created by Wallace's searching for his
father's hidden loot. The Pole and would-be British aristocrat is driven in a Rolls Royce from Elya's Tudor home on Long Island into
Manhattan, where his benefactor lies dying in the hospital. On the
way, Bellow brings the highways, the bridges, and the streets of
Upper Manhattan to the page with the kind of accuracy and feeling
for image that all American writers, no matter how original, have
learned from Hemingway. The streets made greasy by the butchers,
the feel of the Puerto Rican blocks, the look and mood of Columbia
University, and the melting pot of urban drive and melancholy have
the slip, rhythm, tone, and collective force we expect of a master
dishing out his talent with sublime and emotive nuance.

The novel then reaches a high point of violence when the Rolls
Royce comes upon a street hassle. Feffer, an admirer of Mr. Sammler and an academic hustler anxious to photograph the black pickpocket so he can use the pictures on a talk show, is in the street
fighting off the elegantly dressed thief, who is much stronger and
overwhelmingly intent on taking the camera. Shula's ex-husband,
Eisen, is there, standing on the toeless feet that came of being
thrown off a winter troop train after the battle of Stalingrad when
his fellow Russian soldiers reverted to anti-Semitic normalcy, as had
the Polish soldiers who were so outraged when the idea of a Jewish
state in Poland was suggested that they went out killing the Jews who
fought at their side against the Nazis; or the Pole who risked his life
hiding Mr. Sammler but gradually resumed his traditional animosi-
ties once the war was over. The old man and the mad Russian Jew
share the experience of short-term camaraderie, since Mr. Sammler was one of the Jews the Polish soldiers attempted to murder but
was lucky enough to escape their miniature version of the Final
Solution. Yet the short-term, and essential, defiance of injustice that
lasts no longer than the time of extreme conditions is something the
unwillingly deified symbol of survival is grateful for. Earlier in the
novel, Mr. Sammler contemplated Cieslakiewicz, his "savior," and
what his own survival had amounted to in New York:

> The old Pole was also a hero. But the heroism ended. He was an ordi-
> nary human being and wanted again to be himself. Enough was enough.
> Did he have a right to be himself? To relax into old prejudices? It was

only the "thoughtful" person with his exceptional demands who went on with self-molestation—responsible to "higher values," to "civilization," pressing forward and so on. It was the Sammlers who kept on vainly trying to perform some kind of symbolic task. The main result of which was unrest, exposure to trouble. Mr. Sammler had symbolic character. He, personally, was a symbol. His friends and family had made him a judge and a priest. And of what was he a symbol? He didn't even know. Was it because he had survived? He hadn't even done that, since so much of the earlier person had disappeared. It wasn't surviving, it was only lasting. He had lasted.

Both his age and his experience make Mr. Sammler the patriarch of the family line, the Pere Goriot of his moment, the soul of his circle and of all the extensions, elaborations, and refinements the most gifted Jews had brought with them through the forced displacements of their history and the willful immigrations to a place that promised the chance to rise above the dark and bloody shadow of a discrimination made all the more absurd by its denial of individuality to the members of one of the most contentious groups in the history of the world. These people cut the teeth of their endless variety on argument, high and low, the constant disruption of warring interpretations, the struggles to realize the meanings of the singular life in a briar-patch world where the thorns of tragedy and disillusionment were recognized as basic to the human tale but were fought, nevertheless, over and over and over, sometimes with the cantorial song so basic to the cry of flamenco and so much a long-distance cousin of the American blues, sometimes with the social and economic theories that toppled empires, sometimes with the rude humor of vaudeville and the urbane tunes of Tin Pan Alley, sometimes with labor organizing and the legal briefs that challenged traditional patterns of prejudice writ into law, sometimes with the hard work and shrewd decisions across the professions that lifted raggedy immigrants to the finest environs money could buy, and almost always with the willingness to pant and drool for a mile if given the opportunity to move an inch. That patriarchal representation of the tribe is Mr. Sammler's unwelcome position but it carries the irony that he is understood and taken seriously by no one other than Elya, who lies in the hospital, suffering the emotional abandonment of a contemporary Lear—which is also to say a Goriot—expiring as his children screechingly fiddle and fret over the inheritance they will or won't get. The role of the civilized man is, finally, to fight for a compassionate consciousness that is neither sentimental nor overwhelmed by the stark and brutal facts of a world known to move with almost whimsical suddeness from the elevated to the barbaric.

The precise, technological magic of Feffer's camera and the ugly pieces of his own "art" that Eisen carries in a baize bag become symbols of elevation and barbarism entertwining in a moment of bloodshed. When Mr. Sammler gets out of the Rolls Royce, leaves his air-conditioned symbol of aristocratic privilege and steps into the hard stone of the street, he asks Eisen to do something in Russian, the two of them suddenly foreigners in a situation where the locals, both black and white, have chosen to be no more than spectators, not one moving to do anything. Here the earlier images that have had many variations come together—Raskolnikov smashing an ax into his landlady's head and Eisen's recalling the Russian front, seeing "men too insignificant to waste bullets on, having their heads smashed by shovel blows." The monstrous, sharp-edged lunks and the thick abstraction of a tank are swung inside the bag Eisen tightly clutches, knocking the pickpocket down with a terrible blow that is followed by another. A third, perhaps a killing blow, is stopped by Mr. Sammler, appalled by Eisen's cheerful readiness to crush the man's skull. As the old man summons the muscle to grab Eisen, we realize that, after all of the musing, it surely comes down to mad or to civilized action. The mad action echoes back to Eisen's response in the hospital—"How can art hurt?"—when Mr. Sammler told him his heavy creations shouldn't be pushed on Elya because handling them might tire out the very sick man. Eisen's retort to Mr. Sammler's disgust at his violence in the street pulls up their common experience, "You can't hit a man like this just once. When you hit him you must really hit him. Otherwise he'll kill you. You know. We both fought in the war. You were a Partisan. You had a gun. So don't you know?"

This scene is also an exceptional metaphor for the complexity of race relations at the time. While the pickpocket represents the street version of the criminality that Mr. Sammler sees all about him, manifesting in almost every member of his family, he is also an apparent allusion to the priapic version of black "manhood" that slithered from behind the black power movement's fly and throughout the "revolutionary black art" in which white men were so often rendered as impotent or homosexual or terrified of what we recently saw in redux on a Spike Lee T-shirt, advertising one of his movies — "Jungle Fever: Fear of a Big, Black Dick." The thief's flashing of his privates also predicted Eldridge Cleaver's shot at fashion designing just a few years after the publication of *Mr. Sammler's Planet*. While the revolutionary rapist was spurting out his Marxist rages in Paris, he also tried to huckster some "real men's pants," which featured large, dangling, black, cotton-stuffed penises. (Could this bold appropriation and extension of the European codpiece be the ultimate black revolutionary reference to the cotton fields back home?) Beyond that, through the machinations of Feffer, there is a merciless criticism of the Jewish opportunists who sold real and imagined black pathology under the banner of "serious discussion," while the only thing serious was the intention of buttering their own bread with controversy. The kind of black "leaders" who made their money ripping off or intimidating middle-class whites, and the outraged Jews of the late sixties who reacted to the separatism of black power by going into Zionism, are brought together in a hard and shocking metaphor of that rift when the Stars of David, those religious symbols of the group, almost become murder weapons in broad daylight on a city block in sophisticated Manhattan.

Throughout the novel, and on to its conclusion, when Mr. Sammler is further shocked by the money grubbing and the self-centeredness of his relatives, from his own daughter to Elya's children, we see all of these people reflecting a time when the possibility of riches remade the rules and the lowdown dirty blues of city life was played out across all lines of social distinction. Yet Mr. Sammler's evolution from the kind of autocratic remove that makes him both a near-racist and a man who looks upon all mortal foolishness with hostile condescension is a very high moment in our literature. This old man, he plays his way through what become the three-tiered challenges of the past and the present — the spiritual nicks and gashes that smart inside his scars and inside those that he sees on others; his own evasive knack for packaging the omnidirectional rush of life into brilliant but airless categories; the unpadlocked wackiness that threatens to knock his will to its knees. Fighting free of the sorrowful bitterness left by the thoroughbred and mongrel dogs of war that endlessly gnaw at the decomposing bodies and crack the bones of the many dead he's seen, Mr. Sammler comes on home.

This old man pushes himself closer and closer to all the muddy human hearts around him. He learns to summon the heroic feeling of compassion through the stern memories of his own shortcomings. The thick, red blood of the black pickpocket lying wounded and helpless in the street turns him into a man before Mr. Sammler, who feels again the butt of the Nazi rifle against his own head and knows that it partially blinded him to the humanity of others. The thief is no longer a dandified puma or an animal, but a human being vulnerable to the hysteria at the nub of injustice. We are not asked to forgive the pickpocket his sins, assuming that "society" gave him no choice and that he shouldn't be punished. The point is far more subtle: the thief is on the receiving end of force so excessive that it reduces the potency of the law by snarling into a ruthless werewolf of totlitarianism right before the eyes of the onlookers.

In the hospital, Mr. Sammler's feelings towards Elya's daughter change. Angela, whom he has always looked upon as one sort of a tramp after another, is recognized as a woman trapped inside the splendor of her own orifices and the childish ways of an era that coats itself with a phony knowingness, strategically avoiding the needs of the soul by compulsively satiating the senses.

Emboldened by his identification with the desperate ambitions that can twist the human spirit into a hill of fishhooks, Mr. Sammler looks into all of our mysteriously human faces with his Cyclopean eye until he recognizes—as Goriot did on his deathbed—how easily we begin the breakdown when we infantilize our children by spoiling them rather than showing them the most responsible kinds of love. Standing over the corpse of Elya, the old man closes out the book with what amounts to a splendid recasting of Lear's last words. The meter is the same but the message isn't. What protects the world from the eradication of its humanity is the willingness to empathize with the range of mortal triumph, mortal folly, and mortal pain. This transcendent willingness allows us to say, even to the dead, "we know, we know, we know." *Mr. Sammler's Planet* is the sort of achievement we will appreciate as long we are willing to explore the chaos of our world and accept the humbling truths about the parts we all play in its making.

AN INTRODUCTION TO
GERALD EARLY

This introduction was given to the Academy of American Poets in New York City on January 29, 1991.

There is a metaphor that fits what Gerald Early does—his first and last names' lead letters: GE. Those acquainted with the technological advertisements made possible by television and radio will never forget how various American companies trumpeted the absolute necessity of their precision engineered technology for sale, those mechanical wares that made it possible for any citizen of these United States to be part of the modern age. General Electric, or GE, was one of those companies, and the idea that light controlled in a promethean leap beyond the past was one of the things that lengthened our distance from a history of technological shortcomings was a familiar one. We had come a long way since torches, since strings were set in molds soon to filled with hot wax and later to be lit as wicks, a long way since those dangerous gas lights. Now, at the flip of a finger an entire room could suddenly be lit without a flame in sight, and like that room, so would whole cities defy the night through the workmanship this company could boast. General Electric. Light as a general fact, a large part of the identity of modern life.

Gerald Early is bringing a broad reach of intellectual light to a number of subjects that have often been pushed into the darkness that results from clichés. The cliché is sort of a portable form of darkness, something like intellectual burnt cork. It dismisses actual identity in favor of gargoyle entertainment, the sort of entertainment in which the subject is never the equal of the speaker, is only the servant of a fantasy so addictive it would be painful to kick the habit of introducing it into conversation or writing. That is what Gerald Early does so well: he rubs off the burnt cork or goes into the tar pits and pulls up the bones and then puts them together and from them builds models that let us know what something lost to that devouring mass of darkness actually looked like. His is an enormous contribution to an era in which so many things are seen so imprecisely.

To the general sweep of his concerns, Gerald Early brings an electric lyricism that ennobles the condition of the essay, his chosen lamp to carry in search of honest understanding. He has obviously burned enough oil in the midnight hour to expand upon what must have been at one time a primitive level of linguistic illumination but that now looms before us as his very own literary power station, full of transformers and coils and the humming, clanging rhythms that signal the ability to send calibrated force across the limitations and superstitions of our society in the very same way that Ralph Ellison and Albert Murray remember radio waves smacking down segregation and making the jazz and dance band broadcasts, for instance, national experiences in the most democratic sense possible.

What Gerald Early does so well is juxtapose sources and references. As a pharmacist of my old neighborhood loved to say of himself, Gerald Early can "go from the alley to Buckingham Palace—and back!" He is a writer whose sense of human complexity allows him to understand America's body and soul as they move across class, race, and geography. Since he has written so well about boxing—as well as the best who have ever written about it—he is obviously not afraid of blood or pain or of the grand fascination we will forever have for this form of what Budd Schulberg calls "show business with blood." There is neither fear of the body and its pains as well as its glories, nor fear of the convoluted soul of this country that is sometimes so luminously exposed through the bell of a saxophone in the hands of Sonny Stitt. Age does not intimidate him and he, unlike so many who have fallen before the sword of rock-and-roll social science fiction, obviously looks forward to the point at which he will be proof of one of his own dictums, "Never try to beat an old head at anything, whether it is doing the dozens or doing the dukes."

It is that aspiration to wisdom and the will to knowledge of the sort that mixes the soul with hard-core scholarship as opposed to the pornography of indocrination that have made Gerald Early's *Tuxedo Junction* such a wonderful moment of literary brawn and blazing songsmanship. He exhibited the intellectual muscle and the ability to croon out his glowing ideas in sentences that were sometimes parallel to stanzas taking form between capital letters and periods. Try this out for a man turning on klieg lights in the darkness of the American racial night: "Indeed, what is race in America but the Melvillian doubloon hammered in our consciousness that bedevils us endlessly and turns anything it shines upon into a metaphor as well." Listen to the luminescent report of these syllables as he takes down a well-known boar of the evening with intellectual tracer bullets: "For Mailer, the black is always the id-dominated beast, the heart of the white man's darkness; and always, in Mailer's tone, there is that juvenile penis envy that might as well be hate because it amounts to such an insulting kind of love." Here is an artistic understanding that allows for a defense against the destruction so many face when they cater to the burnt cork of any insufficient trend:

> Monk did not play anything new; he sounded very much like a man at peace with himself. He had allowed electronics and the avant garde to pass him by as if he were standing still. Monk, unlike the old R&B singers who perform at revival shows, was not living in the past. If anything, he had been grappling with the meaning and the measure of his artistic past, which is why he felt so compelled to repeat it without ceasing. He had paid dues in the ass-kicking business of music making. He had been an original, so he certainly did not need to be novel."

In repudiating Bigger Jim Collier, who has biographically tarred and feathered both Ellington and Armstrong, Gerald Early pulls a rapier of light:

> Collier is simply measuring black culture against a white cultural norm and, inasmuch as black culture resembles any poverty culture, it would appear that middle-class Euro-American culture is superior, at least materially. But poor black folk counterstated the deprivation they suffered by emphasizing in their rituals a refulgence of style. Although the poor black could not read, he did possess speech, so that through a com-

plex manipulation of this medium, blacks created their theater in their barbershops and churches and their history and traditions in their folk tales, folk beliefs, jiving, and signifying. Armstrong was not the product of an inadequate culture; if he had been, there would have been no emotional or psychological sources to support his becoming an artist.

Perhaps what most distinguishes Gerald Early and the general but orchestratedly specific electricity of his work is the understanding that we all, as Americans, regardless of the shortcomings of a history that has had to address ethnic complexities unlike those of any other society of world significance, are the products of a far from inadequate culture. Of course, Gerald Early is not naive and knows well how many decoys and hurled buckets of tar we must recognize for what they are—and avoid. He is as critical of silly ideas in one camp as in another, as willing to search with the lamp of his essays in any group, history, culture, or technique for honest manifestations of human meaning. Because of that we should all be very happy that this American virtuoso knows the meaning of bringing together the gift for language and the honor necessary for art to be the result of what Duke Ellington called "the world's greatest duet." Though Ellington was not referring to the indelible duet of talent and honor, what he said about the couple he was referring to equally applies to what we learn when reading Gerald Early. For Ellington, "the world's greatest duet" was "a man and a woman going steady." He also said that the "blues is the accompaniment" and that "if neither one of them feels like singing 'em, the blues just vamps 'til ready." Thank you.

BEYOND AMERICAN
TRIBALISM

Like our economy, our cities, and our universities, our long fiction has been in trouble for years. The problem is as much spiritual as intellectual, for we need a far, far richer sense of the inner lives that give our nation its particular complexity. And because all Americans make their elevating to wacky variations on a set of essences, those essences need to be delivered with high and subtle style, a feeling for the labyrinths of our history, and a sense of the shifting dialogue across race and class, sex and geography, myth and fact. Most novelists duck the job, preferring to sink down into explications of ideology and statistics; or they hop the latest cattle car of academic convention from France; some even embrace the least revealing aspects of our popular culture, never determining what the relationship of the street is to the truly sophisticated expression of our protean national consciousness. If nothing else, they bushwhack the reality of our lives from behind barricades of ethnic and gender franchises.

But Leon Forrest has accepted the task of capturing our culture and has produced a novel that provides a signal moment in our literature, one that was largely missed when it arrived last year. With an equal level of ambition, he responds to the standards of fiction and the breadth of thought found in the work of Ralph Ellison, Albert Murray, Saul Bellow, William Faulkner, Herman Melville, James Joyce, Thomas Mann, and Marcel Proust. The resulting success of *Divine Days* is as startling for its narrative risks as for the sustained power of its author's literary will. Having spent twenty years working his way to this point through three earlier novels—*There Is a Tree More Ancient Than Eden, The Bloodworth Orphans,* and *Two Wings to Veil My Face*—Forrest has now moved to the forefront of American literature. All of the previous experiments and partial successes now read as a triptych of an overture to this masterwork.

Not one to satisfy himself with an imposing gift for mashing together the rural and urban sensibilities that make epic the Afro-American language of our cities, Forrest has a big feeling for literature at large, and this 1,135-page novel reads the way a whale eats, swimming forward with its massive mouth open to ensure the continued substance of its bulk. Forrest gives us characters, tales, set pieces, sermons, rhythms, images, jokes, and a vision of our culture's mythic size we rarely encounter in this day of the little world, the little thought, and the devotion to a defeatist vision imported from Europe in the wake of the one-two punch of the world wars.

Even so, Forrest is no New Age Good Humor Man. He understands how we are duped by color, how unexamined or hysterical ideology often blinds us like intellectual mustard gas. But rather than crawl into that trench where engagement lies traumatized, Forrest successfully captures the struggle for the Afro-American soul that took place during the middle sixties. That soul has the feeling of multitudes and is a prism through which the spectrum of our nation at large appears: no matter how accurate the Afro-American texture, *Divine Days* provides us with a metaphor as resonant in its general meanings as it is commanding in the nuances of the particular.

Through the world Forrest summons with one brilliant thematic variation after another, we are able to see the struggles our democracy has in facing up to the prickly relationship between the individual and the masses. He artfully shows that the resentment we feel when faced with inevitable tragedy is what sets us up for the "happy endings" promised by purveyors of snake oil in every arena from the religious to the secular, the political to the psychoanalytic. The popularity of the intellectual, economic, spiritual, and physical surgery guaranteed to produce a "new you" is also fresh meat for the leaders of cults that stretch from the academy to the street corner. Our difficulty in combining intellect with style and style with intellect results in our accepting eloquent but empty-headed theories or being overly impressed by manner when we should also be looking for content. Our shallow, hand-me-down revisions of history and culture tear us from the transcendent grandeur of our human heritage, deny the endless miscegenations that complicate our national identity, and set us up for so many sucker blows that we end up culturally punch drunk. Finally, we can become so sanctimonious that we feel engagement is below us, or we can sneer at engagement because we have become convinced that every horror and disappointment is held in place by an invincible conspiracy.

These national themes come forward in the novel as the profane and empathetic flexibility of the blues spirit does battle against the various puritanical visions that stem from either the most restrictive versions of Christianity or the totalitarian cults that combine ethnic nationalism with religion. In one corner is Sugar-Groove. Sugar-Groove is a Mississippi-born half-caste and road runner whose mutating legend is a gift to the Chicago black people ever willing to spin a tale about him or listen when a fresh one arrives. Though it is not immediately apparent, Sugar-Groove dies seeking the meaning of life. He wants to get next to the light that symbolizes both the bittersweet richness of his cultural background and the courage to face the burdens of existence with tragic optimism. That affirmative courage sells out neither to innocence nor cynicism; it is the source of the wounded and optimistic love call heard in the pulsive swing of blues and jazz. That wise and enlivening principle has made the people as charismatic as the music.

In the other corner is W. A. D. Ford. Ford is the demonic force that rises from the recesses of black American culture. Through Ford, *Divine Days* looks without a blinking eye into mad orders and confidence men such as the Nation of Islam, Father Divine, Daddy Grace, and Jim Jones. Ford possesses ominous charm and knows that those black people who feel most intimidated by the intricacies of a society demanding great sophistication often harbor the desire to be part of an elite at any cost. Their rage, insecurity, envy, and bitterness can be manipulated to the point where they will end up accepting every repression of vitality in the interest of order. Overwhelmed by so many choices equaled by so many responsibilities, they will submit to one source for all direction. "They were absolutely mindless before his powers," Forrest writes of two potential Ford followers, a borderline street walker and a waiter, both marvelously drawn in their sass, pretensions, sorrow, and paranoia.

Though the spiritual contestants are quite clear, nothing functions very simply in *Divine Days*. The novel takes place over a week in the night world of Chicago's South Side, but much more is going on than a few guppies warring in the miniature aquarium of a pimp's platform shoe heel. Forrest weaves his complexities with a multihued fishing tackle that will not break under the demands of his epic ambition. His people have complicated family lines, and their experiences, their educational backgrounds, their interests, their terrors, and their hopes cross many different lines of color and class, religion and career. Freed from the small talk of the contemporary provincial, the characters of *Divine Days* move across the country and around the world. Having done or wished for or failed at many things, they have much on their minds and memory trunks full of corkscrews and bent objects.

Joubert Jones is perhaps the hero, at least the narrator, a playwright just returned from two years of military service in Germany. Joubert intends to write a play about Sugar-Groove and has previously worked at bringing Ford's evil to the stage. This conceit allows the many literary allusions to work naturally, and Joubert's job as a bartender in his Aunt Eloise's watering hole supplies the novel with the rich breadth of characters either met during visits to the Night Light Lounge or remembered through the hooks of association.

The characters function in a narrative that is built upon *Invisible Man* in as original a way as that novel was built upon Richard Wright's *American Hunger*. (That is: the published *Black Boy* and the then-unpublished second half, which took the narrator to a disillusioning North, the book ending with his decision to become a writer and an allusion to the last lines of Tennyson's "Ulysses.") Forrest is taken by Southern experience and the seditious elements in the North that also infringe on individual identity. For Wright and Ellison, the conservative and brutal demon of racism was extended by the radical Northern demon that dismissed human specificity in favor of rote political theory. Setting his novel in 1966, Forrest brings us to the brink of the destruction of the Civil Rights Movement by the politics of black power. The writer revels in the vitality, humor, religious depth, sensuality, and lyricism of black American culture but sees its radical enemies as black nationalism and the romance of Africa, both of which are finally so disappointing that they destroy one of his characters, just as bitterness over the shallowness of The Brotherhood did in Ellison's Todd Clifton.

The work's exceptional strength arrives through the virtuoso fusion of idiomatic detail and allusions to the worlds of literature and religion. Though the playwright narrator will push his own sound into the mouths of people when he feels like it, Forrest knows so well the diction, the living patterns, the aspirations, the courtship styles, the dangers, and the brands of humor from the alley to the penthouse that he is quite free to deliver his black American world with three-dimensional authenticity, while creating an antiphony between that universe and—to give but a *few* examples—Shakespeare (especially *Othello, Hamlet, Macbeth,* and *King Lear*), Poe, Hawthorne, Joyce, Melville *(Moby Dick,* "Benito Cereno," and *The Confidence Man),* Homer, Cain and Abel, Osiris and Set, Oedipus, Icarus, and Saint Paul. Having done a marvelous variation on it earlier, Forrest even tips his hat to Ellison's short story "Flying Home" for his finale. Those allusions allow Forrest to layer his renderings of the weights and wages of identity, murder, manipulation, greed, exploitation, ruthlessness, irresponsible uses of power, madness, and the heartbreak of the doomed romance. There are also copious references to black American writing, opera, boxing, popular songs, blues tunes, movies, cartoons, and the various kinds of technology that either support or destroy memory, threaten or sustain life.

As Joubert observes, interacts with, and contemplates the condition of the world he's in and the worlds he's known, Forrest critiques as often as he celebrates. In a masterful sequence, Forrest brings together criminals, church ritual, and the honoring of dubious martyrs. However much Joubert might be moved by the singing at the funeral of Aaron Snow, a scurrilous black drug addict shot to death by a black policeman, the narrator doesn't mistake the hot rhythm for substantial reflection: "They had all gone too far with this mushy-minded-mercurial palaver, in which the punk was elevated to a man on stilts, and turned into a kind of outlaw, as hero. I found myself disdaining the eulogizers, by and large, and pitying the blindness of the kids in the audience. . . . Oh, well, it is some burden to be known as a soulful people. Whoever heard tell of such chosen people, as also known for moderate lamentation? This was mindless celebration!" But it doesn't stop there. Soon "even the life of Emmet

Till was echoed out here in the chapel in several statements concerning Aaron Snow." The concluding speaker announces the establishing of a scholarship "to do honor to Aaron Snow."

Joubert's pursuit of the facts about Sugar-Groove, the folk hero at war with the dictatorial W. A. D. Ford, makes *Divine Days* a Melvillian detective story of shifting styles. The following of clues opens up the novel to much irony and humor, erotic attraction and sexual repulsion, tragic disillusionment and hard, ruthless violence. The literary flat-footing pulls in elements of the gothic, the tall tale, the parable, the philosophical argument, the novel of ideas, the history lesson, the novel of manners, and the sort of close observation Balzac, Mann, and Hemingway would admire. The technique of the novel is as musical as it is bold. Forrest prefers to lay his symbols out clearly so that the reader consciously watches him do his stuff the way an audience listens to jazz inventions on a standard song. He often sets up motifs—phrases, characters, colors, natural elements, conflicts, images, and so on—that form a chorus structure. With each successive chorus, the variations become more and more complex until they are either resolved or abruptly come to a conclusion, only to be picked up later. He also likes the extended dialogue, calling upon the precedents of Plato, Doestoevsky, Mann, Faulkner (especially "The Bear"), and the competitive invention of two jazz players foaming their creations at each other in four-bar units or entire blues choruses. Lengthy passages of evocative narrative in which the symbols are carefully submerged make obvious how well Forrest knows that the surreal nature of American experience often declares itself best when rendered accurately. The orchestral control from the first chapter to the last is apt to make our most serious novelists both grateful and envious.

As with every very long and great novel, there are passages that don't sustain force, fall into excess, or blubber into sentimentality. But, like a liberating hero who must rise over interior shortcomings, Leon Forrest never fails to regain his power and take on the details necessary for a difficult victory. *Divine Days* should capture the souls of all who truly love books and feel our national need for freedom from the rusty chains of an intellectual and asesthetic slavery that maintains itself by adding link after link of clichés.

HOW DID THEY
LIFT MY LOOT?

Barbara Probst Solomon's
Transcendent Detective Story

Gabe couldn't help noticing how she bloomed when she talked about money . . .
She savors it so, why didn't she make more of it? Go into it herself. Why did she
fiddle with medieval history?

Smart Hearts in the City

1.

Barbara Probst Solomon's famous essay about the posthumous, high-handed editing down of *The Garden of Eden* mightily shook Scribner's voodoo Hemingway industry when it was published in a 1987 issue of *New Republic*. That investigative essay impressed the way first-class detective work always does, supplying the pleasure of witnessing the covers pulled off a serious fraud. But her 1991 novel, *Smart Hearts in the City*, is a banana peel that can slide us out of our customary disappointment with the short range and the low ambition of contemporary American fiction. Still in print, it provides an illuminating pratfall from smugness because we are all accustomed to fiction that shrinks our understanding of this country by avoiding the evidence of those things seen just about everywhere—in our politics, our mass media, on our menus, our campuses, our showroom floors, in our department stores, our malls, our bureaucracies, the lobbies of our hotels, our movie theaters, at our airports, on our highways, in our advertising.

Going her own way, Solomon gives us a special vision of New York laid down with epic moxie. Like the big guns of the nineteenth century, she wants to make palpable the smell, the texture, and the presence of class, place, history, law, business, and dreams as they arrive through the visions, rituals, and ambitions of the society. Yet her pace, like our age, is faster than the stroll and the trot of last century's fiction. Ingeniously using modernist techniques, Solomon shoots for that high point of American understanding achieved by *The Great Gatsby*, where poetic precision summoned the weight of an age with the kind of accuracy Flaubert developed in the wake of Balzac—characters and situations that swelled in the juices of the reader's brain the way those small kitchen sponges do when they touch water.

Above all, Solomon knows that everything in our American story, every piece of our lives, is finally the result of our individual personalities and our interplay with the multiple realities that push against us from the universe of dollars and cents. In our world of unavoidable business dealings, we find ourselves part of the protracted war against corruption that raises the fundamental question of civilization under capitalism. That question—*How do we bring together morality, ethics, and the profit motive?*—is not only clear, it also provides plenty of imaginative and dramatic latitude for *Smart Hearts in the City*, which calls up more than fifty years of American life and history with stirring and hilarious attention to informing distinctions and representative anecdotes.

There is exceptional command of structure, thematic variation, the manipulation of symbols, foreshadowings, and echoes that resonate throughout the length of the tale, which is divided into three sections, a literary version of the musical ABA form. The first and third are set in 1986 and move over a period of about three and a half months. In the second, which spans the thirties and the forties, we are allowed to peep in on an American childhood of a special kind, one that evolves into an adolescence of interracial camaraderie and sexual initiation, then an expanding adult sophistication that tears loose from the snakeskin of protracted innocence as the hard blues of race, bad luck, and greed so inevitably intrude.

However elegant, sophisticated, and earthy the tone of this novel might be, it is also that most American of urban tales, a detective story. We follow the adventures of a middle-aged widow, Katy Becker, whom we meet on the Fourth of July, 1986. Her son, Matt, is away at school and she is ambivalent about what constitutes her love life. Lonely and mulling over her difficulties, she drives down to the World Trade Center, near Battery Park, where the fireworks are going off and her spirit is moving toward its own version of a Declaration of Independence, a document of feeling and engagement that will write itself in her epiphanies and her actions as the tale progresses. Katy is already at war, refusing to be trodden upon and battling to win back an inheritance left by her dead husband, Lewis Eichorn. The estate has been stolen by her brother-in-law, Beanie, who sits on the modern colonial throne of an international real estate empire.

Katy's lawyers aren't willing to dig into the case with enough passion. As with the prototypical American protagonist, she has to do it herself, to make a way where there seems no way. She becomes her own private eye, falling back on the improvisation and the mother wit that are so basic to our history. The pursuit of clues explaining exactly how she was bilked and how the money was hidden takes Katy across a wide stretch of Manhattan life, downtown to uptown. As she assesses both the filthy and the fancy, Katy discovers what coal miners know, that inside those dirty holes are the lumps that can illuminate. Conversely, our lady is rattled but not intimidated by the baleful rot found on shelf after shelf when she forces open the doors of the expensive refrigerators that are the private homes and show places of those who coldly finance the right cause of the moment with one hand, glorying in all the congratulations, while picking pockets with the other.

At first, spoiled and aloof, the widow Becker is not up to the task. She has to force herself free of a spiritual slump and a naive disdain for the details of finance she shares with many intellectuals and liberals whose handling of their business is sometimes self-destructively sloppy. In order to find the combination of facts that will unlock the mystery of Beanie's lowdown downtown doings, our feline private investigator has to return to the geography of her family's American beginnings, which are so much the richer for not being what we might expect. In effect, she does just what Ralph Ellison admonished white Americans to do—investigate the Negroid elements of their own "whiteness." (Fitzgerald did this by using the lyrics of W. C. Handy's *Beale Street Blues* as the thematic outline for his tale of wild partying, illegality, violence, adultery, false identities, clayfooted idols, and the mixing of classes in *The Great Gatsby*.) Katy goes uptown, north and home to Harlem, where the secret information she needs lies in a riddle of dummy companies, foreign investment, and real estate. Closing in, Katy must call upon all of her resources and relationships, everything she knows and every emotional debt or scrap of loyalty.

Her recognition of how she came to be who she is reveals to Katy the way to go and what to do. Encased in wad after wad of velvet and trapped—stuck—inside a stone of privilege is a fighting sword that Katy has to tug free, sweating, bleeding, and wailing until she becomes, finally, a woman armed with a combination of maturity, spunk, and cunning equal to her years. A central pleasure of the novel is the certainty with which Solomon shows us just how Katy's background provided her with the fundamentals of spirit, heft, aesthetics, social awareness, and contempt for personal and general injustice that become so essential when the chips are down.

2.

Katy is of German Jewish descent and was born in a tub of moonbeams and butter—twentieth-century enlightenment and wealth—around 1930. Her childhood home was at the upper end of Fifth Avenue, at 95th Street, where the public school district changed from privileged to a few notches lower as the street continued into Harlem. Her father, Jeremiah, was a World War I veteran and a lawyer with a poetic soul. He made the bulk of his riches during the Depression. His unruffled self-confidence in the face of worldwide economic turmoil charmed forth financial backing from Protestant bankers. But Jeremiah, the oldest of three brothers and patriarch by default, was progressively isolated by his somewhat uneasy emotional response to high, high success—a prelude to the greater isolation that came when he lost his fortune and other wealthy Jews shrank from him as though his fate might be contagious.

Jeremiah's fate might not have been contagious but an oblique version of his discomfort with success was absorbed by Katy, as, near the end, Solomon writes, "Now that she was so close to her goal, she began to lose her nerve; part of her yearned to backtrack to the comfortably more familiar position of defeat."

It is not until Katy integrates the strengths of her paternal heritage —the financial acuity of her father with the intelligence and poise passed on from her mother—does she become the kind of person capable of achieving a difficult victory. As she is kicking herself for never having pushed her late husband to work out his financial affairs because she didn't want to be "the family materialist," Katy realizes how silly she was to "feel like a heel for bringing up such mundane money stuff," reflecting:

> Your second worst flaw? Not looking after your own assets that would have come through your father . . . You could have worked with Jeremiah. You could have taken over everything involved . . . You might have actually liked the business end of things.

Then there is the other side of the Becker household. Katy's maternal family set down its Eastern seaboard immigrant roots in Harlem, where she was taken shopping as a little girl by her mother and her two Southern aunts, learning, little by little, how to discern quality from dross. Observing as though every gradation of her future depends on learning what her mother and her two aunts know, the Becker girl is all ears and eyes.

> She liked listening to her aunts' and mother's chatter—the women spoke in short staccato cuts; without warning they jumped from fish to silks to Hitler: they were sisters. They gossiped cattily about other women they knew who did not come up to their measure. Katy figured out it was important not to look wrong; she immediately understood what was no good from the lowered inflection in her mother's voice. Wearing too many real jewels was a definite sin. The three sisters mocked women who did. "Can you imagine such vulgarity? Wearing big diamonds at lunch!"

Anita, Katy's mother, was much, much more than a snob searching for other women to backstab with her sneers. She had a lyrical but imperious hankering for both the new and the substantial. Anita Becker, to that end, possessed the most important and mysterious gift of the upwardly mobile—good taste so firmly lodged in her eye that she couldn't be intimidated by Europeans. She was a pace-setting model for the circle of *American* women who felt so much envy and respect when in her presence. Beyond that, Anita's liberal politics were attractively counterpointed by her aesthetic curiosity and a capacious ability to keep Indian Path—the Becker's large summer home on Long Island Sound—aswirl with the buoyant feeling of perpetual good times. Of course, both the Fifth Avenue and Connecticut homes of the Beckers were run through by that inevitable conjunction of the understandable and the puzzling, which even the most pampered children experience as they try to interpret the passions, doings, and ideas of adults.

Katy's rite of passage into the world her mother dominates so powerfully through her exquisite choices comes when, as still a little one, she exhibits the gift of the family eye. Pushed, the girl tries to pick the best single piece from a stack of bric-a-brac in an antique shop favored by the trinity of Anita and her two sisters.

> . . . She was scared. She knew, because she had heard, that there was good stuff and bad, but she had no idea how to go about selecting. She saw a small, plain jar, of a blue as blue as the Long Island Sound on a summer day at Indian Path. Tentatively she reached out her hand. She looked at the women for a clue, but they said nothing. She grabbed it. The women immediately shrieked, "She's got it! She has the eye! The eye! The eye! Poppa's eye. Momma's taste." They hugged and kissed her as though she had passed some ancient *rite de passage*, and in their joy they bought more stuff.

That moment has multiple importance. Near the end and twelve chapters later, Solomon reminds us of that childhood experience when Katy rummages through a trunk chaotic with folders of documents connected to her suit against Beanie, searching "with the confidence of a woman who had been told early in life that she had been able to see." The lady gumshoe notices a discrepancy between the street numbers in a photograph of some Harlem buildings and the ones in a rental ad, a discovery that gets her closer to the devious specifics of how she was done wrong, how money belonging to Katy and her son was lifted in an elaborate bamboozle.

The rite of passage in the antique store also sets up another side of her inheritance, the coordinated partnership of the eye, the hand, and the knowing touch, that her grandfather, Saul Jaches, had: "Jil-

lian, Katy's younger aunt, then told her that her grandfather's 'luck'
in America had to do with his 'eye.' " Fifteen chapters later, when
the scent of victory is playing hide and seek with her nostrils, Katy
must go back to that trunk for one more piece of information, this
time functioning without her eyes.

> She seemed to be reading Braille; her eyes were slightly closed, and even
> without looking down, her fingers, darting this way and that, knew what
> was there. . . . She reached down to the floor of the trunk, then slightly to
> the left. She suddenly felt the stiffness of an unusually fat maroon folder.
> Her hands stopped searching and she lifted it out of the trunk.

Beyond the command of onomatopoeia, this passage is a skilled
extension of something we learn about Saul Jaches's coordinated
talents and what amounts to another version of reading Braille.

> According to Jillian, what had separated him from most cloak-and-suiters
> and accounted for his quick success was his ability to draw, to design for
> himself. . . . He drew swiftly, stunningly, with deft, firm strokes; it was
> also said of him that all he needed to do in order to make a woman the
> best-fitting outfit in Manhattan was to wrap his arms around her waist.

The passage also brings together the Gohonk summer home,
Indian Path, and the color blue, which, throughout the novel, refers
to travel on water, to the blue of her first love's eyes, those of mulatto
Brad Culver, to Texas where Katy had lived with her dead husband,
Lewis Eichorn, to musical blues, and a host of other things Solomon
set up in an earlier, sustained, lyrical passage that extends over two
pages. Here is one paragraph:

> There were the colors you saw. Blue is the color of intelligent memory.
> Of his eyes. Of the blue door swinging open at the white beach house in
> Gohonk. Of the Mediterranean, of the cornflowers and bluebonnets
> growing wild in the Austin Hill country, the blue of the East River in
> August, the colors of the old transatlantic French liners, of the Blue
> Mosque, of travel and the smell of Gauloises, and the Motherwell
> Gauloise, and "Blue Moon," and "Mood Indigo," and "The Blues in
> the Night," and "Sugar Blues," and not the blue of "Blue Velvet."

The rest of the passage twists together memories that are dominated by stream-of-consciousness spokes fitting into the hub of Brad Culver, whom we meet in the first section of the novel.

In the present time of the tale, Brad is married and lives on the West coast, "the most prominent landscape architect in the Bay Area," where his Negro wife, Elise, "was always quoted for her pioneering work in child psychology." As have many Americans, Brad takes advantage of the geographical distance between him and his beginnings, inventing whatever autobiography he wants, always choosing to leave the romance with Katy out of his black rap sessions because "She fits into no useable history."

But Katy calls upon Brad to help her move out of Texas and back to Manhattan when her husband is killed in an accident. No matter how conflicted he is and how much his wife resents this Jewish woman's power over him, Brad flies down and helps Katy get things together. He is impressed by the almost martial certitude she brings to the organization and the delegations of responsibility. That certitude foreshadows the strength she will bring to battle with Beanie. Near the end of the first section, Brad tells Katy she has been shredded from the story of his past and she introduces what will be the theme of the second part of the novel, almost teasing to a flame the erotic connection that was never snuffed out.

> She smiled at him as though making a joke. "You could pitch me as a Jewish woman . . . who was the child of two American parents." Her phrase struck her as funny, and she elaborated on it. "Every time has its dirty secrets. The nineteenth century hid sex, in the nineteen-fifties people lied to themselves about the place of money, and now our stinky little secret"—she took Brad's face in her hands, and, smelling of verbena, whispered in his ear, as if relaying to him some sultry bit of news—"is our American childhood." She paused, and added in a stronger voice, "We pretend it never took place. Like we're a bunch of stray ethnics."

In other words, just as whites have so often chosen to deny their relationships to Negroes, ours is a time in which the conventions of "blackness" encourage the simplifying of human experience in the interest of a half-baked "unity." This theme of single-lane minority experience with no curves or detours will be picked up later as Katy examines the way Jews like Beanie manipulate the horrors of history for their own self-aggrandizement.

The first section ends with Katy coming to a snowy New York and telling her father that she is now a widow. We have had the major characters laid out for us and know that some marvelous world centered in the Connecticut summers, a world that both Katy and Brad remember quite differently, is now lost in time and no longer the possession of the Beckers. The family fortune is gone, Anita Becker is dead, and the defeated Jeremiah lives in Manhattan's Volney, his brain partially submerged in the dimming jelly of semi-senility. Brad observes Katy as Solomon triumphantly expresses the majesty of this woman standing up to her task:

> From the car window he watched Katy, Snowball's coat thrown over her shoulders, walk into the hotel. She paused in the entryway, as though remembering something. She removed the dirty white sweater she had been wearing over the muumuu and carefully rolled it into an inconspicuous small ball. Then she pushed the snow out of her hair, put on her cousin's coat properly, stood up straight, and marched through the lobby to the elevator to tell her old man her husband was dead.

3.

The hundred pages of the second section, "A Family Romance," constitute one of the most impressive performances in our contemporary fiction. The central themes are ancestry, inheritance, the American freedom to create an identity, and the many meanings of miscegenation. We learn the stories of Jeremiah's and Anita's families — the bitter sibling conflicts, the dreams, the varieties of taste — observe the celebrations of holidays, and eventually see that there is a melancholy sexual distance between Katy's parents, both scratching their erotic itches with affairs. We are also shown Jews moving into the bourgeoisie and above, though all of the Lower East Side clichés are absent.

This is partially the story of the rise of a class and its influences on the scene and the scene's influence on it. In sum, the making and the makings of Americans. Poetic control of epic events is used to tell us how the grandfathers and uncles and cousins and aunts and friends and in-laws found the appropriate intersections of public appetites and the personal talents necessary to satisfy them well enough for small and large fortunes to stack up. The contradictions of success in business are well handled, as when Katy wonders how her mom and dad, who are so unswervingly supportive of the struggles of workers against their employers, can celebrate so ecstatically after Jeremiah negotiates the purchase of some mining property.

Brad, the olive-skinned, blue-eyed mulatto boy whose father remains a mystery, is reared with Katy and her brother Jim. His mother, the imposing Tartan, may have had an affair with Jeremiah, whom Brad comes to believe is his father. Tartan is from the South and works for the Beckers, who conclude that she and her son must move from Harlem into their Fifth Avenue home so that Brad can take advantage of the public school their children attend, P.S. 6, one of the best in the city.

Brad and Katy, unnoticed by anyone other than Tartan, get closer and closer, falling in love. Almost one of the family, Brad is not embraced the way he would like to be—an equal with access to all of the privileges he sees Katy and Jim slide into, such as private school. It is also true that the Becker household cannot compete with the Christmas dinners given by Tartan's well-to-do relatives on Sugar Hill in Harlem, where Katy consumes food with the same zest she later brings to sex with Brad. The way Brad admires the lobby of that Sugar Hill building foreshadows his becoming an architect, another of Solomon's refined strokes.

Brad's envy and jealousy form a thematic variation on the passions that drive one of Jeremiah's brother's mad. But the mulatto boy's turmoil does not change the fact of "the stinky little secret" that is his and Katy's equally American feeling for the world. The classic or urban fairy tales in books or comic strips, the Wild West, the radio, the heroines and heroes of film, the forbidden books that go far beyond the birds and the bees, and the concrete doings and structures of the world, determine the rhythms and dreams of their youth. They wear the same secret agent rings and, following Gary Cooper and Jean Arthur in *The Plainsman*, they have nicknamed each other Wild Bill and Calamity Jane. When Brad and Katy decide to canoe down the Croton Aqueduct into New York, the teenagers share an adventure on the water that spins its riffs off *Huckleberry Finn* but is far more symbolic of this country's pioneer heritage, so much of it resulting from young men and women standing up to the harsh and dark demands of nature. It is an athletic version of what Jeremiah and Anita have done another way, cutting into the Protestant territory of their summer home, becoming "forerunners" of social integration. Close reading reveals even more foreshadowing: the adventure points to the last section, where "sent up the river" and "sold down the river"—going to prison or being pushed into some form of slavery—are alluded to in Katy's talk and thoughts as the struggle with Beanie reaches the hot zone.

When Brad is accepted to a college in Wisconsin, he feels it is his chance to get away from Katy, to find out who he is and to assert the fantasy of his racial identity, to put all of his confusions and longings behind him. So the second section ends with the death of their romance and Katy's marrying the philosophy professor Lewis Eichorn after she graduates from Barnard. With her Lewis, Katy is on the water again, waving with him from the first-class railing of a ship heading for Europe. Waving back are Jeremiah, Anita, her brother Jim, and Tartan, all representatives of the mulatto coagulations of Katy's consciousness.

After breaking up and going their separate ways, Brad and Katy see themselves in terms of the bottomless past as well as the spectator sensations of mass electronic media that make our time so particular. By middle age, their memories take command and all myths become personal and malleable.

4.

In the third and last section of eleven chapters and one hundred and fifty-six pages, the complexity and detail of the second part are equaled, this time in a world completely adult. Katy has the task of resolving her personal and financial life, getting her man problem straight, and defeating Beanie. She brings off both in ways that are realistic and give us a very special portrait of the almost casual corruption that fish-tailed through the financial world of the middle eighties.

Any verson of the sanctimonious victimhood that pollutes the era
is too simple-minded for Katy. She is always asking herself questions
and fighting off self-pity, though she doesn't pretend that her problems are not pressing against the tip of her nose. The feeling of
responsibility for her son's future keeps blistering the edges of Katy's
mind. What worked for her as a child doesn't get it as an adult.
There is nothing in popular culture connected to being a widow
that speaks to her the way it did when she and Brad were kids. The
plots and the solutions are all the same: "None of the widow films
that Katy had seen had heroines who awake wondering how to pay
tuition; they never seemed *ruffled* economically. Why were these
women so much braver than she? Why didn't they need money?"

As for money in the world around her and the world she fights,
the world where Beanie sits on his throne, Katy sees the present of
the novel through a Balzacian black light that shows all of the moral
muck coating the fine surfaces of a particular strain of the wealthy.
Katy, accompanied by her cousin Snowball, goes to a social occasion sponsored by Beanie, who is the angel of an erstwhile avant
garde magazine, *American Rebel.*

Was the *American Rebel* a medical victim? Or a holocaust victim? Or
any type of victim? Was it new? Bohemian? A rebel? The crowd—
bankers, lawyers, and some arbitrage men, all on its board—were "nice"
Upper East Side. Their money was not so rawly fresh as the Boeskys',
the Steinbergs'; they had just a little less of it, and their names were less
often in the newspapers. Their morality consisted of not being named
Boesky, in not being up for prison. In New York in the eighties this suf-
ficed for honesty.

Beanie, ever the thief, has appropriated European tragedy for a
hustle that covers his own insatiable greed for attention and esteem.
This piece of social flim flam promotes a false vision of parallel
American suffering while putting the real estate tycoon at the center
of a high-class circle.

The air smelled of cumin, saffron, and scorched lamb. Beanie's Morro-
can couaye chef . . . had been stolen from the Mamounia in Marrakech,
Churchill's favorite retreat. He was serving his specialty: mechoui of

unborn lamb smuggled illegally into the States. . . . The guests included two competing art dealers, one expert on nuclear deterrents, a Milano dress designer, one expert on biblical canon, a Channel Thirteen anchor, and two Russian dissidents. The evening's *American Rebel* discussion topic, led by Beanie . . . was: The Mid-century American Jew: True Holocaust Victim. . . . So the Holocaust had become just one more equal opportunity gizmo; in America every victim for himself.

At another point, Katy remembers that 1986 was the hundredth birthday of the Statue of Liberty and works on this theme of uninterrupted European experience from another angle:

It occurred to her that, one way or another, her family had been connected to this city for over a hundred years. Jews confused being Jewish with being, eternally, the freshly arrived immigrant. But other boatloads had docked since they came ashore—hello, Hispanic, hello Korean. Wipe from your eyes the Holocaust gold dust hiding your natural history.

Those are the eighties. Forty odd years earlier, Katy had been an adolescent seductress whose charm pulled Brad into her pantics. Now, in her middle fifties, she has to give the bum's rush to an opportunistic folk singer from Texas who is younger than she is and whose erotic presence in her life has been used by Beanie's lawyers to paint her as a scarlet woman, one who probably called Brad down to Austin for sex while her husband's body was still on the way to rigor mortis. But here Solomon uses her understanding of how classes and ideas cross at the quirkiest times, creating influences beyond the perception of those affected. As Katy attends a ridiculous benefit for every kind of victim or would-be victim under the sun, the folk singer tries to seduce another woman right in front of her, inspiring an anger so obvious the judge presiding over her case notices it with his older sister from across the room. But when the judge puts Katy down, his sister, who has always been a supercilious pain in his backside, attacks him for having prehistoric ideas about women and about sex between consenting adults, all of which, in her scornful opinion, make him fundamentally incapable of presiding over the case against Beanie and giving a grown woman a fair shot. The judge's pestering sister becomes Katy's shadow benefactor and later relishes "every piece of press recrimination she could wave" as she pressures him to lean in Katy's favor when the covers are pulled off Beanie.

Katy also has to resolve a love affair with Mike Braden, a Jewish millionaire whose hobby is sailing and whom she goes to see when told of his wife's death by Snowball. Their romance is direct and adult. Katy knows what she wants when she visits him. The development of feeling between them is rendered with a gutbucket lyricism that balances the subtleties of mature affection and the viscous facts of sex. The affair works for a while but falls apart, haunting Katy as so many elements of her past do. Katy cannot be with Mike as a beggar or the wife of a rich man who ran to him out of poverty. They can only get it back together after she has had her victory over the devil, squeezing from his severed scalp the bloody coins of the pilfered inheritance.

But you set a devil to get a devil, which is where Adam Klager, "the shittiest Mr. Fix-it in Manhattan," comes in. A lawyer who made his name in the red-baiting era, harassing liberals and destroying their careers if it meant another step upward, Klager is dying of AIDS and would like to pull some of the ruthless down with him. Klager's legendary abuses of the law, the willful persecution of the vulnerable, and the readiness to suck off profit from almost any kind of scum is a theme given another variation in Beanie's stealing from Katy and her son. In fact, the dark and the light sides of the law determine how all of the attorneys and judges are assessed by Katy, most of them nostalgic about their public moments of supporting liberal causes way back when. Klager has no nostalgia. He is the devil with his dirty hands on the little balls of details. When Katy visits Klager in a townhouse and office that reeks of spiritual decadence, the expiring demon gives Katy a clue which takes her to Harlem, back to her beginnings.

The lady who has become her own private dick pulls Brad in once more. This time she does it through his mother, Tartan. Tartan pushes her unwilling son to help Katy make her way into Harlem real estate, to serve as a Negro side-kick so that she doesn't have to go snooping uptown all by her white lonesome. As Katy and Brad meet with an uptown realtor, the hostility between the two men is finely nuanced, the Harlem bigwig seeing the West-coast architect as another Negro who fled when he should have stayed and fought, while Brad hears what is said about the rebirth of a beautiful Harlem as no more than word of a fresh batch of fried ice cream. No matter, Katy lays down her family line as social credentials and flirts her way into the latitude necessary to search out what she needs, continuing to investigate the leads in Harlem after Brad has left for good, taking his mother with him, the last remnant of the Becker household and Indian Path.

Before his death, Jeremiah pushed himself up from his senility and went to meet Beanie with Katy, smacking everything they threw at him over the fence. Then, with biblical fury, he rose and spoke to Beanie about betraying his family, gave Katy a moment, a piece of information, an idea that would come back to her when she needed the last whetstone to sharpen her fighting sword. Once she gets it, Katy doesn't call upon her lawyer, Max Shecter, to do the job, to make the most telling incision under the scalp of the enemy. Alone but now pulling up everything from her family and from the wacky fundamentals of popular American culture, where the tough style became a national legacy, the feline investigator menacingly growls as she confronts Ronnie Munche, Beanie's lawyer.

> In her wild adrenaline surge, Katy floated past Max Schecter, past Jeremiah, to listen to her own voice: she reached back into the grade-B movies of her youth, to Cagney, Edward G., Bogart. . . . Ronnie was so distraught . . . that he didn't stop to think Katy's delivery had a nutty, obsessive tinge; in his unconscious, the Cagney style resonated as the Ur-truth of the land.

The lawyer capitulates, spooked by this Calamity Jane reborn forty years later as a Lower East Side Irish thug. Katy's victory is soon coming.

Like the lyrics of *Beale Street Blues* and the end of *The Great Gatsby*, this novel concludes at the water, after something has run dry. In Katy's case, all of the fantasies connected to her remaining a daddy's girl, a brilliant and charming child in a middle-aged body, have been pushed away. Indian Path has long been gone, even cut up into smaller units; Harlem is a garbage can that may or may not become a cradle for new and vital cultural life. Even our lady gumshoe's sentimental and envious moonings about the "Aryan" beauty of her cousin Snowball hit the deck when Katy is shocked by that unblemished blonde's midlife shift in sexuality. Nothing wet with the dewy sheen of perfection is left, and none of it is needed. Like the heroine in *Juliet of the Spirits*, our all-American protagonist lets the little girl in her leave like a favorite toy that doesn't function in the grown-up world.

On a way made solid by her own accomplishments, Katy stands tall in her maturity. She accepts her position as a woman well off and in charge of a foundation that will allow her to maintain the tradition of high-class tithing that Beanie and his bunch had set aside in favor of self-celebration and hustling more bucks through the causes they exploited as cooly as they did anything else. Her journey to the yawl with Mike Braden in the last pages has taken the reader across much of the urban culture of our time as one sort of a worldly person would know it—what they eat, how they vote, what they wear, the music they listen and dance to, where they summer, how they explain themselves to their therapists, which benefits they attend, the tricks that connect the dirty rich to the slime pit of drugs, and so on. The mulatto textures of Katy Becker's world and the many, many ways in which Barbara Probst Solomon has elevated her epic sense of Americana into literature, subtle to raw, is an achievement that should take a lasting place in the writing about the riddle of the human spirit as expressed within the context of this polyglot nation's bittersweet and stinking little secrets.

AN INTRODUCTION TO
MARTHA BAYLES

This introduction was delivered to the New York Institute of the Humanities on November 4, 1994.

What I like about the writer Martha Bayles is the all-American woman warrior quality of her work. It is something we can easily associate with Harriet Tubman and Susan B. Anthony, or see as a perfect metaphor in the accuracy of Annie Oakley. Moral outrage put into brave action by a former slave, intellectual lyricism delivered by a suffragette, and the ability of a pretty Irish girl to keep hitting the target long after everybody else has missed—all have a presence in the American story that we should never overlook in times as demanding of intellectual courage as ours, especially since courage is something we don't usually expect of intellectuals any more than we do of anybody else.

That woman warrior quality is something I first noticed in my petite and gracious grandmother. She was part Choctaw, part Asian, and part African. Not much taller than three fingers of whiskey, her personality under the best circumstances had the heavy charm of the finest Steuben glass. But when something as heated as what we give the legendary title of *Indian Blood* roused itself inside her, another set of traits came into the complexity of the person I understood slowly. Once, when I was about eight and riding somewhere with her, that *Indian Blood* sparked her to stop the car in the middle of the street and press open the glove compartment of the mint green Pontiac she drove with undimmed wonder and magisterial slowness. Her face now rigid with the incantational fury that is a condition of war, her brown eyes as unforgiving as the freshly sharpened edge of a bayonet, she pushed her man's Bulova wristwatch with the stretch band up almost to her elbow and used her right hand to remove the .45 automatic from that glove compartment where she kept her ruby lipstick and her compact with mirror and tan powder, as well a Bible suitable for Tom Thumb, various legal papers, candies, and bobby pins, even, now and again, a bottle of castor oil, and the Juicy Fruit chewing gum she smacked with pride because her teeth were all there and she wasn't worried about any sticky flare-ups. She pulled the hammer back on that .45 with her crimson-painted nail and put it in her lap, rolled down the window on the driver's side and waited for the big man in the rearview mirror who was cursing her for her driving and threatening her with assault. My grandmother was now sublimely relaxed and she fingered the handle of that pistol as familiarly as if it were a chipped button on an old and comfortable housedress. Brown and small, she sat there in her gingham and pearls, playing possum, waiting for him to move up into the close range of the open window on her left where she was ready to explain to him that he was, surely as the sun carries big light the way a field carries a bumper crop, this nasty, foul-mouthed man was on the verge of having his brains carried out of the back of his head faster than a coroner could say, "Dead."

So I have always associated women of integrity with the willingness to fight, whether they were willing to fight with words or with personal style, with weapons connected to the long history of brutal desperation or with the ones that present the intellectual beast of contemporary combat with smartly filed teeth so perfectly aligned the most decadent among us will discuss the shape of the bites, not the pain of the wounds. At this point in her writing career, which has included, among other things, insightful pieces on mass media and contemporary fiction, Martha Bayles has just had published *Hole In Our Soul*, which addresses the European salon rot that has parachuted into American popular music over the 30 years since the "British Invasion" of the Beatles and, especially, the Rolling Stones.

Surely, our popular music has always been vulnerable to our own national sense of sentimental expression, our celebrations of and

laments for sugar-coated crystalline figures that come into prominence whenever—which is almost always—we are dismayed by the
rough and tumble demands of our democracy, where our humanity
and our intellect are put to greater tests of empathy, deduction, and
imagination than those of any people in the history of the world. Far
more often than not, we Americans are both sappy and flinty; we
love to be maudlin and pretend we are hard-boiled, primarily
because compassion and toughness are so central to our history and
to what we have brought off as a gumbo nation of ever more complicated inputs of human style, choice, and direction. But the qualities of compassion and toughness usually find themselves dyed in
deep purple when they are put into the mass codes of our electronic
and entertainment culture. They become corny.

As a Negro, it has never really been a surprise to me that Negroes
could also be corny, but I must admit that some of the things that I
see in the extremes of popular entertainment have a corniness I
would never have previously believed was so all-American. We supposed minorities in our most naive states would like to believe that
there is some sort of majority corruption or lameness that we are
invulnerable to, that we're included *out of*. But the angels, the devils, and the vast majority of spirits between those two unsturdy points
of identity, have always believed in what we now call "non-tradi-
tional casting." So it is to the good that Martha Bayles, unlike those
literary critics who put high-class seals on the bottles of bathtub corn
liquor Toni Morrison produces, has no sentimentality about
Negroes. Her understanding of the antiphonal response between so-
called black and so-called white, so-called white and so-called black,
is superior to most of the commentary we get on the subject.

Far more than the bulk of Americans who purport to know about
the high points of this culture, she understands—as have Constance
Rourke and John A. Kouwenhoven and Ralph Ellison and Albert
Murray—the positions of democratic consciousness made possible
through the aesthetic achievements of Negroes in our national
music. I do wish she had a deeper understanding of contemporary
developments in jazz, but you can't get every present you want in
one package. Regardless of my inevitable carping, she achieved so
much in her book that there was a tizzy at the palace of the *New
York Times,* one that led to rock critic Jon Pareles being given the hit

man job of reviewing *Hole In Our Soul* for the Sunday Book Review. When they come at you like that, the way Bob and Charlie Ford got Jesse James, you can be sure that they are afraid of you. Without further ado, I introduce to you one of the hardest working people in the show and tell business of big-hearted intellectual clarification—Martha Bayles.

BLUES FOR JACKIE

The inaccurate idea of extremely separate realities that make collective experience a sentimental fantasy hadn't set in when Jackie Kennedy and her husband moved into the White House. In that America, for all its segregation, a sense of community was at work and the ideals of the nation were being forced to come alive, like stone monuments of mythological figures, or the weeping statues of the Virgin Mary, even the storybook toys on display when lights are low and the shopowner has gone home.

She appeared as a national presence in a time of turmoil and elegance, when the threats of nuclear missiles and universal destruction were in the air, when extraordinary young people of the sort we rarely see now were surging forward in the Civil Rights Movement, when the idea of a homemade American aristocracy was being taken seriously, when Khrushchev, in one of those terrible suits that then distinguished Russian leadership, ostentatiously slid his chair closer to that smiling Kennedy woman.

The blue-collar Negroes I grew up among took a liking to the Kennedys because they thought the Eisenhowers were dull and that Ike was on the golf course too much when he should have been doing his presidential job. Mamie Eisenhower was the sort of homely white woman Negro females loved to make fun of, from the way they dressed to the way they spoke. Most of those Negroes remembered when the radio voice of FDR had brought the nation through the Depression and World War II. Wanting some more of that, they went with the Kennedys over the Nixons.

The Kennedys had spark and Jack had grown into a handsome

man, a male swan rising out of the Billy the Kid version of an Irish duckling he had been when he was a young senator. His lady, whose myth went back to Lafayette's time and whose maiden name was Bouvier and who wore those marvelous Chanel dresses and spoke perfect French, well, she added strut and mustard to the White House. Gatherings of domestic workers in my mother's kitchen would admire her poise and clothes, something they had learned about from working in the homes of the extremely rich but the less than famous.

Because of their positions of service, those domestics knew more about how it really worked at the top than middle and upper middle class white Americans. They knew that that neither the blues nor stupidity nor callousness nor any of the maladies of human life fall down before money. So their experience made them high-quality critics of those privileged Americans who would be aristocrats, most of whom, like rock and movie stars, had *only* money—no grace, no manners, no taste—and were forever lost in the praises of those intimidated by their positions.

They thought Jackie Kennedy was the real thing because she had what they were confident all aristocrats, no matter their social stations, had to have—the ability to bring rich human warmth to refinement, which was very different from the flatiron pretension of the professionally repressed. Those domestics also knew that elegance is a form of courage, a way of standing up to the inevitabilities of disillusionment, decay, dissolution, and death.

When she sat in that limousine with Jack Kennedy's brains in her hand, her life crossed a line into blues territory that few of the privileged or the destitute ever know. Her face had the stupor of shock as she stood next to Lyndon Johnson while he was being sworn in on Air Force One. Jacqueline Bouvier Kennedy had reached across a century to take the hand of Mary Todd Lincoln, to experience the gangster politics of murder most foul. She was then put to the televised measure of public mourning, and in the ritual of Jack Kennedy's funeral, Jackie Kennedy's grief took on the majesty associated with Bessie Smith or Mahalia Jackson or Mary staring at the body of her son when he was taken down from the cross. She became all human sorrow. And she called the heart of the nation home.

Part Three

THE MIGHTY

SOUND AND

SWINE AND

TRANSCENDENCE

MARTIN'S TEMPO

This eulogy was delivered in April 1992 at a small memorial ceremony held in Virginia for the jazz and cultural critic Martin Williams, who had just left the living world and whose influence on my generation's writing about jazz was extremely large. Williams, who was born in Richmond, Virginia, in 1924, was one of the best who ever did it. He was always encouraging young writers to investigate the roots of jazz and had a rare grip on the value of artists across generations. Williams loved jazz as a unit and played no stylistic favorites because he hadn't been duped into believing that art "progresses." While Williams was quite aware of the essential Negro-American components of jazz, the material he wrote was pleasantly free of two tendencies in jazz writing—the ogling at noble savages and the reduction of music to aural sociology in rhythm and tune. Williams developed the skill to describe in clear language what constituted the art of jazz as he heard it. He was an editor who encouraged the writing of jazz books and was always working at something that helped document the art and expand respect for it, whether on college campuses or in the varied and important jazz work he did at the Smithsonian Institution. His critical interests extended across American art at large, and his last book, Hidden in Plain Sight, *was his attempt to step up next to John A. Kouwenhoven, who hit the longest balls on intellectual record. Martin Williams was one of those men whose passion, discipline, and intelligence helped define and give direction to the arena in which he worked. In every way, he was "made in America."*

An early law we all learn is that the velocity of destruction is much faster than the velocity of creation. We see this when a match is set to some paper or a wave does in a sand castle or some clumsiness results in a broken glass. All of the time that went into making those things, yet they are destroyed so quickly. We know, too, that no matter how boring the slowest days of our lives seemed, they were all on the express, not the milk train. The entire trip is over so soon. But what jazz has done, with its improvising attention to the details of memory, imagination, experience, passion, and design, is make the velocity of creation equal to that of destruction. No other art in our time, or perhaps in the history of Western performance, has done so much at such a superficially destructive speed.

I think that is why Martin Williams was so taken by jazz and why he dedicated his life to it and why he stood his watch through all those years when so few outside the community of the musicians themselves knew what it was. He understood the American miracle of the music and the wonder it brought to the arsenal of expression we use against the fall from consciousness to endless darkness that is the fate we all share. Martin knew that something had been added that could detail the passion of human life as it is given sense by aesthetic order. He bet his life on it and he tried to get as many others to bet theirs as he could. In that sense, Martin Williams was on a mission and one that few felt strong enough to join.

He was one who stood his ground against the Goliaths of contempt, of racism, of sloppiness, of disregard. He was dedicated and he was prickly, so knowing him could be inspirational one moment and similar to wrestling with a cactus at another. There was wit and sadness to the man, an affirmative grasp of the sensibility that enlivens the blues. In blues there is what I call tragic optimism, a vision that doesn't avoid the many shortcomings human beings are capable of but one that affirms in its very rhythm and its lyricism the bittersweet wonder of our lives. Perhaps that is what Martin meant when he described King Oliver's playing as containing "communal anguish." Of course, the idea of community is itself a form of affirmation, a recognition that we are all in this express drama of human existence, and a recognition of the fact that we can speak in some recognizable way of the wages and the elevations wrought by experience.

Martin Williams embraced it all. He wrote of television, of film, and of comic strips. Understanding the brutal pulse and the vitality of our culture, its fanciful conflation of folly and deep feeling, its irreverence, its hysteria, its unexplainable nobility, he became a high priest of perhaps that most invaluably human religion, the religion of integrity. In the process, Martin developed a language to describe the art of the invisible, which is music. He took it upon himself to learn what was necessary to render the feeling of jazz with the charismatic eloquence demanded of signal understanding. His was the way of dedication, and he would be moved by nothing other than the details of the meaning of the human heart in the motion of revelation we know as swing.

Like Thelonious Monk, whose work he loved so much, Martin was willing to stay out there, working often alone, creating small communities, and instructing by example. He was like no one any of us ever knew before and like no one we will ever meet. For a music so given to individuality, it is perfect that he was here. Martin, we will miss you, the tenderness of your spirit, your grit and your vinegar. Your intellectual progeny may be small, but then, so was the stone that felled Goliath. You understood the velocity of that stone and knew it as one of creation. And in every encounter, you were willing to hand over a stone that had to move at the velocity of destruction in order to create the space against death that is the essence of human memory made eternal. You honored your time and you swung it and we will never deny all that you have done and all that you inspired. God bless you now, for you were surely blessed while you were alive.

BEALE STREET REDUX:
TOM CAT BLUES
&
PASSING FOR WHITE BLUES

These two pieces, one published in The New Republic, *the other in the* New York Daily News, *were responses to the controversy dusted up by Charles Murray's* The Bell Curve. *The first appeared in an avalanche of attacks on Murray, which I knew would focus on race, so I shot for an overview based on traditional antagonisms, the metaphor beneath the skin. The second went after the idea of race in our society and raised some too frequently ducked observations about mutual social histories. Together, they form something of a diminuendo and a crescendo.*

1.

Ours is a country in which the responses to failure are often nearly the same as the responses to excessive success: low-boiling resentment and explanations of why the other guy without as much or the one with more should either stay down there where he is or be debunked for getting so much better a line of comforts.

The truth is hard to swallow as a fat piece of broken glass if you ask me and besides I heard tell that if you just look at it and don't mess around and just be honest about things and don't let anybody push you until you keep your mouth good and shut especially when it comes to the truth and let everybody know that it doesn't matter how much you try it can't amount to anything more than what it is which is something we all just have to face up to and let the chips keep on keeping on because it couldn't be any kind of way different than it is and trying to say something else won't even come close to making it so because there happen right now to be people who go to the schools way up yonder and they study this kind of stuff and you couldn't even get them to lie about something if you paid them because being honest is what the hell they spend all their damn time trying to be as it is. I mean Jesus H. Christ and the angel that tickled the hyena out of heaven!

The other side is, perhaps, somewhat different.

You mean to tell me I should take them serious when they try to tell me that just because they can afford this and they can afford that we should be willing to bow down to them and kiss whatever they put in our faces when it stands to reason that if they were all that why are their kids as bad as cancer and how come their wives are always laying down and looking up at somebody else and besides that let me tell you some people who are friends of the family who have a son working out of town in one of those real expensive hotels will give you the chapter and the verse on what the so-called Mr. Man of that big fancy house does when he goes to town and besides which if you put the entire bunch of them out here in the wind with the rest of us they'd get knocked over and roll away before you could say I told you so.

The panoramic lyrics of W. C. Handy's "Beale Street Blues" refer to a class-mixing world of secret lives, illegal celebration, potential disorder, and nostalgia. They formed the basis of the themes F. Scott Fitzgerald rendered in *The Great Gatsby*, a masterpiece that continues to clarify just who we are. In a fat book Tom had read—*Oh, Lord!*—that the lower races were going to rise up in cannibalism, licking their chops and ready to gnaw those at the top into a dead and bloody mess. Something had to be done about it. In his fantasy, Jimmy Gatz thought that upper-class identity could easily be achieved through name changes, claims to social pedigrees, expensive emblems, and big parties.

Neither the nightmares nor the dreams were right. Mistakes of one sort or another caked up the blood. It all came down to paranoia, counterfeit elegance, the corruption of national ideals and athletic games, the endless stomach the masses have for rot and gore, and our stubborn belief that we should be able to sit in our sandboxes and strike those next to us or those at the edge with the costly shovels and buckets that were made way up in high places. Even so, as the blind man on the corner sings in "Beale Street Blues," "I'd rather be here than any place I know. It's going to take the sergeant for to make me go."

2.

Because *The Bell Curve* raises the question of whether or not the majority of Negroes are doomed by their genes to be less intelligent than white people, the furor is understandable. The complaining noise is pompous, or paranoid. The pomposity is no surprise because we have developed a pulp set of reactions to the subjects of race and privilege that drain the blood from discourse. The paranoids always assume that there is a very dark corridor somewhere beneath the ground and around this corner and that exist a smoke-filled room in which white men of great power decide what design of steel-toed boots they're going to kick deep into the bottoms of so-called minorities.

Both pomposity and paranoia miss the issue. The real issue is what we mean by "race" and what we mean by "white" and by "black." It is perhaps understandable that when obviously mixed-bloods like Elijah Muhammad, Malcolm X, Rap Brown, Angela Davis, Louis Farrakan, and so on began to triumphantly call themselves "black" that we were on a path in which the evidence of what our eyes saw was supposed to take a secondary position to what we were being told.

The blood definition of Negroid was updated up from slavery and segregated restriction so that "a little dab will do you" could once again determine a closed racial category. Others see us Americans as culturally connected. Psychoanalyst Carl Jung observed that white Americans walked, talked, and laughed like Negroes, while Africans usually think of Negro Americans as dark-skinned white people.

No matter your definition of Afro-American culture, there is, quite frankly, no Afro-American race. The miscegenations have been too multiple, which is proven by almost any family gathering or by the seeming impossibility of light-skinned children being born now and again to dark-skinned parents, the recessive curve balls howling their ways into the world, striking out all expectations. What race could range in skin tone from pale to eggplant? None that anyone knows of.

Above all else, there is the fact that all so-called white ethnic minorities initially found themselves living behind a hostile set of stereotypes so close to the ones imposed on Negroes that those white ethnics were, in essence, socially black themselves. From the middle of the nineteenth century through the Ellis Island rush that began in the 1890s, new arrivals were met not with open arms but with pomposity and paranoia.

This is a fundamental American irony. Especially since those who said such nasty and biased things about the immigrants were themselves the descendants of convicts, witch burners, backwoodsmen, indentured servants, slave owners, carpetbaggers, scalawags, and the rest of the social mess out of which the democratic aristocracy of achievement arose. American meant blood and class weren't balls and chains.

Yet the stereotypes about the immigrant Irish, the Germans, the Italians, the Jews, and whomever else you want to list defined them as innately stupid, filthy, thieving, drunken, lascivious, and so on. The imposed iron mask of prejudice kept them out of certain neighborhoods, schools, private clubs, churches, and professions. That iron mask was one of negative blackface, the burnt cork of limited access.

Unlocking that iron mask was central to social mobility and is part of the arduous pioneer history of white ethnics expanding American democracy beyond the superstitions of prejudice. So the proverbial "nigger in the woodpile" was their early immigrant social history in America—and they know it.

This means that whenever anyone from a group formerly considered innately disreputable tries to uphold or justify any form of prejudice, especially under the guise of science, that person is truly "passing for white." One could say that social mobility, at its worst, allows for that smug masquerade, white ethnics hiding their blackface social experience under the bed. As for science, in the November 1994 issue of *Discover*, Paul Hoffman writes, "race accounts for only a miniscule .012 percent difference in our genetic material."

So the next time you hear some descendant of white immigrants talking about race as a limitation, remember that that person's forebears were social darkies and that he or she is only trying, desperately, to pass for white.

BIGGER JIM'S DUKE

On December 17, 1987, James Lincoln Collier, author of forty books, addressed and took questions from members of the Duke Ellington Society and a number of others who had come to see and hear the man responsible for a controversial biography of the organization's namesake. After delivering a lecture about jazz criticism, his own life, career, and research methods, Collier emphasized the importance of a new standard of jazz criticism, one demanding that, "If we are going to write about jazz, we should be writing about jazz as accurately as possible. It has forced those of us who are writing about jazz to come up to the mark, to come up to the same kind of scholarly standards that are applied to people who are writing about Beethoven or Wagner or Monteverdi or name it. I think this is the essence of it." Placing his own work in that context, Collier also said, "I write books for Oxford University Press. Oxford University Press is the world's oldest continuously running publisher. The English think very well of themselves and they insist upon anybody who writes for them coming up to a certain kind of standard. Whether I like it or not, if I'm going to write for Oxford, I have to follow certain kinds of standards and scholarly practice." Soon, he opened the meeting to questions and discussion.

What became embarrassingly obvious in that meeting is made even clearer upon reading the book: essentially, Collier's *Duke Ellington* is pulp scholarship, the work of a mind neither up to nor willing to take on the task of explicating the life, work, and context of a genius long obscured from view by intriguing mystery. It is an astounding example of putting on intellectual airs. Though Collier is never less than willing to accuse Ellington of laziness, pretension, perpetually hasty preparation, and ignorance of the components necessary for successful extended composition, those are actually the problems his own aspirant revisionism displays over and over.

In order to avoid any real work, Collier bootlegs the supercilious opinions of John Hammond and the hysterical dismissals of late Ellington by the French critic André Hodeir, truncates quotes that would lay his assertions low, evades the challenge of in-depth assessment of the last thirty years of Ellington's work, and uses a mask of informed disdain to hide his dishonesty and his lack of the technical skills any serious analysis of the sort he pretends to be making would require. The upshot is an elaborate con: a great amount of effort has been put into a ruthless charade. The pernicious extent of the charge is such that it must be refuted through close examination, primarily because it amounts to a scandal of no small proportion and reveals how much an unscrupulous writer can get away with when purporting to do scholarly work in the arena of jazz.

The bulk of detail, wrapped in a stubborn baling wire of unsubstantiated opinion, is in the first half. Then, to cover either his own shiftlessness or the rush to meet a deadline, Collier coats his prose with a sneering gloss and hurries to the finish, dismissing large bodies of experience and aesthetic expression as a poorly chosen way of life or proof of artistic erosion. Where one might expect illumination of an exceptionally intricate world and personality, the reader is given a dishonest cartoon vituperatively drawn.

Every complexity of Ellington's life and world is misinterpreted or willfully distorted, while the methods of his art and its range are perceived superficially at best. Collier believes that Negroes are inevitably victims of inferiority complexes, whether lower or middle class, and that they are never given to the potluck and will of human personality as much as to the imperatives of responding forever, even in the free air of art, to supposed white standards. "American blacks," writes Collier, "exist in a side culture running parallel to the mainstream, very similar to, at times joining, but never entirely part of the central culture. As a consequence, blacks have always been seen by the white majority as somewhat different, somewhat exotic, somewhat threatening. Blacks in turn have been forced to view the mainstream culture with two eyes—the one coveting the advantages whites seem to possess, the other angrily trying to reject a culture they have trouble laying claim to."

In order to make his case, Collier reorchestrates a mode of thought that has bedeviled the image of the Negro since the middle of the nineteenth century when minstrelsy split the Afro-American into two basic types, the rube given to barbaric charm and the colored man who would be white but was at a loss for the essentials. Depictions of "aristocratic niggers" who made jackasses of themselves by hopelessly emulating Caucasians allowed whites to maintain feelings of superiority to free Afro-Americans as well as slaves. "Minstrelsy's completely self-centered dandies," Robert C. Toll writes in *Blacking Up*, "who thought only of courting, flashy clothes, new dances, and their looks, epitomized . . . pretentious upstarts at their worst." Even Caucasian patrons of the Harlem Renaissance who thought themselves enlightened "friends of the Negro" tended to prefer the Afro-American who was "true to his origins" over those who fled them out of shame or the intimidation so basic to pathological envy. Primitive Negroes supplied such Caucasians with an escape from the strictures of middle-class convention, setting a boil to the blood of those who felt that civilization was some sort of a frozen lake under which they were interred. Such Negroes were romantic tools, burr-headed clubs used to smash holes in the ice. They could be pitied for their pathos and celebrated for their gaiety and sexual forthrightness. But when Negroes chose paths different from an imposed vision of black "purity," assuming they could expand their origins on their *own* terms, they were warned to avoid "the slippery pond of Western civilization," as a paternalist of the Harlem Renaissance admonished those on her payroll.

As Collier will have it, his subject's very baby carriage was rolled on that slippery pond. Born in 1899 in Washington, D. C., Ellington supposedly bought into a way of living and looking at the world that was passed down by white Victorians. "Upwardly mobile blacks cultivated the genteel mode endemic to the Western world; it demanded a rather formal manner of dress and deportment, coupled with an abhorrence of sexual display, drunkenness, and the open emotionalism thought to characterize 'foreigners,' lower-class blacks, and working people in general." For such people, the arts represented a way to "turn the mind to higher things and away from depravity and debauchery."

Of Ellington's parents, "aspirants after the genteel norms of the Victorian middle-class," Collier writes, "People like them, black and white, expected their children to do well in school, keep away from lower-class children, stay out of trouble, and deport themselves like little ladies and gentlemen." This is a perfect example of the writer's cultural illiteracy: what class *doesn't* want its children to do well in school, stay out of trouble, and deport themselves like little ladies and gentlemen? And as far as social thought goes among the lowly, there is a big difference between lower class and *low* class, the latter meaning that one is bad news not because of economic shortcomings but because of objectively bad behavior. Any community with a heritage of Christianity as strong as the one that existed when Duke Ellington was a young man would have that vision across the board, especially since the experience of bondage and the capriciousness of racism had taught most that the meanings of good and evil weren't determined by color, class, or money. Were Collier aware of that, he would understand how Christianity and democratic aspirations were fused with Afro-American culture.

Collier implies that what he perceives as Ellington's later biting off more than he could musically chew was rooted in the black middle class's "putting on airs." In this particular case that theme is given a "like father, like son" variation. The great musician's father, James Edward Ellington, called J. E., worked as a butler for a wealthy society doctor and was himself known for charming speech and aristocratic carriage, whether he had the money or not. "Given this attitude," goes the book, "the young J. E. would have been quick to emulate the style of the family. He learned about wines and food and about the most renowned makes of flatware and china . . . J. E. knew what a gentleman was, and he was determined to be one. There was an element of pretentiousness in this, but we can only respect his insistence that he was as good a man as any. Duke Ellington was not raised in a wealthy home; at times money was tight, in part because of J. E.'s desire always to have the best. But he grew up, paradoxically, knowing a good deal more about champagne and Wedgwood than most youngsters do, and it is clear that J. E.'s feeling for the elegant, however superficial, became part of Ellington's way of seeing the world."

Clearly, Collier is incapable of understanding the way social evolution takes place—that in a democratic society even those formally excluded from positions of conventional leadership or status often recognize the universal aspects of cultural elements considered beyond them by those the society favors. The idea of Negroes aspiring to things prejudiced whites thought theirs and theirs only is not proof of the human will to expand beyond what is given, but evidence of the wages of racism, of an imposed inferiority complex. Rather than adding something, such Negroes are seen as attempting to escape from the hellhole of post-slavery quarters.

But the bale of racism toted by Collier's Negroes comes through strongly in his description of early Ellington trumpeter Arthur Whetsol, who was also from Washington, D.C.: "He adopted the attitude common to many blacks of his time that they must earn the respect of white society by behaving honorably and with dignity." This is racist because it implies that Negroes could act "honorably and with dignity" only if they were trying to impress white society. It is also a subtle perversion of a statement Ellington made in his memoir, *Music Is My Mistress*, about what he was taught in grade school by a Miss Boston:

> When we went out into the world, we would have the grave responsibility of being practically always on stage, for every time people saw a Negro they would go into a reappraisal of the race. She taught us that proper speech and good manners were our first obligations, because as representatives of the Negro race we were to command respect for our people.

The Edward Kennedy Ellington fashioned by Collier could neither earn nor command respect in any true sense. He is a charming but superficial young man whose primary interests are preening, partying, and picking up women. Lazy, he neither finishes high school nor takes the discipline of learning to be a musician seriously. "One reason he never worked harder than he did at his music was that, at this point, he saw music primarily as a way into the spirit of the new age—the high life, to put no fine point on it."

By reducing Ellington's social beginnings to a toy version of culture and asserting that the maestro lacked seriousness, Collier is able to pretend that the young musician was barely competent. Ellington's modesty and wit throw Collier, and he accepts the oft-told joke that the inevitable appearance of a beautiful lady at the lower register of the piano was what drew the apprentice performer into professional music. In fact, music was something Ellington had feeling for above all else. He had no choice because he was so moved by it.

In *Music Is My Mistress*, Ellington repeatedly provides autobiographical corroboration of Malraux's observations about artistic calling, laid down in his *The Voices of Silence*: over and over the maestro describes his being pulled deeper and deeper into music by the experience of hearing it played superbly. Most important, the young Ellington sensed his dual heritage of the primitive and the sophisticated early on. His recollections of the sessions where local Washington piano players gathered shows how clearly he heard the potential of combining the homemade and the trained:

> . . . each would take his turn and display his own unique devices. Doc Perry and Louis [Brown] were the Conservatory Boys but they also had profound respect for the cats who played by ear, and in spite of the fact that their techniques were as foreign to each other as Chinese, they lauded them, praised them, and there was the most wonderful exchange. Everybody seemed to get something out of the other's playing. . . . It was a wonderful, healthy climate for everybody.

There is the foundation of his entire mature style and the intention behind his hiring musicians whose styles and sounds would seem to almost automatically conflict with or detract from one another.

Collier prefers an insidious caricature to any of that: Ellington's charm, not his musical seriousness or talent, gets him where his artistic merits never could. The password is "middle-class manners," and this is essential to his image of Ellington the Manipulator who will later be described as a bandleader who played his "men like a card shark manipulates the deck" or controlled them as a ring master would trained circus animals. Of course, the card shark is a fraud and a cheat, and the animal tamer has blanks in his gun. According to Collier, Ellington's own grandiose sense of himself, passed on to him through his father's superficial sense of elegance, drove him to charm and manipulate masterfully even when he was ignorant of what he was getting credit for.

As Collier would have it, the international community of musi-

cians, listeners, and writers who have praised Ellington, as well as
those who commissioned him to write sophisticated longer works,
were somehow all duped. Paradoxically, Ellington even duped himself. Claims Collier, "his naïveté lay in the fact that he did not realize there were things he did not know." No matter how great
Ellington is finally, he is also much less than cracked up to be by
"all" concerned. But James Lincoln Collier won't be taken in: he
understands music much better than Thelonious Monk, Dizzy
Gillespie, Tadd Dameron, Miles Davis, John Lewis, Charles Mingus, and Gil Evans, can hear Ellington's compositional limitations
better than people like Leopold Stokowski, who commissioned
extended works from him, and has analytic skills superior to those of
classically trained musicians such as Maurice Peress, a conductor,
composer, and orchestrator whose public lectures on the quality of
those extended works are obtainable.

Here is where John Hammond and André Hodeir fit into Collier's overview, the former primarily for claiming that Ellington lost
touch with his roots and made an enormous mistake when he began
writing extended pieces, the latter for his vision of jazz as music in
which the best work is usually done during a musician's youth.
Though important to jazz history as record producer and promoter,
as well as early champion of Billie Holiday, Benny Goodman, and
Count Basie, Hammond was also a paternalist and pompous busy-
body who wrote of himself, "I was, after all, my mother's son, not
quite free of her proselytizing impulse or the certainty of knowing
what was good for other people." But Collier owes Hammond so
much that he describes him as "an idealist, ever quick to sniff out
deviations from purity, a good many of which he detected in Ellington's work."

Hammond thought little of Ellington's longer compositions and
harshly criticized as "arty" and "pretentious" the 1935 recording of
Reminiscin' in Tempo, one of Ellington's first extended pieces. Collier acknowledges Hammond's dislike of the composition, but the
scholarly biographer hadn't the subtlety to pick up the fact that
Hammond was also the unnamed critic whom Barry Ulanov
described in his own biography of the maestro as being floored
when he later heard the piece performed in Chicago at the Urban
Room. Ellington didn't mention the name of the work, which the

critic, moved to the point of awe and near trembling, said was *"it!"* Helen Oakley, who was with Hammond when it happened, told this writer, "The critic was Hammond all right. Duke and I often laughed about that afterwards."

It is also important to Collier that Hammond wrote in his memoir, *On Record,* "I did not consider Ellington a first-rate pianist. I considered him a supreme jazz arranger and a great although limited composer." Following him, Collier says, "Duke, in my view, was a good jazz pianist, but not a great one." Then, faced with the testimony of his excellence by a number of important musicians, Collier concludes, "It is very difficult, I feel, to make judgments about rhythm players without playing with them." That difficulty has never stopped Collier from assessing musicians with whom he, as an admitted low-level jazz trombonist, has never played. For a supposed scholarly critic to even write that is but another example of Collier's lightweight thinking.

André Hodeir's essays "Why Do They Age So Badly?" and "Why Did Ellington 'Remake' His Masterpiece?" lie beneath Collier's presentation of some very old ideas about Ellington as fresh insights. In the first piece, Hodeir asks why so many jazz musicians fall apart once they reach middle age, turning to clowns or unimaginative parodies of themselves. In the second, outraged by a 1956 version of an accepted 1940 masterpiece, "Koko," Hodeir spurns Ellington by writing, "The Duke has simply lost the remarkable musical sensibility which lay at the heart of his genius, or else he was never really conscious of the beauty of his music." Collier himself believes this and parrots a conventional vision: Ellington developed a powerful style between 1927 and 1939 that reached its greatest realization in the music produced by the band of 1940–42. Then, still overly impressed by Europeans celebrating him as a composer, the maestro floundered by taking on the task of working in extended forms that were beyond his abilities. The beginning of the end was best predicted by the supposedly abortive *Black, Brown, and Beige* of 1943. When bassist Jimmy Blanton died, Cootie Williams, Barney Bigard, Rex Stewart, and Ben Webster left, and trombonist Sam Nanton died, the "true" Ellington sound also expired, never to come alive again.

This vision of Ellington's deterioration is sustained with a

vengeance. The problem was one of delusion. His reception as a
major composer in England when the Ellington band performed
there in 1933 rekindled something from his background: "Duke
Ellington had come from a middle-class home where the word
'composer' almost automatically came attached to the word 'great."
He knew—or he thought he knew—what an artist was and, if that
was what he was, he ought to live up to the role. To a considerable
extent, Ellington was deluding himself about his European reception." Those middle-class manners had ruined him from the start.
The superficial grasp of elegance and position passed on from J. E.
had been a curse upon his son. That sense of life might have given
Ellington such confidence in his own importance that he remained
ambitious, but there was a point beyond which the bandleader and
composer should never have gone: the three-minute performance.
In this tragedy, social environment and class are the fates. The hero
overreaches his gifts through arrogant belief in their invincibility.
He gets out of his place, becomes uppity to a tragic point, and is
pulled down. The pride instilled in Ellington from childhood was
inflated to such an extent by his own vision of self-esteem that he
was tempted to folly.

But that pride and those "middle-class manners" also served him
well, from his days as an apprentice to those of international celebration. "Apparently, he was an ingratiating young man because
several of the older men went out of their way . . . to help him."
Ellington wrote of being invited to the homes of the pianists and
teachers Oliver "Doc" Perry and Henry Grant after they either heard
him play or heard of him. That would suggest that the young Ellington had recognizable talent, which Collier labors to deny, preferring to imply that whatever attention the young musician got had
more to do with his social skills than his artistic soul.

As Ellington began traveling to New York with what would eventually become his own band, struggling at first, retreating to Washington, returning to New York, retreating, finally getting an
important job at Barron's, the premier Harlem night spot, Collier
concludes that "middle-class manners" impressed the singer and
later soul food restaurateur in Paris, Bricktop, who suggested the
Washingtonians to the nightclub owner. Collier appears to have
read the memoir *Bricktop*, but chose not to address her assessment

of the musicians. According to Bricktop, "I really liked Washington, D.C., and every chance I got I went there. One of the reasons was a combo called Elmer Snowden's Washingtonians . . . I met them when I was singing at the Oriental Gardens at Ninth and R Streets, N.W. Later on I partied with them and made sure I caught them wherever they were playing. I'd already been lucky enough to meet some great musicians, but I knew a sound outfit when I heard one. The Washingtonians were something."

This is an important distortion of fact, or avoidance of contrary opinion, and it is basic to what Collier does throughout the book. By reducing Ellington's early success to a surface social technique ("He clung to that almost ritualized tony manner of speech that he had acquired from J. E. This was in part due to his character, his sense of himself as aristocracy; but it was also contrived, something he had learned was helpful in business."), Collier shrinks the Negro world to one in which deportment is more important than substance. In Collier's slightly upgraded Amos and Andy conception, those "middle-class manners" function as social trinkets so impressive to urban bushmen that even remarkable musicians such as Harlem stride piano giants Willie "the Lion" Smith, Fats Waller, and James P. Johnson, are taken in by them. Collier is so ignorant of how relationships among musicians work that he believes the men accepting Ellington as either a prodigy or confidently sending the young piano player out to substitute for them made decisions that had nothing to do with his talent. The implication is that there were no aesthetic standards: all musicians had to do if they were Negroes was to carry themselves in a way that endeared, and success was imminent.

Collier's determination to reduce Ellington and his world leads him to paint the maestro as no more than a careerist whose methods were simple. When Ellington begins to find his direction as a composer, Collier lets the reader know that no aesthetic demon is pushing him: "He was composing not because he was driven by an inner flame, a vision of himself as a black Joyce who would forge in the smithy of his soul the music of his race, but because he wanted his band to succeed." The continual refashioning of arrangements that kept his music fresh and its nuances in flux is made easy: "He would make changes as he saw fit, switching sections around. A piece was never really finished but went on changing for as long as the band played it. This was relatively easy to do; since very little was on paper, it was simply a question of telling the men of the change."

Though Ellington, like all who substantially expand an idiom, had a contempt for the rules that underlie slavish convention, the conclusions he came to that shaped his own style and attended his relentless bending of forms were not the result of a superior musical intellect: "He was driven . . . by temperament, not any careful process of thought. . . ." That last position allows Collier to avoid dealing with the depth of musical thought Ellington exhibited from the late twenties through his death in 1974. Collier is also able to maintain the old sense of jazz as the work of primitives who intuit their art. "Jazz," he sagely informs us, "is more emotion than design," and ". . . architecture is not an important concern of most jazz musicians." Give me that old-time natural rhythm.

Collier then claims that Ellington never really knew enough about music to either innovate consciously or to function as a composer in longer forms of the sort pioneered by the European masters. The intellectual logic is specious. Of his earliest band, Collier concludes, "They were playing . . . the peppy, new dance music that hundreds of bands around the United States were playing," which means that they were journeymen, purveyors of the day's convention. Yet, when the distinctive dissonances began to emerge, the maestro couldn't have known they were there: ". . . in most instances, Ellington broke rules simply because he was unaware of them. He never, even after he was writing extended and quite complex pieces, knew much about formal music theory . . . I am certain that Duke would not usually have been able to analyze his own scores in the way a more formally trained arranger would. . . ." This is pure perversity. At the beginning of the biography, Collier quotes from the clarinetist Barney Bigard's book, *With Louis and the Duke*, but neither acknowledges nor argues with this section of it: "We were playing a concert for the New York School of Music and this professor of music had his class there. We were playing 'Crescendo in Blue' and the professor had the class to figure out what Duke had done as a lesson. They couldn't grasp what Duke was up to and neither did their professor. Duke had to stand out in front of the class and go over what he had just played step by step. He had to explain it to the professor, too." Bigard, the music professor, and the class must have been taken in by Ellington's "almost ritualized tony manner of speech."

However often Ellington made it clear that he was writing Negro music, not attempting to emulate European practices, Collier says of his fifty-minute *Black, Brown, and Beige*, "Ellington did not set out simply to expand the sort of thing he had done with 'Mood Indigo,' 'Creole Love Call,' or 'Rockin' in Rhythm.' He tried, instead, to write something that seemed to him symphonic, using a lot of jazz rhythms and other jazz effects here and there." Collier assumes that Ellington's models were *Rhapsody in Blue* and *Grand Canyon Suite*, then goes on to say, "I have seen this sort of thing happen, again and again: the writer of a much-admired children's book abandons his method when he sets out to write an adult novel and tries to imitate Henry James; the successful illustrator paints in a wholly different style when he does what he considers serious work." To compare Ellington with a praised writer of children's books or an advertising illustrator suggests things about him and about jazz that are uncomfortably close to preconceptions about the capabilities of Negroes and the substance of even their most shining aesthetic efforts no audience member of the nineteenth-century minstrel shows would have trouble recognizing.

Collier's Ellington almost inevitably threw pieces together in the studio because he "lacked the training to sit down at the piano and write a piece cold," which supposedly explains his inability to work in longer forms and his dependence on his musicians to fill the holes he hadn't the imagination to close with his pen. Yet Rex Stewart, an Ellington trumpeter whom Collier describes as "certainly intelligent . . . one of the very few jazz musicians to write seriously about the music," penned this observation of Ellington's discipline in an essay the biographer surely read but, again, doesn't acknowledge: "Many's the time that I have seen him on the Ellington Orchestra's Pullman with his feet propped up and a towel draped over his eyes, seemingly in repose. Then, he'd suddenly jump up as if a bee had stung him, grab a scrap of manuscript paper, a yellow pencil and scribble madly for hours—or sometimes only for a minute. Other times, he has been observed riding in a bus of ancient vintage that seemingly never heard of springs, jounced around like a dodg'em at a carnival, but the Governor wrote on and on, not concerned as we, the members of his band, were with the lack of comfort. As I recall, it was a rare day that Duke didn't write something, even if it was only four bars." Not bad for a lazy guy who was only committed to the high life.

This kind of dishonesty dominates the text, attended by Collier's Cub Scout morality, which functions to demean Ellington's musicians, reducing them to "bad boys" who are verbally spanked for letting down the very middle-class standards of manners and deportment that had so misled J. E. and his son. After all is said and done, Ellington was at the helm of a bunch of drunks, cranks, and eccentrics, with a dope addict or two thrown in. Losers, victimized by Ellington's need for applause and adulation, they have their music stolen by the leader, a meager talent and master trickster whose ability to manipulate made possible his enormous success.

No matter how much Ellington is celebrated for the depth of his contribution to the music, his motives are always external, when not haphazard decisions made on the moment. The first plunger player, Bubber Miley, is hired because Ellington sees that the "sweet" music his band played in the twenties was on the way out and he needed the trumpeter to assure the ensemble's success as jazz became more popular. Lawrence Brown was not hired to add another voice or color, but to get the jump on other bands by first having three trombones in the section. Ellington employs tenor saxophonist Ben Webster in order to keep pace with the big bands that already have featured players of that instrument. Directions are "cooked up," music is "thrown together in the studio," and Ellington's taste in singers is the result of his being "middle class." The remarkable gift that the maestro had for bringing together musical elements that would seem to clash but that were made coherent and fundamental to his sound isn't understood as part of a conception Ellington consciously maintained throughout his career: ". . . rather than think through the critical question of the make-up of the band and whom, specifically, he should get to replace the departing veterans, he would wait for the crisis to arrive and then reach out blindly for whoever happened to stumble in his way in order to smooth the path in front of himself as quickly as possible."

Collier then chides Ellington for not replacing band members with white musicians such as Jack Teagarden, Bobby Hackett, Bill Harris, Lou McGarity, Zoot Sims, Stan Getz, and Sonny Berman, crystal-balling this explanation: ". . . despite Duke's refusal to take a public stand on racial matters and despite his itch for meeting powerful and celebrated whites, he recognized that whites had generally, after all, treated his people brutally and even as late as 1945 showed little inclination to stop. Why should he do anything for white people when they had done nothing for blacks except use them as workhorses and cheat them as frequently as possible?"

No public stands? Two examples. According to his sister, Ruth Ellington, the maestro was playing benefits in Washington for the NAACP as early as 1928, which is how she met the leadership that would later make use of her services. John Hammond wrote in *On Record* of Ellington performing solo piano in a benefit for the Scottsboro Defense Committee at New York's Rockland Palace in December 1932. Given the controversy surrounding the trial of the Scottsboro Boys, Ellington could hardly have been more public.

The musicians he suggests Ellington should have hired wouldn't have fit his tonal tastes and lacked the kind of character that the maestro preferred. To assert that Getz and Sims would have sounded good in the band is further proof of Collier's ignorance. Ellington *never* used Lester Young–derived tenor saxophonists: all of them were variations on the Coleman Hawkins–Ben Webster sound. To say that Lee Wiley or Peggy Lee would have been better for him than Joya Sherrill or Kay Davis is equally uninformed. Which of them could have sung the parts Ellington wrote for Davis on "Minnehaha" and "Transbluesency"?

Rex Stewart's writing is again ignored, this time regarding Ellington's supposed racial animosity toward whites: "Ellington was careful to make certain that no one possessed any parts of his music until he chose so, nor did he permit others access to perform it. I recall only two exceptions that he made—when Charlie Barnet's music was destroyed in the fire at the Palomar, Ellington came to his rescue with the loan of arrangements. Later, he helped sponsor Boyd Rayburn's band with both arrangements and money." Perhaps neither Barnet nor Rayburn was actually Caucasian; maybe they were just passing for white.

When Collier's alternately perverse and insipid ideas don't mar the book, his remarkable shoddy scholarship does. "Astonishingly," writes the biographer, "even though he saw his concert pieces as central to his life's work, he never bothered to put together definite scores that might be played by other orchestras. After his death Andrew Homzy, a musician and Ellington specialist, had an opportunity to go through a trunkful of Ellington manuscripts in Ruth Ellington's possession. He found bits and scraps and pieces that simply defied being put into order."

At the aforementioned Duke Ellington Society meeting where Collier spoke and answered questions about his book, the trumpeter, arranger, and transcriber David Berger accused Collier of confusing two stories that Homzy told the biographer about Charles Mingus and Ellington. Collier testily denied making such a mistake. In an interview with Homzy, this writer was told, "I had a late lunch with Collier when he was working on the book. I had two beers and Collier had about four beers and six white wines. I told him about going through Mingus's manuscripts and how they were disordered and had to be organized, which I volunteered to do for his widow, Sue Mingus. Then I told Collier that I had called Ruth Ellington to get copies of some lead sheets. He confused the two stories and I'm embarrassed to see my name in a book and connected to such an inaccurate passage."

Further, the conductor Maurice Peress pointed out at the same meeting that the scores for almost every one of the concert pieces is available from the G. Schirmer music company. He also said that had Collier called him, he would have gladly helped the writer with analyzing the music, which he knew had been discussed in a very inadequate fashion. "I felt," said Peress, "what you had to say, especially about the concert pieces, was a cheap shot and would need much more time, much more scholarship, and a much deeper musical mind, and someone to look at the music."

Much more time and deeper musical thought were neither intended nor possible. At the Ellington Society meeting, Collier defended his glib dismissals of the last thirty years of Ellington's work in thirty pages by saying that Oxford University Press would not have published his book if it contained another one hundred pages. A little checking reveals that Collier fell short of doing all that he could to meet the challenge of his subject. Ellington musical scholars like Herb Pomeroy, Bill Dobbins, and Gunther Schuller were never interviewed, especially about the later work, and a number of reviews have already shown how little Collier himself knows about the European techniques and the harmonic conventions he accuses Ellington of not understanding well enough to achieve what he set out to do in his extended works. His insistence on discussing suites as though they were symphonies is also exemplary of his mock disdain.

"Bigger Jim" evades the issues facing any true biographer of Ellington: the determined development that exceeds that of any other jazz musician, the unrivaled range of moods and techniques, the creation of masterpieces, long or short, in every decade. Contrary to numskulled convention, Ellington's greatest period might well have been from 1956 to 1970, when he had mature players who could bring greater depth to his music than ever before and when his ability to extend himself resulted in an unparalleled number of astonishing albums that include, as examples, *Such Sweet Thunder*; *Black, Brown, and Beige* (with Mahalia Jackson singing an overwhelming "Come Sunday"); *Newport 1958*; *Anatomy of a Murder*; *Indigos*; *Piano in the Background*; *At the Bal Masque*; *A Midnight in Paris*; *The Ellington Suites* (containing "The Queen's Suite," "The Goutelas Suite," and "The Uwis Suite")"; *The Nutcracker Suite*; *Paris Blues*; *Afro-Bossa*; *The Popular Duke Ellington*; *The Far East Suite*; and *The New Orleans Suite*. As Martin Williams has noted, no assessment worthy of its subject has ever been made of late Ellington, and our all-American maestro from Washington, D.C., remains one of the most formidable challenges facing American biography and musical criticism.

ON THE CORNER:
THE SELLOUT
OF MILES DAVIS

The contemporary Miles Davis, when one hears his music or watches him perform, deserves the description that Nietzsche gave of Wagner, "the greatest example of self-violation in the history of art." Davis made much fine music for the first half of his professional life, and represented for many the uncompromising Afro-American artist contemptuous of Uncle Tom, but he has fallen from grace—and been celebrated for it. As usual, the fall from grace has been a form of success. Desperate to maintain his position at the forefront of modern music, to sustain his financial position, to be admired for the hipness of his purported innovations, Davis turned butt to the beautiful in order to genuflect before the commercial.

Once given to exquisite dress, Davis now comes on the bandstand draped in the expensive bad taste of rock 'n' roll. He walks about the stage, touches foreheads with the saxophonist as they play a duet, bends over and remains in that ridiculous position for long stretches as he blows at the floor, invites his white female percussionist to come, midriff bare, down a ramp and do a jungle-movie dance as she accompanies herself with a talking drum, sticks out his tongue at his photographers, leads the din of electronic clichés with arm signals, and trumpets the many facets of his own force with amplification that blurts forth a sound so decadent that it can no longer disguise the shriveling of its maker's soul.

Beyond the terrible performances and the terrible recordings, Davis has also become the most remarkable licker of monied boots in the music business, willing now to pimp himself as he once pimped women when he was a drug addict. He can be seen on television talking about the greatness of Prince, or claiming (in his new autobiography, *Miles*) that the Minneapolis vulgarian and border-line drag queen "can be the new Duke Ellington of our time if he just keeps at it." Once nicknamed Inky for his dark complexion, Davis now hides behind the murky fluid of his octopus fear of being old hat, and claims that he is now only doing what he has always done—move ahead, take the music forward, submit to the personal curse that is his need for change, the same need that brought him to New York from St. Louis in 1944, in search of Charlie Parker.

Before he was intimidated into mining the fool's gold of rock'n'roll, Davis's achievement was large and complex, as a trumpet player and an improviser. Though he was never of the order of Armstrong, Young, Parker, or Monk, the sound that came to identify him was as original as any in the history of jazz. His technical limitations were never as great as commonly assumed, except when he was strung out on drugs and didn't practice. By January 1949, when he recorded "Overtime" with Dizzy Gillespie and Fats Navarro, he was taking a backseat to nobody in execution. By May 1949, when he traveled to France and was recorded in performance, he was muscling his way across the horn in molten homage to Navarro and Gillespie, the two leading technicians of the bebop era; he was three weeks short of his twenty-third birthday and already had big-band experience with Billy Eckstine and Gillespie, already had stood next to Charlie Parker night after night on bandstands and in studios.

The conventional idea that Davis discovered that he couldn't play like Gillespie, and proceeded to develop a style of stark, hesitant, even blushing lyricism that provided a contrast to Parker's flood of virtuosic inventions, is only partly true; a methodical musician, Davis systematically worked through the things that were of interest to him. Eventually he personalized the levels of declamation, nuance, melodic fury, and pathos that are heard, for example, in Parker's "Bird of Paradise." But first he examined Gillespie's fleet approach and harmonic intricacy, which shaped the dominant approach to bebop trumpet. From Gillespie, he learned bebop har-mony and was also encouraged to use the keyboard to solve prob-lems; he even took from Gillespie an aspect of timbral piquancy that settled beneath the surface of his sound. But Davis rejected the basic nature of Gillespie's tone, which few found as rich or as attractive as the idiomatic achievements of the Negroid brass vocabulary that had preceded the innovations of bebop. Davis grasped the musical power that comes of having a sound that is itself a musical expression.

He moved in the direction of a refined *and* raw understanding of tonal manipulation based in the blues. His early problems with pitch demanded that he focus first on the quality, the weight, and the accuracy of his sound. Once he established control over his tone, Davis's work began to reflect his affection for the resources of color and nuance heard in Armstrong, Freddy Webster, Harry Edison, Buck Clayton, Rex Stewart, Navarro, Dud Bascomb, and Ray Nance. But his extraordinary discipline led him to strip everything away, striving for a sound that was direct in its clarity, almost pristine in its removal from the world of Negro trumpet tone. On that clean slate, Davis later added dramatic timbres and attacks.

Next Davis chose to work out a style that was superficially simple, that was rarely given to upper-register explosions or to the rhythmic disruptions that the boppers had built upon the droll games that Lester Young played with the beat. On his first recording as a leader in May 1947, Davis already had the dark, warm sensuousness that he later extended and refined. By using Charlie Parker on tenor, rather than on his customary alto, Davis got a richer texture, the sort of thickness that he favored in his later quintets; and a number of writers have heard premonitions of the tonal concerns, the phrasings, and the moods of "The Birth of the Cool," the highly celebrated but essentially lightweight nonet sessions that Davis steered a few years later.

But the essential influence on Davis's first recordings as a leader was still Parker. The saxophonist's 1946 recording of his "Yardbird Suite" with Davis as a sideman shows precisely the ease that characterizes the playing and the writing of the trumpeter's own session, especially "Half Nelson" and "Milestones." On that first date, Davis not only plays quite well himself, but uses the mood of the material to inspire Parker to reach for an emotional projection that the saxophonist rarely called upon. Davis resides comfortably in the middle register as he improvises through the difficult harmonies of his compositions, sailing and swinging in almost seamless legato eighth notes on "Little Willie Leaps" and inventing a meticulous thematic improvisation on "Half Nelson." Harmonically his notes say bebop, and he works toward the layered sound that has a top, a middle, and a bottom, all the while understating a thoroughly felt joy as he nearly swings the ink off his tail.

Equally important were a number of other recording dates under Parker's leadership. There are examples in the ballad sessions of the winter of 1947 of the softer approach to sound and ensemble, as when Parker plays delicate and soaring obligatos behind Davis on "Embraceable You," "Out of Nowhere," and "My Old Flame." Even earlier, as the flutist and composer James Newton points out, the contrapuntal Parker writing of "A-Leu-Cha" and "Chasin' the Bird" brought to bebop qualities that Davis's "cool" nonet explored. By "Marmaduke" in 1948, Davis is much closer to the almost purely melodic style of quiet but calling intensity that became an important aspect of his musical signature.

Then came "The Birth of the Cool." Davis's nonet of 1948–50 played little in public and recorded only enough to fill an album, but it largely inspired what became known as "cool" or "West Coast" jazz, a light-sounding music, low keyed and smooth, that disavowed the Afro-American approach to sound and rhythm. This style had little to do with blues and almost nothing to do with swing. That Davis, one of the most original improvisers, a man with a great feeling for blues, a swinger almost of the first magnitude, should have put "cool" in motion is telling. Indeed, it is the first, premonitory example of his dual position in jazz.

Heard now, the nonet recordings seem little more than primers for television writing. What the recordings show us, though, is that Davis, like many other jazzmen, was not above the academic temptation of Western music. Davis turns out to have been overly impressed by the lessons he received at Juilliard when he arrived in New York in 1944. The pursuit of a soft sound, the uses of polyphony that were far from idiomatic, the nearly coy understatement, the lines that had little internal propulsion: all amount to another failed attempt to marry jazz to European devices. The overstated attribution of value to these recordings led the critical establishment to miss Ellington's "The Tattooed Bride," which was the high point of jazz composition of the late 1940s. Then, as now, jazz critics seemed unable to determine the difference between a popular but insignificant trend and a fresh contribution to the art.

Davis began making his truest contributions as a leader in the 1950s. The Prestige recordings from 1951 to 1956 have been reissued in a single package, and it constitutes one of the richest bodies of work in small-group jazz. One hears Davis consolidating influences, superbly cross-weaving improvisational styles and instrumental approaches, in his own playing and in that of the musicians he brought together. The quintet included John Coltrane and a rhythm section that was nearly as important to jazz of the fifties as Basie's was to that of the thirties.

In the early fifties, inspired by Monk, Armstrong, Young, and Holiday, Davis learned to strip away everything not essentially musical. He maintained the harmonic sophistication of the bebop school, but picked only the most telling notes for the construction of his melodic lines. He recognized that the smooth swing of Basie and the territory bands used pulsations that, for all their flirtations with the beat, were never jerky. In this work Davis sublimely combined the unsentimental detailings of tone, emotion, and attack of the blues; the joy and the surprise of Armstrong and Young that melodically rose up over the tempo and meter of ensembles in the thirties; and the idealistic but earthy sensuousness of the romantic balladeer.

One of the more interesting things about Davis during these years is that he brought together musicians with varied tastes in sound. As early as 1946, when he recorded "Yardbird Suite" and "Ornithology" with Parker, the smooth, vibratoless sound of Parker was contrasted by the heavier Coleman Hawkins–derived tone of Lucky Thompson's tenor. Davis himself had worked with Hawkins, and used tenor players rooted in Hawkins's work (such as Thompson and Sonny Rollins) until he hired Coltrane. But his alto choices were always Parker derived, such as Jackie McLean and Davey Schildkraut. Just as he was interested in bringing together the essences of blues-based trumpet and ensemble swing with the lessons of the bebop movement, Davis also seemed to want to fuse the tones of those different schools in his ensembles.

Thus, in 1951, he brought McLean and Rollins together for a sextet recording, the instrumentation foreshadowing the six-piece group he later led with Cannonball Adderley and Coltrane. Davis played with confidence on the blues, gave poignance to the ballads, swung with very individual articulation on McLean's "Dig." But perhaps the high point of the session was Rollin's tenor on "It's Only a Paper Moon," where his gruff and ghostly sound reached startling levels of lyricism and fresh phrasing. For the next three years he was playing marvelously, with J. J. Johnson, Jackie McLean, Jimmy Heath, Horace Silver, Gil Coggins, Percy Heath, Kenny Clarke, and Art Blakey on Blue Note Records. And in 1954 Davis reached one of his first peaks as a bandleader and a player. In March he recorded a version of "Old Devil Moon" that had an arranged and recurring vamp that anticipated the sound of the Coltrane rhythm section of the 1960s.

In April he brought together trombonist J. J. Johnson, tenor saxophonist Lucky Thompson, pianist Horace Silver, bassist Percy Heath, and drummer Kenny Clarke. According to Silver, Thompson had written arrangements that didn't come off, and they did two blues numbers, a fast and a slow blues, "Walkin' " and "Blue and Boogie," to avoid a failed day in the studio. The results were signal achievements. The weight of the ensemble sound is perfectly balanced and darkened, Davis's and Johnson's broad brass tones melding in unison with Thompson's thick, breathy tenor; Silver's percussive attack and the ideal mesh of Heath's bass notes with Clarke's cymbals and drums form perhaps Davis's first great rhythm section. On the swift "Blue and Boogie" the trumpeter moves over the horn with grace and pride, his last two choruses a response to the emerging challenge of Clifford Brown.

In December Davis used Heath and Clarke again, but instead of horns he brought Monk's piano and Milt Jackson's vibes. The overtones of Davis's trumpet and the ringing of Jackson's metal keys achieved another superior texture (this one foreshadowed the electric piano on *Filles de Kilimanjaro*, the trumpeter's last important jazz record some fourteen years away), Davis's abstraction of the melody of "The Man I Love" reached back in conception, but not in execution, to Parker's classic transformation of "Embraceable You." Because of the trumpeter's problems with Monk's style — contrapuntal, icily voiced, given as much to ongoing improvised arrangement as to chordal statement—Davis asked the pianist to "stroll," or lay out, during his improvisations. The musical effect is systematically wonderful, however much Monk was irritated. Monk's improvisations are easily the highest expressions of originality and profundity in all of the Prestige sessions.

They are also the peak of piano playing on any Miles Davis recording. Monk brings a motivic brilliance, a command of inflection and timbre, and an idealistic lyricism that are unexpected in their purity. His playing is as far from European convention as bottleneck guitar work. His melodic response to Davis on "The Man I Love" is startling. And on "Swing Spring," Davis pulls off what must be one of his best spontaneous decisions. Featured first with just bass (Percy Heath) and drums (Kenny Clarke), he jumps back in after Jackson has finished his improvisation and Monk is about to play. Monk stops immediately, and Davis plays again with Heath and Clarke, choosing to use a patented Monk phrase for his last chorus. He builds upon it and finishes. Monk then picks up the phrase and invents one of his most masterful recorded performances. It is, quite simply, one of the high points of jazz.

As Davis developed into the next phase of his bandleading and his improvising, he continued to expand on blues, pop songs, Kansas City swing, and the conceptions he personalized from Parker, Monk, and Ahmad Jamal, whose 1955 arrangement of Gould's *Pavane* provided the structure for Davis's 1959 "So What" and the melody for Coltrane's 1961 "Impressions." When he formed his great quintet in 1955, with Coltrane, pianist Red Garland, bassist Paul Chambers, and drummer Philly Joe Jones, Davis not only improvised marvelously eight times out of ten, but also wrote particularly imaginative arrangements. Much of the praise that this quintet has received is deserved. It was a unit that had invincible swing at any tempo, that utilized the possibilities of group color with consistent intelligence, that stoked fire as ably as it crooned. No small part of Davis's achievement was his rhythm section, an ongoing, spontaneously self-orchestrating unit of piano, bass, and drums that delineated the forms of the tunes, responded to the improvisation of the featured horns, loosened and tightened the beat, and swung with an almost peerlessly precise attention to color and the varied possibilities of harmonic-percussive drama. Still, what made this band so wonderful was Davis's breadth of emotional expression. His sensibility drew on the entire sweep of jazz feeling, from the playful to the tender to the pugnacious to the aloof to the gutbucket-greasy and the idealistically lyrical.

When he moved to Columbia Records in 1957 and *'Round About Midnight* was released with the same musicians, Davis was on the verge of becoming a star, a large influence, a matinee idol, and a man destined to sink down in a way no one — himself least of all — could have imagined. Columbia Records, with its distribution and promotion networks, its record club, the air play its products received, and the ink it could generate outside the jazz press, started the most significant leg of Davis's march to celebrity. The trumpeter soon saw his performances and his recordings become emblems of taste in contemporary art.

With Nat Cole and Sidney Poitier, moreover, Davis became part of an expanding vision of American glamour in which dark-hued Negroes were admitted into precincts of romance and elegance that had previously been almost the exclusive province of light-skinned Afro-Americans like Billy Eckstine. As Betty Carter observed of Davis's matinee-idol appeal, "Miles wasn't a power trumpet player, he was a stylist. He had a soft, melodic approach that made him very popular with women. Women really liked him the way they liked Dexter Gordon, Gene Ammons, Ben Webster, Johnny Hodges, and all of those guys who knew how to play things that had some sweetness in them."

Davis also benefited from a shift in audience taste that harked back to the popularity of the glowering, sullen, even contemptuous nineteenth-century minstrel characters known as Jasper Jack and Zip Coon, who sassed and sometimes assaulted the plantation white folks. Davis's bandstand attitude originated in the bebop generation's rejection of Armstrong's mugging and joking, in a trend of aggression that opened part of the way to what became blaxploitation ten years later (and now causes whites who confuse their own masochism with sensitivity to celebrate Spike Lee). The result was superbly described by Ralph Ellison:

. . . a grim comedy of racial manners; with the musicians employing a calculated surliness and rudeness, treating the audience very much as

many white merchants in poor Negro neighborhoods treat their customers, and the white audiences were shocked at first but learned
quickly to accept such treatment as evidence of "artistic" temperament.
Then comes a comic reversal. Today the white audience expects the
rudeness as part of the entertainment.

A story about Davis from this period may be apocryphal, but it
has poetic truth. It has been related that one night a European
woman approached Davis at the bar in Birdland to tell him that she
loved his music, that she bought all his records, even though they
were quite expensive in her country. Davis is said to have replied,
"So fucking what, bitch?" As the stunned woman walked away, the
musician with Davis said, "Miles, you really are an evil little black
sonofabitch, aren't you?" And the trumpeter replied, "Now the bitch
will buy *two* of every one of my records. When you have stock in
Con Edison and make all the money I make, you have to act the
way people expect you to act—they want me to be their evil nigger,
and that's what I'm ready to be."

These first developments in ugliness aside, Davis's achievement
in those years was genuine. It drew not only on the detailed idiomatic
thought of his own musical conceptions, but also on his interaction
with his musicians. Just as Davis had been deeply impressed by the
spare side of Monk's decidedly Afro-American approach to instrumental technique, and by Monk's immaculate sense of thematic variation, so Coltrane, when he left Davis to work with Monk in the
summer of 1957, was inspired to push beyond his superior bebop art;
Monk remade Coltrane substantially, and even the sixteenth-note
rhythms that the saxophonist worked on until the end of his career
were introduced by the pianist's formidable "Trinkle Tinkle." Thus,
when Coltrane returned to Davis's band in 1958, he brought materials that elevated the intellect, the surprise, and the fire of the group.
In fact, as the 1960 Stockholm recording shows, the saxophonist was
blowing the trumpeter off his own bandstand.

But Davis understood how to use Coltrane. By now he was fully
his own man. The album *Milestones* shows how well he understood
that a jazz recording should emulate a strong forty-minute set in a
nightclub. Though the under-recorded piano greatly reduces the
power of what is quite mighty swing, the recital shows just how

much of a bopper Davis still was, and how strongly he believed in the blues as an organizing tool for the overall sound of a recording. Four of the six pieces are blues numbers; each is approached differently, utilizing varied tempos, big-band effects, saxophone exchanges of entire choruses, drum breaks, harmonization, unisons, antiphony. With the title work, moreover, Davis began his exploration of modal materials—limited harmonic structures that relied on scales—and pointed toward *Kind of Blue*, perhaps his most influential album and certainly one of his finest achievements.

In the interest of accuracy, however, it is important to recognize that Davis's publicity, and the cult that has grown up around him, inflated his work out of proportion. As a trumpeter, Davis was constantly challenged by Clifford Brown, who died, at the age of twenty-five, in an automobile accident in 1956. By 1953 Brown was being hailed as "the new Dizzy." His extraordinary technique, his large sound, his unlimited swing, and his heroic combination of melancholy and grandeur brought an Armstrong-like bravura to the bebop trumpet. Brown's recordings show that he possessed qualities of beauty that Davis would never equal. Had Brown lived, Davis would have had to deal with another force of unarguable potency. It is the influence of Brown, not Davis, that has dominated the instrument, from Donald Byrd and Lee Morgan through Freddie Hubbard and Booker Little, and now Wynton Marsalis.

Other strengths of Davis's have been overstated too. His idea of the small group was, finally, no more sophisticated than John Lewis's, Charles Mingus's, or Horace Silver's, and he was rarely as imaginative in his arrangements. Though his fame grew, he had yet to explore the kinds of metric innovations that obsessed Max Roach. And as the Dizzy Gillespie–Sonny Rollins–Sonny Stitt sessions of December 1957 reveal, especially in the playing of Rollins and Gillespie on "Wheatleigh Hall" and of all three on "The Eternal Triangle," the Davis group on *Milestones* was far from the last word in swing or fire.

As for formal innovations, both George Russell and Mingus examined modal forms before Davis, and each made use of pianist Bill Evans (who became important to the next stage of Davis's development). Rollins's *Freedom Suite*, from the summer of 1958, exhibits a much more provocative and successful conception of group rhythm and extended form than anything Davis had produced. (What Rollins did with tenor saxophone, bass, and drums has still to receive the critical recognition it deserves.) And compare Davis's much-lauded improvisation on "Sid's Ahead" from *Milestones* of 1958 with Louis Armstrong's "Wild Man Blues" of 1957: you will hear a vast difference in subtlety, nuance, melodic order, and swing. As fine a player as he had become, Davis could not even approximate Armstrong's authority.

Still, of all the trumpet players who came to power during and after the first shock waves of Parker's innovations, Davis seemed the one who would eventually come the closest to Armstrong's emotional gravity. As he proved with his eerie, isolated, and mournful playing for the score of the murder thriller *Escalator to the Scaffold*, and in the better moments of his collaborations with the arranger Gil Evans (*Miles Ahead*, *Porgy and Bess*, *Sketches of Spain*), he had a talent for a transfixing musical logic and a scalding melancholy. It is true that those albums with Evans also reveal that Davis could be taken in by pastel versions of European colors (they are given what value they have in these sessions by the Afro-American dimensions that were never far from Davis's embouchure, breath, fingering); if Davis's trumpet voice is removed, in fact, a good number of Evans's arrangements sound like high-level television music. But these infirmities pale before the triumphant way that Davis summoned a range of idiomatic devices far richer in color and in conception than those of any of his fellow beboppers.

In the liner notes of *Porgy and Bess*, Davis noted a movement in jazz away from harmonic complexity toward simpler structures that emphasized melodic invention. In early 1959—the watershed year in which Ellington recorded *Jazz Party*; Coleman, *The Shape of Jazz to Come*; Coltrane, *Giant Steps*; Monk, *Orchestra at Town Hall*; and Mingus, *Blues and Roots* and *Ah Um*—Davis made *Kind of Blue*. Here the modal movement reached a pinnacle, precisely because Davis understood that blues should be the foundation of any important innovation in jazz. The record, which uses his sextet with Coltrane, Cannonball Adderley, and Bill Evans, has the feeling of a suite. It is dominated by the trumpeter's compositions. (On one piece where straight-out swing was called for, Davis used Wynton Kelly instead of Evans; but on the softer pieces the things that Evans had learned from Debussy, George Russell, and Mingus issued in voicings of simple materials with intricate details.) The set realized all of the possibilities of cool jazz without sinking into the vacuous, the effete, and the pretentious.

By 1960 Coltrane and Adderley had left to lead their own bands, and Davis began to cope with a jazz scene of expanding technical and emotional means. Davis's playing continued to grow in power and intensity, but for all his success he was no longer the center of the discussion. The centers, instead, were Coltrane and Ornette Coleman, who were inspiring charlatans as well as serious musicians. It seemed possible that the crown would slip from Davis's head, that he might be relegated to the neglect experienced by many of the older masters. Former Davis sidemen were leading the most imposing small bands of the day—Coltrane, Silver, Blakey, Adderley, Rollins. Musicians he had been associated with, such as Monk and Mingus, were either refining, or adding to, the art, especially to its formal scope. In terms of pure bebop, Gillespie's quintet with James Moody was playing extraordinarily well, as was the Modern Jazz Quartet, with its lyrical use of percussion and harmony instruments. When his second great rhythm section of Wynton Kelly, Paul Chambers, and Jimmy Cobb left him in 1963, Davis had to rebuild for what became his last great period.

He soon found the musicians who provided the foundation for his final creative years. With *Seven Steps to Heaven*, Davis introduced George Coleman on tenor, another of the fine tenor players who had followed Coltrane into the band, and the rhythm section of Herbie Hancock, Ron Carter, and Tony Williams, the force that was to shape the orchestration and the propulsion of his next phase. The band with Coleman made its finest music in concert performances, released as *Four*, and *My Funny Valentine*. Wynton Marsalis has noted that on the many fast numbers of *Four*, Davis produced unorthodox phrases that are technically challenging and demand unique fingerings. *My Funny Valentine*, by contrast, and particularly the title tune, captured Davis in a moment of heroic intimacy that he rarely reached again.

When Wayne Shorter joined him in the fall of 1964, Davis had what has been considered his best group since the *Milestones* ensemble. In January 1965 the band recorded *E.S.P.*, and the music still sounds fresh. The trumpeter was in superb form, able to execute quickstep swing at fleet tempi with volatile penetration, to put the weight of his sound on mood pieces, to rear his way up through the blues with a fusion of bittersweet joy and what Martin Williams termed "communal anguish." The rhythm section played with a looseness that pivots off Williams's cymbal splashes and unclinched rhythms, Carter walking some of the most impressive bass lines of the day, and Hancock developing his own version of the impressionism that Evans was making popular.

Shortly afterward, Davis went into the hospital for surgery and didn't return to work until late in the year, when he recorded *Live at the Plugged Nickel* in Chicago. At the Plugged Nickel he and his musicians were staring right in the face of the period's avant-garde, spontaneously changing tempi and meters, playing common or uncommon notes over the harmonies, pulling in harsh timbres, all the while in a repertoire that was roughly the same as the trumpeter had been using for a decade. Again, as with *My Funny Valentine*, the pieces were remade. Shorter was in such startling form that his improvisations remained influential through the 1980s. Davis himself seemed to be having trouble with his instrument; his authority on *E.S.P.* is rarely heard. His "Stella by Starlight," however, with its masterful touches of brass color, is one of his supreme late efforts: it swells with intimacy, voices an elevated bitterness that seems to argue with the human condition, then rises to a victorious swing.

The remainder of Davis's studio recordings with that band drew on the chromaticism of Warne Marsh and Lennie Tristano, who influenced Shorter and Hancock—and, to the surprise of almost all concerned, on popular dance music, on rhythm and blues and rock 'n' roll. Though the albums vary in quality, though they sometimes lack definitive swing or cohesive fire, even the weaker ones have at least a couple of first-rate performances. The range of ideas heard from the rhythm section put it in line with the best of the day, and Shorter wrote many fine compositions, especially on *Nefertiti*. But the clues to Davis's course were in his own pieces, in "Stuff" and in much of the work for *Filles de Kilimanjaro*. His extended "Country Son," which features perhaps Shorter's finest studio improvisation with Davis, revealed that he was capable of a flirtation with pop rhythms. He was headed, in fact, in the direction of Motown, the English bands, and the black rock of Sly Stone and Jimi Hendrix.

"Mademoiselle Mabry," on *Filles*, is a brilliant example of Davis's ability to elevate pop material. An innovation in jazz rhythm, it is an appropriation and an extension of Hendrix's "The Wind Cries Mary," and proof of what Davis might have done had he kept control of his popular sources, rather than succumb to them. The borrowing was in perfect keeping with the tradition begun by Armstrong's alchemical way with banal popular songs. In fact, what Davis does with popular influences throughout this recording shows off his sophistication and his ability to transform yet another universe of music in his own image.

That Davis was able to initiate what became known as fusion, or jazz rock, and with it to inspire musicians as different as Hancock, Rollins, Hubbard, and Coleman, shows what a powerful position he had in the minds of Afro-American jazzmen. Jimmy Heath described his position this way:

> Miles led the way for a lot of people because he was one of the ones who got through. He had the fine clothes, the expensive cars, the big house, all the magazine articles and the pretty girls chasing him. He seemed like he was on top of *everything*. Then you had all of this rock getting all of the press and it was like Elvis Presley all over again. Miles stepped out here and decided he was going to get himself some of that money and a lot of musicians followed his lead. It was like if Miles had led the pack for so long they didn't know how to stop following him, even if the music wasn't any good.

And then came the fall. Beginning with the 1969 *In a Silent Way*, Davis's sound was mostly lost among electronic instruments, inside a long, maudlin piece of droning wallpaper music. A year later, with *Bitches Brew*, Davis was firmly on the path of the sellout. It sold more than any other Davis album, and fully launched jazz-rock with its multiple keyboards, electronic guitars, static beats, and clutter. Davis's music became progressively trendy and dismal, as did his attire; at one point in the early 1970s, with his wraparound dark glasses and his puffed shoulders, the erstwhile master of cool looked like an extra from a science fiction B movie. He was soon proclaiming that there were no Negroes other than Sonny Rollins who could play the saxophone, and that musicians like Ornette Coleman and

Mingus needed to listen to Motown, which was "where it was at." Many hoped that this would be only a phase, but the phase has lasted twenty years. In his abject surrender to popular trends, Davis sank the lowest in 1985 in *You're Under Arrest*, on which one hears what is supposed to be the sound of cocaine snorting. His albums of recent years—*Tutu, Siesta, Amandla,* and the overblown fusion piece that fills two records on *Aura*—prove beyond any doubt that he has lost all interest in music of quality.

As usual, where Davis led, many followed. His pernicious effect on the music scene since he went rapaciously commercial reveals a great deal about the perdurability of Zip Coon and Jasper Jack in the worlds of jazz and rock, in the worlds of jazz and rock criticism, in Afro-American culture itself. The cult of ethnic authenticity often mistakes the lowest common denominator for an ideal. It begets a self-image that has succumbed to a nostalgia for the mud. What we get is the bugaboo blues of the noble savage, the surly and dangerous Negro who will have nothing to do with bourgeois conventions. (This kind of Negro has long supplied the ammunition for the war that many jazz and rock critics have waged against their own middle-class backgrounds.)

Davis's corruption occurred at about the time that the "Oreo" innuendo became an instrument with which formerly rejected street Negroes and thugs began to intimidate, and often manipulate, middle-class Afro-Americans in search of their roots, and of a "real" black culture. In this climate, obnoxious, vulgar, and antisocial behavior has been confused with black authenticity. This has led to blaxploitation in politics, in higher education, and in art—to Eldridge Cleaver, Huey Newton, and the Black Panthers; to black students at San Francisco State demanding that pimps be recruited to teach psychology classes; to the least inventive and most offensive work of Richard Pryor and Eddie Murphy; to the angry cartoonish coons of Spike Lee and the flat, misogynist, gutter verse of Ice-T and racist rap groups like Public Enemy.

Davis provides many unwitting insights into such phenomena in his autobiography, *Miles*, written with Quincy Troupe. His is, at least in part, the story of a jet black Little Lord Fauntleroy attracted to the glamour and the fast life of the jazz world during the period when heroin was as important to the identity of the bebop generation as LSD was to the youth culture of the late 1960s. The book draws a number of interesting portraits—of Dexter Gordon, of Sugar Ray Robinson, of Philly Joe Jones—but it is overwhelmingly an outburst of inarticulateness, of profanity, of error, of self-inflation, and of parasitic paraphrasing of material from Jack Chambers's *Milestones*. Would Simon and Schuster publish such a book, without sending the manuscript to any number of experts for evaluations and corrections, if it were written by a white man? Perhaps the editors assumed that since Quincy Troupe is a Negro, he should know.

Davis's book is divided against itself. His sensitive and lyrical recollections of experience are constantly overwhelmed by his street corner poses. The trumpeter's desire to be perceived as the hippest of the hip has destroyed his powers of communication. This is particularly unfortunate, since his story falls far outside the clichés of jazz and racial lore. His father was a successful dentist and a gentleman farmer who reared his children to have a high sense of self-worth. Davis recalls riding horses and living on a 300-acre estate; there was a cook and a maid. It was a world as full of sophistication as it was of superstition, as full of privilege as prejudice.

Davis tells of what he heard about the St. Louis Riot of 1917, of his father's looking with a shotgun for the man who called his son a nigger, of a preference Negro bands had for light-skinned musicians that blocked a young friend of his from working with Jimmy Lunceford, of the way women started throwing themselves at him as he grew into his late teens. His involvement with music is well described, as are the personalities of many musicians he grew up with, some of whom fell by the wayside. There are powerful evocations of certain aspects of the times: of how drugs took over the lives of musicians, of the difficulties musicians had negotiating the territory between the cult world of bebop and the more general kind of success enjoyed by Ellington. And some of what is probably Troupe's best writing has nothing to do with music; the brief section on Sugar Ray Robinson sheds unexpected light on the influence of boxing on Davis's playing. If one listens to Davis's jabbing, suspenseful, aggressive improvisation on "Walkin' " from the 1961 Black Hawk recording, one hears not only Monk, but also, we can now say, Robinson:

Sugar Ray Robinson would put an opponent in four or five traps during every round in the first two or three rounds, just to see how his opponent would react. Ray would be reaching, and he would stay just out of reach so he could measure you to knock you out, and you didn't even know what was happening until, BANG! you found yourself counting stars. Then, on somebody else, he might hit him hard in his side— BANG!—after he made him miss a couple of jabs. He might do that in the first round. Then he'd tee-off on the sucker upside his head after hitting him eight or nine more times hard in the ribs, then back to the head. So by the fourth or fifth round, the sucker don't know what Ray's going to do to him next.

Once our memoirist gets to New York, however, the book begins to lose itself in contradictions and obscenities. On one page Davis will say that Parker was "teaching me a lot about music—chords and that shit—that I would go play on the piano" when he went to Juilliard, and then a few pages later that "Bird didn't teach me much as far as music goes." Davis claims that he became the musical director of Parker's group, but Max Roach, who was also in the band, vehemently disputes the claim. (It is proof, he says, that the trumpeter has "become senile.") Davis recalls being taken to Minton's in Harlem for the great jam sessions by Fats Navarro, whom many considered second only to Gillespie, but then says, "I would tell him shit—technical shit—about the trumpet." Jimmy Heath has a rather different memory of what Davis did or did not learn from Navarro: "Fats ate Miles up every night. Miles couldn't outswing him, he couldn't outpower him, he couldn't outsweet him, he couldn't do anything except take that whipping on *every* tune."

On things racial, it's impossible to figure out from this book what Davis really felt. "I could learn more in one session at Minton's than it would take me two years to learn at Juilliard. At Juilliard, after it was all over, all I was going to know was a bunch of white styles: nothing new." But only one page later he says:

I couldn't believe that all of them guys like Bird, Prez, Bean, all them cats wouldn't go to museums or libraries and borrow those musical scores so they could check out what was happening. I would go to the library and borrow scores by all those great composers, like Stravinsky,

Alban Berg, Prokofiev. I wanted to see what was going on in all of music. Knowledge is freedom and ignorance is slavery, and I just couldn't believe someone could be that close to freedom and not take advantage of all the shit that they can. I have never understood why black people didn't take advantage of all the shit that they can.

Of the interracial couples that he saw in the clubs on Fifty-second Street, Davis observes:

> A lot of white people, though, didn't like what was going on on 52nd Street. . . . They thought that they were being invaded by niggers from Harlem, so there was a lot of racial tension around bebop. Black men were going with fine, rich white bitches. They were all over those niggers out in public and the niggers were clean as a motherfucker and talking all kind of hip shit. So you know a lot of white people, especially white men, didn't like this new shit.

And then, explaining why he didn't want to do an interview for *Playboy*, he declares, "All they have are blond women with big tits and flat asses or no asses. So who the fuck wants to see that all the time? Black guys like big asses, you know, and we like to kiss on the mouth and white women don't have no mouths to kiss on."

Davis's treatment of women is disgusting. He details the way he destroyed the career of his first wife, Frances Taylor, who was a dancer, and later, claiming that black women are too bossy, he cites Taylor as an example of the way a good colored woman ought to be. He volunteers tales of slapping Cicely Tyson around, though she was probably responsible for his not dying from a binge of cocaine that spanned nearly six years.

The cavalier way that Davis imputes drug use to black musician after black musician is no less objectionable. (He claims repeatedly that the white jazz press didn't start paying attention to white guys being junkies until Stan Getz was arrested, but Leonard Feather has shown that in fact white musicians got the bulk of the attention for using drugs.) And the morality of the trumpeter's memory is oddly selective. About a woman who helped him during his time as a drug addict, Davis says, "I was seeing this same rich white girl who I'd met in St. Louis; she had come to New York to check me out. Let's call her 'Alice,' because she's still alive and I don't want to cause her trouble; plus she's married." And the customers of a white call girl were "very important men—white men mostly—whose names I won't mention." It seems that militant Inky respects the privacy of those mouthless, gluteus minimus white women and those white johns more than he does the dignity of his fellow musicians, some of whom were his very close friends.

One of the most disturbing things about *Miles* is its debt to Jack Chambers's *Milestones*, a critical biography written in two parts between 1983 and 1985 and now available in one volume from Quill. Pages 160–61 of *Miles*, for example, look alarmingly like pages 166–67 of *Milestones*. (There is even a cavalier reference to Chambers as "some writer.") Davis and Troupe:

> Bird had an exclusive contract with Mercury (I think he had left Verve by then), so he had to use a pseudonym on record. Bird had given up shooting heroin because since Red Rodney had been busted and sent back to prison at Lexington, Bird thought the police were watching him. In place of his normal big doses of heroin, now he was drinking an enormous amount of alcohol.

Chambers:

> . . . the man behind the pseudonym was Charlie Parker. Parker was under some pressure, not only because he had an exclusive contract with Mercury, but also because the trumpeter in his band, Red Rodney, had been arrested and committed to the federal prison in Lexington. Parker believed that he was being watched by narcotics agents, according to Ross Russell, and he had given up narcotics for the time being and was consuming large quantities of alcohol instead.

Much of the material used in *Milestones* and again in *Miles* comes from interviews done over the years. Troupe denies using any of it, then says that "the man can quote himself," then blames the publisher for "messing up" by omitting a discography and a bibliography, and by not checking facts.

But the important point, finally, is that *Miles* paints the picture of an often gloomy monster. It is full of stories that take the reader down into the sewers of Davis's musical, emotional, and chemical decline. Once the rage at his cruelty and his self-inflation has passed, we are left aghast at a man of monumental insecurity who, for all his protests about white power and prejudice, is often controlled by his fear of it, or of any other significant power. (One example of many: Davis asserts that he never listens to white music critics, and blames many of the woes of the music business on them, but then he admits that once they had him worried that he sounded inferior to Chet Baker, who was his imitator.) Obsessed with remaining young, and therefore willing to follow any trend in pop music, Davis is now a surly sellout who wants his success to seem like a heroic battle against the white world.

To that end, this former master of musical articulation often reduces himself to an inarticulate man. Davis has worn the mask of the street corner for too long; he thinks, like Pryor and Murphy and Lee, that his invective gives him authenticity. Gone is the elegant and exigent Afro-American authenticity of the likes of Ellington, at ease in the alleys as well as in the palace, replaced by youth culture vulgarity that vandalizes the sweep and substance of Afro-American life. The fall of Davis reflects perhaps the essential failure of contemporary Negro culture: its mock-democratic idea that the elite, too, should like it down in the gutter. Aristocracies of culture, however, come not from the acceptance of limitations, but from the struggle with them, as a group or an individual, from within or without.

DIZZY GILLESPIE

When he died recently at seventy-five, Dizzy Gillespie wasn't in the middle of anything that had the jazz world hanging from the bell of his up-angled trumpet, but his passing was mourned because Gillespie's was the last of the minds that had been central to the bebop movement of the middle forties. When Gillespie went, so did the memory of how it all actually came about, what he, Charlie Parker, Thelonious Monk, Kenny Clarke, Oscar Pettiford, and the others did in Harlem clubs, hotel rooms, apartments, and walking down the street as they talked music. One of those who provided jazz with a fresh set of options, Gillespie could see every room, every uniform, recall the smells, the colors, the meals, the ways the instruments gleamed or lay dully under the light, hear the chords as the unusual notes were added, recollect the styles of clothing and the way Negroes and whites wore their hair and talked during those years, how it felt to become the most recognized member of a movement that bloomed right out of his trumpet and Charlie Parker's saxophone, out of the different way pianos, basses, and drums formed the inspiring and supporting unit of the rhythm section. With their vibratoless tones, their willfully dissonant harmonies, and their race horse tempos, the beboppers remade the small jazz unit and Gillespie led the first big band to make thorough use of what was the freshest material since Duke Ellington had come to power. Over the years, Gillespie worked in many different formats, exploring his interest in exotic rhythms and making—whenever he could afford it—his own variations on the context of trumpet soloist and jazz orchestra that Louis Armstrong had pioneered in the early thirties.

Gillespie is also mourned because he embodied the essence of his art. In his walk and his facial expressions, the movements of his hands, the sound of his laugh, the tonal flexibility of his voice, the bored to molten cast of his eyes, the way he danced on his bandstands and the position his body went into when he was on fire and the trumpet had no limitations, Dizzy Gillespie carried and projected the moxie, the curiosity, the wit, and the pathos that enliven the world of jazz. Like Louis Armstrong, he was aware of the spiritual muscle necessary to hold himself in place with the gymnastic elegance called for when executing an unwavering iron cross, one hand in the ring of tragedy, the other in the ring of comedy. The travels, the parties, the many rehearsals, the endless train of nights across the globe when he was made welcome because of the heat he could put through a cold brass instrument, the high casualty list of talent he had seen knocked across the line into death by self-inflicted or social blows, and the humor both light and of the gallows brand were taken into Gillespie's electrons. When he arrived, the epic was there.

Like a number of the American geniuses who affirm the democratic ideal, Gillespie came not from the polished fish bowl of the academy, but, at least partially, from the ocean itself. He was homemade and a scholar of his art, a man who sweated his way to a pinnacle of velocity technique, harmonic sophistication, and rhythmic intricacy that hasn't been surpassed. With his cheeks swelling like those of a brown wind demon, he played the trumpet with such power and finesse that he took a position—after Louis Armstrong and Roy Eldridge and before Clifford Brown and Miles Davis—as one of the five most influential players of his horn in the history of the national music.

Even under ruthless scrutiny, Gillespie becomes a mythic figure, because his accomplishments were of such exceedingly large size that they would seem to have been accomplished by some Crockett-like combination of fish and fowl, man and beast, sinner and saint, angel and devil, bear and antelope. He was a supreme musical intellectual, whose fire and evangelical willingness to personally deliver musical details made ensemble sense out of what might have been no more than an individual horn style. Many are the stories of his sitting down and showing piano players how to accompany and what chords to play, bass players the nature of the new harmony, and drummers the rhythms compatible with what he and Charlie Parker were playing. The Harlem apartment he had on Seventh Avenue during the forties was a conservatory where the young and curious came to find out what the increasingly formidable trumpet master was putting together. Fifteen or twenty musicians used to be seen walking with him through the streets, listening to his advice and singing the notes he was explaining to them.

In keeping with the necessities of the night world in which jazz was made and the wit that has carried the Negro through the protean configurations of our society, Gillespie was prepared. Born in Cheraw, South Carolina, in 1917, he became a professional in an environment where anything could happen. His humor was boundless. His temper was quick and his response could cut to the bone. The pranks he loved to play and the confidence he had in his dissonant harmonic ideas sparked the antipathy of certain older musicians when Gillespie was making his way during his early twenties. But the young trumpet player who had initially been influenced by Roy Eldridge continued to search the piano keyboard for what he needed to get him where he wanted to go. A bottle was thrown against his head because he refused to play something on the piano for a white man during a Southern tour with Earl Hines in the early forties. Above the Mason-Dixon line, that man might have experienced another side of Gillespie. He was good with his dukes. He carried a knife and once nearly slashed off the arm of a Northern redneck.

Bassist Al McKibbon worked with the trumpeter's bebop big band in the late forties and remembers a night when they were playing a dance at the Savoy Ballroom in Harlem. McKibbon's wife was at the edge of the bandstand and Gillespie, ever spontaneous, jumped off the bandstand, took her in his arms, and went on to win the jitterbug contest. Four or five years ago at a New York club a woman in the audience turned out to be the same partner with whom he had won first prize in Manhattan's largest Latin dance contest two or three decades earlier. "Man, did we *practice!* Oooh. And when we got there, we were *ready.* I'll never forget that night. Oh, it was *so* wonderful."

Such Americans are both numerous and rare. They are numerous because so much of our national tale is the story of their arriving from such surprising places and so indelibly imprinting our culture with both their personalities and the impersonal facts of their accomplishments, proving their work both inimitable and beacons of universal possibility. They are rare because few of even the great American individuals have had as invincible an effect on the way we define ourselves as Gillespie did. He rose from the position of an odd fish to a star surfer riding the high, high curving water of a trend, sank into the position of those miracles taken for granted, but periodically returned to view, dripping with new wisdoms, beckoning as others followed him on the thin boards of art and entertainment that those who make their names in jazz must ride, atop the roller coaster waves of public taste, swinging all our blues in a fickle brine where they are forever at peril.

TRUE BLUE REBELS

The efforts of young jazz musicians pose a vital alternative to the vulgarity and ineptitude of contemporary popular musical trends. On almost any night in New York, you can walk into jazz rooms like Bradley's or Iridium or Visiones or Sweet Basil or Small's or the Village Vanguard and hear them at work, or watch them studying someone like master saxophonist Jackie McLean, as a gathering did recently at the Blue Note's bar.

These are the truest rebels on the music scene because they have made up their own minds and are going in directions other than those dictated by MTV and BET. The art they are mastering demands far more skill and substance. André Malraux defined their ambitions when he said, "A culture is reborn when men of genius, seeking their own truth, wrench from the depths of centuries everything that once resembled that truth, even if they aren't sure what that truth is."

Malraux spoke of events that took much longer than they do in our world, where mass media technology spreads ideas, techniques, imitations, and decadence at unprecedented velocities. In our time, 1894 is almost as far away as 1694 was to those of the ragtime era. Today, we have become so accepting of spiritual rot, the sado-masochistic rituals of action films, and the obnoxious pornography of the Madonna–Def Comedy Jam era that the sort of young people who are coming into jazz might seem startling.

Following the lead of musicians like Wynton Marsalis, Wallace Roney, and Mulgrew Miller, all of whom appeared fifteen years ago, these are the troops of a renaissance. They are in their teens or their twenties and they share with Marsalis, Roney, and Miller an appreciation of jazz achievement across the decades, from Jelly Roll Morton and Louis Armstrong to John Coltrane and Ornette Coleman. Unlike those Malraux spoke of, they are more than sure what the truth is.

Nicholas Payton, Abraham Burton, Ali Jackson, and Kevin Hays don't walk around with their shoes untied, their pants falling off, caps sideways. Karen Farmer, Vanessa Rubin, and Renee Rosnes never give the impression they're turning tricks on the side. They represent a movement of young people who aren't trying to emulate the bad taste of pop stars and gangster rappers.

"In order to discover this music and learn how to play," says twenty-year-old Nicholas Payton, "that wouldn't be necessary. You're trying to help bring honor to something, not degrade it or degrade yourself. You're not trying to be a teenager or be like some older person who wants to be a teenager. You're looking for something else, but it's not easy. It separates you from your own generation, not in a bad way but a good way.

"To the average teenager, jazz has no place in their social life. It won't help you get with a woman or with a man; it won't necessarily make you any money. So they think, 'What good is it?' To play jazz today, you have to be able to withstand all the pressures and study. You have to be willing to take your chances and sacrifice. But if you love the music and understand the depth of it, you don't have any choice. It's too good to turn your back on."

Because these young musicians aren't hog-tied by the conventions of commercial youth culture doesn't mean they are the sorts of icy academicians the worst of the jazz press—which is the bulk of it—thinks they are. They are humorous, down-home, and soulful more often than not—no matter their points of social origin. If not, they wouldn't be important.

They suffer no feeling of a generation gap. It is not unusual to see them in the company of older musicians, asking questions and learning. Or they will excitedly discuss something just discovered on a classic recording. In their desire to reach the standards set by Louis Armstrong's progeny, they symbolize the resurgence of the democratic art of jazz and predict the increasing freedom from decadence we will see in American youth over the next few decades.

IN THIS HOUSE,
ON THIS MORNING

In the Sweet Embrace of Life

1.

The liturgical pearls of our culture originated with the chattels who loved percussion and never failed to remember the eternal drumbeats of human affirmation. Often expressing their needs in secret, with the moon for a steeple, they softly sang music that had possession over a lofty and grand melancholy. Socially motherless children, unclaimed by the protective wing of the law, spiritual eagles who could be treated like flies, they also crooned because, in the sweet embrace of life, their souls were happy. That heroic, transcendent joy caused the less advanced to mistake them for naive creatures. Even so, after bondage they developed their ceremonial flair for musical depth. In so many houses, on so many Sunday mornings, their souls taught all who heard that the freedoms of the heart come of compassion and gratitude, gratitude felt even while seeking light during the long darkness of injustice. The stomping of their feet against the dirt of the earth's drumskin or against the wooden drumskin of the church floor, their clapping in the alto, tenor, and bass registers of their palms, and the lucid intensity of their exaltations brought the flesh and the spirit together in an understanding that the heroic soul is the only alternative to the decadent orchestration eternally wrought by folly, corruption, and mediocrity.

That liturgical drama of song and percussion, of eloquence and incantation, of the sun and the moon rising in absolute light and

fullness from the bottom of the social valley, added an unsentimental spirituality to this culture, a fresh language for the dialogue
between the all-too-human and the divining, enlivening spark of the
invisible. So whenever we feel that old and noble closeness to the
soul of all meaning, we are again returned to the essence of the spiritual autobiography that was first enunciated in song of grand and
lofty melancholy, in song accompanied by the percussion that had
custody over the indivisible rhythms of existence. We feel the
warmth and the calm, the compassion and the integrity, the sense of
tragedy as well as the will to transcendence that is the moral essence
of courage. In all, we know the illumination that is the sweet
embrace of life.

2.

On May 27, 1992, Wynton Marsalis premiered a long, immoderately
soulful, and often astonishing work in Avery Fisher Hall at Manhattan's Lincoln Center. There had been a graduation ceremony held
in the hall earlier and the concert began at 9:00 instead of 8:00, the
first notes coming out of the musicians' instruments near 9:30, due
to the usual seating delays and an introduction by Ed Bradley, in
which he referred to Marsalis as the most important figure in American music. Some surely bristled at that, either out of jealousy or
resentment of the fact that Marsalis has become a success on terms
of his own and continues to develop what is perhaps the richest single musical talent of the last half century.

Without precedent, Marsalis has gone on to conquer two quite
different musical traditions, performing European concert music
with a freshness and audacity that matches his achievements in jazz,
which are, however, much larger. As a performer of concert trumpet
pieces, he is one of the two or three best in the world. In jazz,
Marsalis has proved himself not only the greatest trumpet player of
the last thirty years but also the greatest bandleader since the peaks
achieved by the Modern Jazz Quartet, Miles Davis, Art Blakey,
Horace Silver, Charles Mingus, Ahmed Jamal, and John Coltrane.
He now adds to those marvels the fact that his is perhaps the most
imposing compositional talent in contemporary American music,
regardless of idiom.

The breadth of those gifts was stated so overtly in the premiere of

In This House, On This Morning that there was a special sense of community felt in the standing ovation that followed the last notes. The two-hour work had given the audience a panorama of human feeling rising through a form shaped in emulation of an Afro-American church service. One knew that evening in that hall that the talents of Wes Anderson, Todd Williams, Wycliffe Gordon, Eric Reed, Reginald Veal, and Herlin Riley provided Marsalis with one of the greatest ensembles in the history of jazz. Those musicians had also set the tone for the piece before the first note was written. Says Marsalis:

> Almost everyone in the band grew up playing church music, and what truly spurred my desire to write this music was the many hymns and shouts that they sing on the bus as we travel, at sound checks before concerts, and after meals. With the demise of a viable blues tradition in popular music, most of the younger jazz musicians learn the expression necessary to play music either in church or from someone close to them who happens to be a musician. In the band, everyone, with the exception of Todd Williams, comes from a musical family, and all of the guys, with the exception of Wes and me, grew up playing in church. Reed's father is a preacher and you can hear the reality of that in his playing. Listening to all of them made me want to put that feeling in a long piece and reassert out here the power that underlies jazz by constructing a composition based on the communal complexity of its spiritual sources.

The piece demanded everything of its players—passion, virtuoso technique, top-of-the-line reading skills, and the sense of extended form in which each improviser develops the essences of the theme and the particulars of the preceding player's spontaneous variations. Though the structural accomplishments were as numerous as they were formidable, Marsalis and his men executed a victory far beyond the technical. They arrived at that place where the wick of the soul caught fire, casting a large and variously shaped light through the wonderfully designed lamp that was *In This House, On This Morning.* That fiery wick spoke its brightness through the bush of silence and darkness with such aesthetic authority that Pearl Fountain, Marsalis's housekeeper and a veteran of many, many long mornings and evenings in church, said of the performance, "God visited you all last evening."

The band went into the studio the next day and the results are here.

3.

The arrival of this work might surprise those who have developed a toughness adequate to face the many disappointments of this era, a period in which the decadent and the inept are celebrated as though the loss of purity into darkness is an achievement. With pop music being played in Afro-American churches, distinguished only by religious lyrics, we know that things are in bad shape, that the flame of the tradition that gave our modern age an original, subtle, and incinerating heat has come to sputter even in the temples where the soul is a central subject.

Because *In This House, On This Morning* so thoroughly expresses the meanings behind the ceremonial imperatives of Afro-American rhythm and tune, the soul is given its due. What we hear is a work that steps right up next to Duke Ellington's *Black, Brown, and Beige* in its ambition and in its command of material. Ellington was always at war with the minstrel limitations of popular Afro-American imagery, seeking to express the range of the Negro spirit that had so influenced the richest aspects of our national identity and that had given so much to the modern vocabulary that expresses the life of our technological era, an epoch in which our machinery is a set of Corsican twins, one good, one evil, forever at war. In this period of overweening decadence, when the opportunistic cesspool of vulgarity is either misconstrued or deceptively celebrated as a fountain of vitality, Marsalis is the point rider in a renaissance of younger jazz artists who would reverse the fall of our aspirations by returning a revolutionary high-mindedness to our ongoing democratic discussion of life's meaning. He seeks to reiterate in his own terms the very elements that gave our American culture such grand vitality in its better years.

This work is part of that vision. Marsalis recognizes the artistic and structural possibilities of the Afro-American church ritual, just as the masters of the European Renaissance saw so well what could happen when they brought the complex human insights of the biblical tales together with the mastery of perspective. *In This House* brings the broad spiritual perspective at the root of jazz together with the intellectual achievements that have taken place in an art built upon the melody, the harmony, and the rhythms of the blues. Marsalis is capable of this because he knows a truth quite profound: the blues is the sound of spiritual investigation in a secular frame, and through its very lyricism, the blues achieves its spiritual penetration.

4.

I wanted to express the full range of humanity that arises in a church service, from deep introspection to rapture to extroverted celebration. The form, supplied by Reverend Jeremiah Wright, is a typical Afro-American church service. It just so happens that the form he told me had twelve sections, like the measures in one chorus of blues. I found that the break following every four sections gave the piece three movements. Within this form, I also drew on my own connection with many types of church music and music of various sorts. So *In This House* has a wide range of things, beginning with "Devotional" and ending with that country feeling of community when the food comes out after all the aspects of the ceremonial have been completed. The last part, which is sort of an emotional and cultural coda, is called "Pot Blessed Dinner."

Overall, what I wanted was to give musical structure in my personality to the communal elements that transcend any single place. Even though the form is definitely American, I wanted to open the interpretation up to all kinds of musical approaches. That's why the piece has the emotion of traveling and visiting many different kinds of churches and many different kinds of services, from the highly refined all the way to the backwoods, way down in the country. *In This House* moves from the feeling of the black American church to the study of Bach chorales, even the feeling of ritual in ancient religious forms and the sounds one hears when in Middle Eastern countries. By using the blues as a fundamental element, I was also able to ground the music in our culture while stretching it onto an international plane. But that's natural to jazz because it builds upon the blues and upon swing. The percussive sensibility of the blues comes from African-based music, and the melodic and textural characteristics can be found in folk and spiritual musics all over the world.

The blues is central to what I'm doing with the structure here. The basic harmonic progression of the blues comes from the "amen cadence," I, IV, I, which we have all heard used so many times in and out of church music to conclude a piece. So it's basic to our hearing. Now the blues is I, IV, V, IV, I. If you don't have the V chord you can still have a blues, but without the IV chord, no blues. So my intention was to reconcile the secular nature of blues expression with the spiritual nature of its sources. It is also another example of my interest in one of the main achievements of jazz, which is fusing the Apollonian and the Dionysian, the intellectual/spiritual and the sensual. The momentum of the piece is based in Albert Murray's description of swing as "the velocity of celebration." That means that the sound of praise is in the rhythm too.

5.

A close observer of Marsalis is Marcus Roberts, who worked with him for five years. Recently, Roberts had to perform this composition when Eric Reed, now the regular pianist in Marsalis's group, was ill. He knows it well and has some very important observations about this grand offering:

What is amazing about this piece is how it gets all the way down into the *depth* of the church service. This music is about soul, soul as pure as it comes. If it wasn't, somebody like Marion Williams wouldn't have anything to do with it. People like her don't play around. That's why the first thing I find remarkable about it is that somebody who didn't grow up attending regular Baptist church services could capture so authentically the *feeling* of that experience. Right here, in this incredible piece of music, Marsalis gets to the heart of the issue better than most people who participate in it on a weekly basis.

This has a special meaning for me because I remember when Marsalis used to call me and ask me to show him some gospel chords, since he knew that I had grown up in the church. He knew I knew the church, and I do know the church. I know how it feels, I know how it goes. I've played in the church Sunday after Sunday. Now he's developed from those phone calls all the way to what we hear in the third movement, where everything he has set up in the first two movements comes together. The architecture is total on every level. There's nothing missing. That's why it captures so perfectly a church service, which is always an attempt to bring the entire meaning of life into structure, an attempt to face our shortcomings, be thankful for our blessings, and recognize the wonder of the works of God. Marsalis didn't miss a thing. He got it just right.

But what he did that will stand forever in *musical terms* is that he brought off the key to what I would call true innovation, which is when you find basic solutions to basic problems through profound achievements. In that respect, this piece represents a step forward and backward at the same time. It's totally modern and totally basic. The harmonic sophistication is just as profound as the grooves. Think about *that.* So are the melodies, the orchestrations, all of it—extremely sophisticated and basic. Whatever you want, wherever your musical taste comes from, there's something in there for you. So the achievement is that it moves us along with all the complexities of our own time while it also recaptures the early essentials laid down by masters like Jelly Roll Morton, who *always* got the very most out of his bands, compositionally and improvisationally. That's why it towers above anything I've heard written since the death of Duke Ellington. Nobody writing music today could have done this except Marsalis. *In This House, On This Morning* brings a lot of knowledge together and it also gives us another insight into how jazz form and structure are being rediscovered.

Now you know how things go in this era. It may take a while for some people to get with this piece. But when they *do* get to it, they will discover that this piece represents the finest use of a band with this extreme level of talent. He wrote very brilliantly for all the men in that group, and they performed it very brilliantly. You can play it after Dizzy Gillespie and Charlie Parker, Jelly Roll, Miles Davis with Coltrane and Cannonball, Coltrane with his own band, Monk—whatever you want to play—and there'll be no drop in quality. In fact, the extended achievement is unequaled for a small jazz band by *anybody.* Two hours of music this tight, this well organized? No one's ever come close to that.

You see, Marsalis was sent here on a mission and that mission is made much clearer in this particular composition. Not only is there an incredible development of the harmony from the first section to the last, but Marsalis has this phenomenal understanding of how to put rhythm with melody and *with* harmony so that *the grooves have thematic relationships as well.* That's *extremely* rare. It allows him to develop different things in isolation, in fragments, in counterpoint, in different registers and rhythms of the band at the same time. No doubt about it: this is music that is deeply felt, well thought out, and right to the point for the entire two hours.

Like I said, only Marsalis could have done this. If somebody else could have done it, we would have already heard it done. This is a masterpiece, which is how blessings make themselves manifest in art. Yes: Marsalis took the whole idea of jazz composition a long ways forward with this one. True lovers of music and true students of music will understand what I'm talking about immediately; the rest will catch up sooner than we might think. Something this great can only be denied for so long.

6.

It is Sunday morning. The regular believers and the visitors are gathered. They have come for the particular purpose of feeling affirmation, which is the force that touches them with the value of existence and is the sword that raises itself against denigration. There are the old who have heard and observed the power of the Word for many years. There are those younger who have come into adulthood learning the strength that results from faith and the will that it allows. There are children, some shy and quiet, others barely restraining their boisterous inclinations, still others who wonder if they someday will be in the choir or become deacons or stand before the congregation passing the Word of light that will dispel the doubting darkness.

The first movement opens with "Devotional." Led by one deacon and followed by whoever is present, this is the informal praying and testifying to God that takes place before the beginning of the formal service. In the masterfully voiced abstractions of this prelude, we hear the main themes and harmonies that will be developed throughout the work. The band superbly executes all the elements—the keening, the deep voices, the tambourine rhythms, the chords, the ringing church bells that will recur throughout, sometimes on the piano, sometimes on the bells of the cymbals, sometimes in the bass, sometimes from the horns.

Next comes the beginning of the service, "Call to Prayer," a bold appropriation of the Middle Eastern sound of the Holy Land, which speaks across the ocean to blues and swing, creating a conversation between the duple and triple meters upon which the rhythms of the work will develop over its entirety. In the hot dialogue with the perpetually marvelous Todd Williams, Marsalis once more proves himself the king of avant-garde jazz trumpet with a remarkably audacious performance that no one else could bring off, or has ever approached. Formally, the trumpet exchanges extend by one bar, the tenor by two, the trumpet on one chord, the saxophone harmony extending downward, its progression the same as that which the bass will play in the last section of this movement. The notes of this bass progression are also used in the third movement, forming the melody "In the Sweet Embrace of Life" as well as the chords. The two-part interlude that precedes the final trumpet statement foreshadows "Representative Offerings" in the horn writing and "Hymn"/"Scripture" in the brief piano waltz. The transitional material for trombone—delivered over a ringing bell—perfectly fuses the oppositional aspects of the trumpet-saxophone exchange into a single line as the music shifts to the next part.

"Processional" depicts the choir, the deacons, and the minister coming down the aisles and taking their places at the front of the church. This is always a moment of jubilation, with the robes flowing and the sound of a mighty song beginning in the back of the church, choir members smacking tambourines as they walk, the deacons and the minister turning and smiling at the congregation. This part presents material that will be given variation in the second movement's "Hymn," "Scripture," "Prayer Response," and "Altar Call." The improvisations by all of the horns have superior swing, clearly supported and inspired by the high-style rhythmic command of the extraordinary rhythm section.

"Representative Offerings" are the petitions from the minister to God. This is where the minister's voice first comes forward, asking for grace, for support, for strength. This section is influenced by Ellington's *Afro-Bossa* and *The New Orleans Suite*. Marsalis had in mind

> Something exotic, something out of the ordinary, something that carries
> you into the other world that the minister is addressing. It's also about
> the fact that whenever people offer other people something in the Bible,
> it's always something exotic. Like Duke pointed out—apes and peacocks
> were what the Queen of Sheba brought to Solomon.

Wes Anderson's feature begins as a response to a drum rhythm, then inhabits the entire environment of the piece with the level of soul, thematic invention and control, harmonic bite and rhythmic fluidity possessed only by the great reed players. The same must be said of Todd Williams, whose two features—one on clarinet, one on tenor—emanate from an equally radiant foundation of talent.

Purity is the essence of this movement's last part, "The Lord's Prayer," a variation on the sound of a Gregorian chant, broken up into octaves and done in the chorale style of Bach with blues harmonies. For all of that, it extends upon material from "Devotional" quite clearly at the same time that the elemental "Altar Call" is foreshadowed within all of this sophistication. It is also significant that the notes of the bass progression again form the melody to which the words "In the Sweet Embrace of Life" are sung during the main sermon in the third movement. Here Marsalis's harmonic originality comes forward with its full weight, sounding unlike Ellington or anybody else. At the conclusion, the alto saxophone line refers back to the movement's opening statement of the soprano saxophone, while bells are rung on the piano and the bass.

The second movement opens with "Hymn"—"an allusion to the kind of hymn you might hear sung in somebody's house. Its form is ABCCBA, with the breaks allowing me to ring bells on the piano." Eric Reed is the central improviser, performing with the lilting optimism and determined swing he calls upon throughout the piece. "Scripture" is self-descriptive. It features the lyrical eminence of Wes Anderson and refers back to the hymn. This section ends on a reverse "amen cadence."

"Prayer" is in three sections. The trumpet gives the "Introduction to Prayer," Marion Williams sings the prayer ("In This House"), then there is a "Choral Response" separated by a short piano and bass interlude. For his part, Marsalis reaches a rare level of melodic majesty, stretching his horn in to the area of elevated sound we associate with the humbling authority of Mahalia Jackson. Williams then sings with the spiritual breadth that creates a line from the human heart all the way to the explanatory star at the center of creation. Bells ring, forming an interlude leading to "Choral Response," which consists of material that comes from "Devotional," "Call to Prayer," "Representative Offerings," and "Scripture." After a trumpet feature of peerless rhythmic complexity, there is a brief section for trombone and alto in which the saxophone foreshadows "Altar Call."

"Local Announcements" take place when the congregation is told of forthcoming picnics, fund-raisings, births, the arrivals of messages from vacationing members, exceptional performances by students in schools, the winning of scholarships to college, and so on. Marsalis says:

> It starts off like a four-part barbershop quartet, representing a country, down-home church. Then individuals take solos that would represent announcements. After that, the bass sets the ambience with the slapping technique and they all come together in a part that celebrates how religion brings people together, recognizing their individual souls and their relationships to others.
>
> "Altar Call." This is where you get everybody to pray for specific members of the congregation. Some go forward to the altar for the prayer, then return back to their seats. This has two sections. In the first, each horn comes in one at a time. Once each of the horns is in, we go back through each measure the opposite way, which is like people going up to the altar and returning to their seats. Here I'm using a pentatonic bass. Next, I want the feeling that comes when the members of the congregation are deep into the religious emotion and are responding to each other with great fervor. During these two choruses, which are blues, we also hear a drum solo. After the statement of the line, Todd Williams is featured. This movement ends with fragments from the entire piece, giving us a cross section of feeling and musical elements.

Those two choruses of blues writing, almost eerie in their grasp of the molten Negro religious voice—the ghostly moans, the humming, the chanting—reach as far down into the soul of the matter as anything coming from this cultural source. We hear what Anthony Heilbut was referring to when he wrote in a *New York Times* review of a 1992 book about Thomas A. Dorsey: "Moans, with their relentless blue tonality, provide the basis of black song: spirituals, gospel, blues, and jazz."

The third movement is a whopping culmination. Now the preacher is at the pulpit, his robes rustling like the wings of justice, his voice winding up with the spirit as he gets to his rhythm, that rhythm finding a confident lope that makes the text of his message smolder into the light of a low fire. Slowly, with its measured confidence spiking up into higher and higher flame, the incantational message starts to billow and shoot its percussive cracklings and explosions into the air, the air now a horse galloping downward, its flanks jerking under the spurs of light made fiery by the divine jockey of revelation, that mighty jockey leaping the mount over all the obstacles to recognition as the mysterious makes itself first audible, then visible, descending at a swifter and swifter clip, soon lowering the thunderous pulsation of its power into human flesh, moving through the hair, the sweat, and the twitches until it arrives in the infinite valley of the heart; then that man or that woman, now in the aisle, now moving like one of the brass circles shaking on a tambourine, is lifted higher and higher and higher by the aggressive structure of connection that is the immortal light of the soul called into the hot, calming, and perpetual arms of the Holy Ghost.

The sustained quality of the writing and the playing gives this moment classic immediacy, the feeling that something new is achieving such feats right before us that it will be toasted and remembered until the end of the world. Reginald Veal's startling bass solo is the beginning of the sermon, the preacher clearing his throat and selecting the elements that will lead us into the theme. Veal seems to appropriate the kind of playing heard from Son House on "Pearline," which is to say that he sidesteps the flamenco clichés that can strum a listener into a coma. When the piano comes in, with the same progression from "Call to Prayer" and "The Lord's Prayer" of the first movement, we hear the main theme of the main sermon, "In the Sweet Embrace of Life."

> The form comes from something I was told when I asked a reverend known for preaching hot, fiery, country sermons what his philosophy was. He said, "It's very simple. Start off low; go slow; get higher; catch on fire." So this part is structured on that conception, a sermon in three sections, which I call the "Father," the "Son," and the "Holy Ghost." Each section is a little faster and higher than the one before, going up a half step, from A to B flat to B natural. In the fast section, where the Holy Ghost arrives, the piece goes up yet another half step, to C, for the trumpet solo.

Player after player improvises or executes parts with an introspective-to-spirited authority that holds boredom at bay, surprising with some unexpected expression of quality at every bar—Veal, Riley, and Reed swinging and grooving their way into the upper echelons of the pantheon, all of it reaching the peak of the sermon with a hat-muted trumpet feature, an inflamed rhythm section, and shouting horns that project an intensity unusual even for jazz.

Next, we have "Invitation," where new members are brought into the church. This features Wes Anderson, in one of the great contemporary improvisations, a sensation of nuance, formal command, and emotional complexity. His work is followed by a glorious ringing of bells, an interlude for the thematic rhythms of Herlin Riley's tambourine, more bell ringing, then a feature for the singing keyboard of Eric Reed. This section builds through horn improvisations to an elevating counterpoint that slides into the chant of the next section.

"Recessional" captures the choir and the deacons coming back down the center aisle, the ceremonial reverse of "Processional." It is a 7/4 chant, with hand clapping, a fusion of the duple and triple meters that have served thematic roles throughout the work. Todd Williams is the luminous tenor voice. "Recessional" melts into bell ringing by the horns. The concluding melodic statement from the pulpit, "Benediction," is delivered first by Todd Williams. A brief ringing of bells leads to the theme in harmony, eventually giving way to the bass playing the line while the horns ring bells.

"Uptempo Posthude" takes us out into the afternoon with the congregation, first milling and speaking in the aisles, amening and making observations about the message, celebrating the good feeling that comes when one witnesses the widening light of the truth. Now, with a long sermon done, the visitation of the spirit clear to all, the wonders of the universe still ringing in mind through the metaphors just witnessed—song, speech, human animation—those regular members, those newly declared members, the old, the young, and the in-between, leave satisfied, for they have experienced, in miraculous variety, "The Sweet Embrace of Life." The only thing left to do is go somewhere comfortable, put feet under the table and satiate the appetite for down-home cooking, "Pot Blessed Dinner." The only thing one need do after rising from the sumptuous stupor into which this masterwork will take the listener is to start again and again, absorbing more and more of the organic order that is the soul of all art and the definition of all craft.

Part Four

OFF THE

WALL:

MOVIES

TOWARD A CINEMATIC
LANGUAGE OF
DEMOCRACY*

This statement concerns the open sky of aesthetic challenges that the serious black filmmakers who have come of age on this national soil need to meet. But, to begin things, I need to air out some fonk fuming from the intellectual shortcomings of our time. Most contemporary writing about Negro American art forms an obstacle to clear aesthetic thinking. It is largely a confusion of ethnic politics, sociological justification, clichés about gender limitations, and the sentimental romance of exotic retentions, none of which speaks to the marvels and dilemmas of our present condition. In such writing, art is almost never the issue, nor is the fact that the work of United States Negroes is, first and foremost, American. What we usually get is a lot of ranting about injustice, a German-derived nationalism (as all nationalism is—read Herder), and a set of flimsy aesthetic briefs borrowed from the French obsession with the mud, all of which forms a desire to defend the most brutal and uncivilized among us, as if that defense will protect us from the burdens of civilization and the complicated consciousness that comes of the embattled bulwark against disorder that is the bourgeoisie at its very highest. We need neither intellectually counterfeit attempts to give pedigrees to Snoop Doggy Dogg nor maudlin discussions of the horrors that come of one's erotic plumbing. We have an epic duty that should never submit to anything less than the largest possible metaphors for human life in our time, or in any other time we actually understand. We should speak of our lives as modern men and modern women with as much accuracy as possible, using the par-

*This paper was delivered in a somewhat different form on the final panel of the Pan African Film Conference at New York University in the spring of 1994.

ticulars of our experience to add complexity to the world of metaphors one steps into whenever creating art. Such qualities will only come of solid conceptions and the discipline brought to the mysterious fact of talent.

There is a very close relationship between classic American film and jazz, this nation's finest Afro-American music. The energy, the startling twists of direction, the disdain for pomposity, and the percussive climaxes of pratfalls, explosions, smashings, and collisions that gave riotous forward motion to the improvised slapstick comedies of Sennett, Chaplin, Keaton, and Lloyd were visually akin to the extemporized melodies, the new tonal colors, the building heat, and the incantational surprises central to the fusion of primitive vitality and sophistication that defines jazz. There was also a perfect aesthetic symmetry to the two arts because of the way the individual and the mass were defined within the shape and feeling of both forms. Close-ups and crosscutting parallel the relationship between the featured soloists and the conversing, woofing, snapping, and crooning brass and reeds in big band jazz. For the film actor, the close-up allows intimacy of expression, the use of the particulars of the face and the eyes for a manipulation of feeling beneath the makeup. That is the same moment for the improviser whose feature allows him to step out in front of the band and make obvious the individuation of tone, the melodic and harmonic imagination of the improvised line, the rhythmic identity, and the ability to work with and against the force, the support, and the taunts of the ensemble, large or small. When most successful, the individual and the orchestration enforce the meaning of each other within both art forms. Consequently, the very execution of each art supplies us with exceptional democratic metaphors.

Watching the slapstick comedies we also see the daredevil bendings of reality into an unpretentious and often joyous surrealism, a quality central to what Louis Armstrong did with popular tunes through the features he made essential to the conception of jazz. The most influential grand master of the improvised musical close-up, Armstrong added an invincible set of aesthetic options to American and world music as he stretched, contracted, twisted, and satirized those songs with his trumpet and his singing. Going the way of genius, Armstrong removed the corny elements that coated popular songs and replaced their adolescent depth with mature, adult passion, from the comic to the tragic. Armstrong's innovative improvisations turned popular songs into individualized abstractions and his phrasing introduced the pulsation of swing, the most revolutionary rhythm of the twentieth century. He adapted his material with the same freedom the best filmmakers brought to the novels, plays, and short stories they remade for the screen.

Yet we must always remember that Armstrong did what he did not because of some ludicrous genetic memory of African abstraction but because he had to face the problems of making sense of the concrete rain forest that is the American city. No matter how deeply Negroid, his lyric gifts were firmly based in the twentieth-century agenda of all serious artists in the modern world. In Armstrong's case, he achieved charismatic distinction through the innovations necessary to give the accuracy of eloquence to the expression of the life of human feeling in the United States. He brought a fresh aesthetic order to the language of democracy, which is the language of individual and collective possibility. In so doing, Armstrong gave voice to what the best of this nation's films expressed—the bittersweet song of the American heart, which is the song of the world. This blues-derived melody of emotion dares to answer the impersonal dangers of our society with a protean metaphor for the human soul. It is what America offered to the world—a sense that we could, no matter how harsh and complex the urban landscape seemed, not only hold it at bay but also meet its measure and triumph over the adversity that could so easily alienate. We could heat the cold, technological force of the metropolis with human energy and make it sing and make it dance. If nothing else, we could supply substantial recognition of the endless dimensions of joy, sorrow, and ambivalence that prove and provide our human commonality. That recognition is itself basic to the highest kind of affirmation.

This is the spirit the Negro actress Anna Deavere Smith uses to animate her play, *Twilight: Los Angeles*, where she performs forty-two parts—male and female, black, white, Asian, Hispanic, rich, poor, policeman, criminal, etc. That daredevil lyricism not only expands our understanding of our American passions but also stretches acting into another dimension. "Who," Deavere Smith is asking, "can wring out all of the rhythms of America better than I can? Who is better prepared than I am, this Negro woman, to express this national epic of conflict, of blood, of murder, of compassion, of humor buffoonish, subtle, ironic, unintentional; of tragedy, opportunism, and heartbreak?" Her very willingness to bust the box of imposed ethnicity we expect from both the light and the dark sides of the street and the boy and girl bathrooms is a high moment of democratic awareness. This awareness takes on the originality of an artist expressing her right to sing the blues across the lines our most unimaginative would draw into the flesh of the human heart. This is what the most serious black filmmakers should strive to achieve within the infinite terms of their individual personalities.

Of course, the struggle for success in the mass technological show business of film will always be hard. The struggle to achieve artistry in mass media will be even harder. But ours is a heroic tradition and victory is always a combination of recognition, execution, and luck. We have been Americans a long time—slaves, Indian fighters, cracker-shooting Union soldiers in the Civil War, scholars, inventors, politicians, pioneer men and women, musicians, dancers, carpenters, mechanics, surgeons, jockeys, builders of cities, of schools, and so on and on. The story of America is our story, and the almost inexorable elements of race can enrich the tragic-comic, flippant and optimistic, romantic and violent thing we mean when we say Americana. To sell out to the nationalist politics of skin tone is to do a disservice to our moment. What we need to address is how a set of aesthetic propositions will develop a cinematic language in which narrative, dialogue, image, cutting, and color provide an accurate orchestration of Americana in the many ways we know it.

In order to do that, we have to recognize that the grand job facing Negro American filmmakers is appropriating the contagious pantheon of heroic themes and issues that have made Hollywood the capital of international dreams. There is incredible space for invention because the three-dimensional black character is absent from so much of this country's cinema. Even so, until we have met the measure of the very best American films—westerns, detective stories, romantic comedies, political dramas, sports stories, rags-to-riches tales, tearjerkers, and so on—we will not have done our jobs. We will not have made real in our own terms Sergio Leone's observation that American film, because it had to speak across so many boundaries within its own culture, became an international language by realizing its own national identity. What I find essential is the development of a democratic vision of cinema informed by the rich variety of Afro-American experience, from the streets to the suites, from the barely human brutality of those depicted in gangster rap to the chilling and heating spiritual elegance embodied by Mahalia Jackson singing "His Eye Is on the Sparrow."

If we are to understand the language of democracy, we need to personalize what John Ford achieved. I don't mean his style; I mean his ideas. The issues of arrogant and irresponsible power, class and racial prejudice, the mulatto realities of ethnic and cultural identity, are some of the themes this remarkable artist works with in his finest films. In his westerns especially, Ford made clear the difference between the healthy, unsentimental American irreverence that increases democratic possibility and the anarchic ruthlessness that threatens our freedom. We need to emphasize this because the remarkable degree of vibrant civilization achieved by black Americans is under attack by the anarchic among us, those who have the same contempt for civilized values as Ford's marauding cowboys. To the good, there are black screenwriters and filmmakers who understand this quite well, for they attack the same kinds of things that the worst of rap music celebrates. Whether we are talking about films such as *Deep Cover* or *House Party*, *Sugar Hill* or *Menace II Society*, the issues Ford often addressed are already present. This is very important because the charismatic relationship Afro-Americans have to this society can be as irresponsibly decadent as it can be high-minded, joyous, soberly critical, and cautionary. We have as much responsibility for the health of our democracy as anyone else. We have known its failures and we have inspired a good number of its triumphs.

All societies must face the inevitable shortcomings of folly, corruption, and mediocrity, and the role of the artist is to alert the audience to those shortcomings, illustrating why and how they triumph, why and how they are momentarily held back. If we take on the challenge of bringing to cinematic art the fruits of mastering those challenges, we have the potential to enrich the Hollywood language of international dreams in the very same way that Louis Armstrong and his children enriched American music and the music of the world. As a close reading of our history shows, no opportunity is beyond the disciplined talents of the best among us, regardless of class or gender.

MENACE II SOCIETY

Excellent. He's enterprising, aggressive,
outgoing, young, bold, vicious. He'll do.

Minister of Interior, A *Clockwork Orange*

Given the small number of truly good works arriving from the spiritual sweatshops of our mass media, no one should be shocked to find that the quality of art we get in black films is as low as that in all other popular cinema. This has little to do with the iron fact that only golden ages provide the illusion of genius arriving in hordes. In such golden ages, a small number of people with artistic vision are supported by large groups of artisans who give their all to a concern for quality supported by the culture at large. At those times, when a great religion or technical innovations fuse with a national spirit of optimism, grand to hilarious renderings of the universe and the human heart arrive, masterpiece set upon masterpiece, followed by seemingly endless works of less magnitude but high standards and integrity.

Through those popular genres we express our mythic themes, we speak of conflict and achievement, of folly and destruction, of corruption and despair, of our deep uneasiness with order when it is too restrictive and our equal terror of anarchy. We also render the archetypes that fuel the tragic optimism underlying our democratic recognition of inevitable risk and universal potential. So whether the stories are curve balls pitched from the mound of American history or conventions shaped in Hollywood, they are means of democratic access as much as they are affirmations of what we know and battle toward in our civilization. Told over and over, rising sometimes from melodramatic entertainment to the glow of art, these myths and the archetypes within them are essential to what we say and what we know of our culture.

Though all are in their early twenties, Albert and Allen Hughes, the twins who directed *Menace II Society*, and Tyger Williams, who wrote the screenplay, know that lower-class black youth culture is in trouble, especially down there in the street, where the values of the outlaw can reduce life to the trivial level on which empty-headed murderers exist. Unlike what the great American painter Emilio Cruz calls the "lumpen bourgeoisie" of white rock critics and their Negro counterparts, the makers of this film aren't titillated by criminal street life and they don't see it as yet another weapon against middle-class convention. In that respect, they join the writers and makers of previous films such as *Juice*, *Straight Out of Brooklyn*, *Boyz N the Hood*, *New Jack City*, and *South Central*, where we see the other side of the posturing, cursing, and threatening that fans of gangster rap find so satisfying. Though far below the craft and visceral thrust of *Menace II Society*, those films repudiate that world by following its philosophy to its murderous conclusions and join the American tradition out of which *Scarface*, *Public Enemy*, and *Little Caesar* come.

In this film, however, we see a fresh use of the virtuoso cinematography that comes from the world of pop music videos, where the music is like newly made stone axes, children's used coloring books, and adolescent diaries traveling in space ships — brute, childish, and naive visions projected by high-quality artisans of film technique. The South Central characters in *Menace II Society* are surely vulgar elements of the lower depths or given to the ethnic clichés and the sentimentality of black popular culture, but within the context of the film they rise above the conventions their lives explicate. They take their places among the most harrowing aspects of our democratic art.

The Hughes brothers and Williams know, or sense, that the crisis of our time travels from one end of the society to the other, that we no longer live in a world that allows us to believe the amoral brats of the upper echelons are somehow countered by a generous humanity at the bottom. In *Menace II Society*, we see that the loss of faith has seeped from the intellectual palace down to the mental pigsty and that there is a voluminous difference between true elegance and decadence, a difference we should never fail to recognize in our gold rush culture of so much quick success. One aspect of true elegance in our version of capitalism is that it, unlike pretension, gives success a spiritual resonance, allowing the trappings of good fortune to express the complexes and subtleties that make the human soul most vital. But in the living world of gangster rap, drive-by shootings, and crack wars, the materialism made emblematic by diamond earrings, gold chains, expensive cars, and brand names has no connection to vitality; it merely expresses the obsessive attraction to surfaces, the consumerist inclinations of types we would elevate by calling them subhuman.

The characters in *Menace II Society* fall right into the conventions of the traditional gangster film—the touchy brutes with guns, the trashy women, the casual attitudes toward violence, the gaudiness, the obsession with never appearing "soft," the feeling of omnipotence and frustration, the morality limited to a small group of buddies, the contempt for women, the bad guy who wants to go good and dies trying—but the tabloid immediacy and the command of idiom make this film the most powerful portrait of the monsters among us since Martin Scorsese's *Goodfellas*, which wiped away any romantic ideas about the Mafia. Though influenced in themes, characters, situations, and techniques by *Goodfellas*, *Menace II Society* is neither as complex as Scorsese's film nor as wide in its social range, but it benefits from a deft handling of the limited world in which its people live. Yet no matter how compelling these characters might be, the filmmakers have achieved the equally difficult job of making them almost uniformly unsympathetic. Beyond the physical horror of their wounds and their deaths, one never empathizes with these distillations of anarchy in human form.

In effect, the Hughes brothers have succeeded in making a film about the way the urban problems presented by the classic gangster tale have evolved over the last sixty years. It is about the mortal wounds of corruption, as all gangster films of serious import must be—corruption of the individual, the family, the community. The classic gangster is a man of arrogance who substitutes bold, unsqueamish action for patience and discipline; he doesn't ask, he takes. Existing in a tar bucket of the soul, he discovers that the illegal appetites of masses of people will enable him to become rich on the express train, not the local; all he has to do is keep up his nerve and limit his loyalty to those willing to die with him or for him, and he can rise above the limitations of class or the alienation of an immigrant background. In the old films, the way up for the Italian or Irish gangster was through selling illegal booze; in our time, for the lower-class black gangster, drugs up the bucks.

In the 1931 *Public Enemy*, James Cagney's Tom Powers began as a mean-spirited boy who stole, lied, drank beer, hated girls, learned the ways of serious crime from crooked adults, and accepted his policeman father's whippings as part of the price charged for a ticket into the world of willful crime. For Powers (as for Ray Liotta's Henry Hill in *Goodfellas*), those whippings were like the pain an athlete learns is essential to development. As an adult bootlegger whose dark profession included killing, Powers remained suspicious of women and of education. The worst thing a man could be was a "sissy," and he described his honest brother's studying in school as time spent "learning how to be poor."

We see the same attitudes prevail in *Menace II Society*. To "act like a bitch" is to lose all respect, to be relegated to the sub-position of a "ho." As for education, there is only the lore of the streets—adults giving children liquor, showing them how to hustle, cursing in front of them, murdering as they look on. Beyond that, there is the blast of rap recordings and the images arriving from television. Books exist neither for learning nor pleasure. Reflection is foreign to this world of shadows, and the gangster, as always, is the man of action gone terribly astray.

The cinema vérité opening of *Menace II Society* appropriates the style and lighting of the gun battle in *Taxi Driver* as it introduces the main character, Caine (Tyrin Turner), and his friend, O-Dog (Larenz Tate). We immediately see the complicity of adults in the corruption of the young and how the proliferation of illegal weapons makes even the slightest insult an excuse for dealing death. Obviously too young to buy liquor, Caine and Dog go into a Korean store loud and wrong. They soon curse the wife of the Korean storekeeper, who pretends to dust as she apprehensively eyes them, then shout at her husband behind the counter. Caine and Dog take quarts of beer out of the refrigerator, open them, drink, brag to each other of their sexual intentions and contemptuously leave money on the counter. No question is raised about their ages; they are only told they cannot drink the beer in the store and to get out. The law is broken in the selling and the buying. No one is innocent.

Then Dog misunderstands something the Korean says and murders him. In the convention of the films from the early thirties, the first gunshot takes place offscreen as Caine, standing at the counter, guzzles beer. He drops the bottle and turns to see Dog firing at a body hidden by the counter. Dog then snatches the screaming Korean woman and takes her offscreen into the back of the store, where he's heard demanding the store's surveillance videotape. We hear more shots as the camera remains in place, the second killing happening outside its frame. Dog rushes from the back, takes money from the register and the Korean man's corpse, then the two flee. The camera holds its position on the exit door as we hear a car start up and screech off. In the tradition of the 1930 *Little Caesar*, a killing and a robbery begin the tale.

Like *Public Enemy*, Caine's tale is told in episodes rather than through a plot, and the use of blackouts seems a metaphor for the characters emerging from and disappearing into darkness. As they strut, curse, party, and kill, we see the reduction of human beings to slop jars filled with the poisonous sputum produced by the spiritual viruses of our moment. We are even forced to ask whether or not the universal humanism rooted in the idea of an immortal soul applies beyond a certain point—environment triumphs over essence. Caine is, as the street chant goes, "born in a barrel of butcher knives." From childhood, he is surrounded by criminals, drug addicts, murderers, and hustlers, the crudest variations on the ethos of the "me generation." By the time he graduates from a high school that he has attended only half the time, Caine is a drug dealer with a beeper. His father, an indifferent murderer, has been killed in a drug deal, and his mother, a heroin addict, has died from an overdose, leaving him to live with his grandparents. The systematic irresponsibility that would allow a student that bad to graduate combines with the disdain his parents show for child rearing, forming an adversity of policy and individual immorality. It is much easier for Caine to flow with the slime than embrace the Christian values espoused by his grandparents, values he and his friends dismiss on racial grounds—"praying to a white Jesus." But even "the black man's religion" of Islam is sneered at when a reformed buddy preaches it to Caine and his crime crew—"Sharriff was an ex-knucklehead turned Muslim. He was so happy to be studying something he liked that he kept coming at us with it. He thought Allah could save black people. Yeah, right." Doom is the only course on the menu.

Though he is the narrator, Caine is as much a spectator as the audience is, and the narrowness of his world is replicated by the tightness of the frames. Everything is closed in, the world almost a succession of apartment and automobile interiors. Even when Caine joins his buddies at a barbecue in a park, the camera only briefly gives a feeling of open space. The claustrophobic mood rarely lets up and much of the menace comes from explosive personalities moving through small places.

The film explores moral decay not only by taking us through Caine's criminal strata of drug dealing and violence but also by showing which myths are important to the characters and which have lost all penetration. No matter how much Caine and his friends talk as though there is no relationship between them and what others would call "white cultural values," the filmmakers know better. It isn't a matter of color but one of identification. After Caine has been shot, he spends time in the hospital looking at gangster movies, caught by the terseness and the violence. But when he returns to the home of his grandparents, the characters and the plot of *It's a Wonderful Life* are unintelligible. Talking tough and killing are things Caine understands, but the idea that civilized men have a responsibility to face the difficult rather than commit suicide, that they have to acknowledge what their deaths might mean to their wives, their children, and their communities, is a morality tale from the moon.

The importance of television is a statement about media in general and how it becomes a reality many choose to emulate. We know now that gangsters of sixty years ago picked up slang and manners from films about imaginary mobsters. In DePalma's 1983 *Scarface*, when the Cuban viper is first interrogated he explains that he learned how to speak English from movies starring James Cagney and Humphrey Bogart. A videocassette of DePalma's film is constantly running in the home of Nino Brown, the big-time cocaine dealer in *New Jack City*. The black kid who becomes a lunatic killer in *Juice* identifies with Cagney's slaughtering maniac in *White Heat*. In the gangsters' willingness to emulate celluloid bad guys rather than those opposing them, they are all variations on the young fascist creep in A *Clockwork Orange*, where evil provides the only thrill, and even the high culture symbolized by Beethoven's "Ode to Joy" is no more than a soundtrack for barbarism, just as it was within the Nazi matrix. In fact, the occupying fascist army within lower-class black communities is not, as the radical rhetoric would have it, the police but black street criminals like O-Dog, who brags that he will kill anybody—man, woman, child, the elderly—who gets in his way. He is the black extension of sociopaths like Richard Widmark's Tommy Udo from *Kiss of Death* and similar to the killer in *Juice*. But O-Dog does them all one better by becoming a gangster movie star as he repeatedly amuses himself and his friends with the videotape of his murder of the Korean merchant; he even sells copies. Rarely has the relationship between fantasy identification with media and brutal emulation been shown as well.

Where *Menace II Society* breaks off from the traditional gangster movie is in the glamourless world its characters inhabit. In *Public Enemy, Scarface, Little Caesar, The Godfather*, and *Goodfellas*, the criminals aspire to some sort of quality beyond good suits and flashy cars. They go to elegant clubs, wear tuxedos, become equestrians, attend the opera, dine in five-star restaurants, own grand pianos, drink champagne, and so on, trying their best to achieve aristocratic position, however poorly they succeed. The criminals of *Menace II Society* have no aspirations beyond jewelry and cars. They murder and sell drugs but spend their time in squat project apartments, drink beer, smoke reefers, shoot dice, almost always eat fast food, and sit up watching television. In place of having grand pianos, they carry boom boxes. There is no society beyond the one they grew up in. They can sport the trappings of wealth but have no place within their souls or their world to travel. Caine's cousin is murdered during the theft of his BMW, and a few scenes later the thieves are trying to beg up on some free hot dogs from a woman who sells the food in a stucco box covered with the thick bars that express the constant fear of robbery.

Like the classic gangster who falls for a good woman, Caine is inspired by Ronnie (Jada Pinkett), the ex-lover of his crime mentor. A determined single mother who can talk as tough as the foulmouthed around her, Ronnie has a femininity that not only makes her a contemporary pioneer woman in an urban Wild West, but gives her a quality lacking in the black gun molls who are different from their men in dress and genitalia only. Ronnie doesn't give in to simple, racial explanations for surrender to the streets, nor passes on to her small son the kind of facile xenophobia heard from the Muslim kid and his father, whom Caine and the others see as something of a "positive role model." Her plan is to leave Los Angeles for Atlanta with her son and Caine. She is determined to get a new start. Nothing will stop her from climbing out of the bucket of gun-toting maggots that is her neighborhood. Caine reluctantly agrees to go, but the rage that periodically surfaces in him leads to his destruction. He is doomed as much by what he is as where he is.

Menace II Society succeeds because its makers have a love of film itself that has allowed them the facility for storytelling in terse aesthetic terms. By absorbing so much cinema, the Hughes brothers have shown us just how important the media have always been in thwarting segregation. That the terrible circumstances and actions result from both our urban conditions *and* the choices individuals make separates their film from most of what we hear in discussions about race, poverty, and crime. We should be grateful to the Hughes brothers for having such a complex vision of corruption, one in which the Koreans, the crooked, peripheral whites, and the frustrated cops are not responsible for what happens to Caine and his crew, but are players in a tale of decay that touches us all and indicts us all. It is not easy to redefine the myths of the national pantheon, whether from an inside lane or from a point of exclusion defined by stereotypes. But Albert and Allen Hughes have helped clarify our identity while also saying things central to the tragedy of human life in the modern world, where the democratization of violence speeds at a terrifying velocity.

HARLEM ON
OUR MINDS

*Leave Harlem? I am Harlem. This is where I belong. This is where hell is.
I'm going to stay here and meet the devil.*

Clarence Williams III as A. R., *Sugar Hill*

Sugar Hill is a psychologically ambitious portrait of a Harlem drug
boss that benefits from the false glamour and the brutal spikes of
Manhattan. In its alternately swift and lumbering pace, its brutality,
and its startling achievement of tragedy, *Sugar Hill* speaks of the
uncleaned and gilded cages inhabited by those who make their
money most ruthlessly. Much of the film's success results from the
fact that in the urban tale of America there is no larger myth than
that of New York, where the most elegant and the most terrible tales
of human life in our democracy have played themselves out. In that
small space, so different from the plains of our Western heritage, so
much more varied in its possibilities and its temptations, a metaphor
has evolved, one in which the threatening impersonality of concrete,
steel, and glass has achieved lyrical meaning in our jazz, our musi-
cals, and our love stories.

We hear the cry of Manhattan as infinite in its textures and sub-
texts, a sound of battered magnetism rising from a melting pot or
screaming from a cauldron. New York is a technological rain forest,
shooting its business world up in skyscrapers, cramming its residents
in tenements and apartment houses, serving up its fun in big ball
parks or small clubs where the life of the night becomes huge under
the pressure of the passion to know joy. In Manhattan, every group
has learned the limits of its greatness and smelled the spiritual defe-
cation of its affinity for corruption. Innocence is a domain inhabited by those who have yet to talk and yet to understand the protean
flexibility of the con that slides off the hustler's tongue. Manhattan is
the place where vitality arrives with scar tissue, the sign that one has

been the mark and now knows the game. A marvel and a monstrosity, New York allows us absolute knowledge of our modern selves.

That myth of Manhattan maintains itself on one plane, but within that myth, uptown in Harlem, urban rot quite ominously dulls what was once one of the most dynamically glittering jewels in the crown of Western civilization. Largely fled by its embattled middle class when the drug culture turned so much of its cultural blood into pus, Harlem is an emblem of our society's decline, of our inability thus far to sustain such an engine of spiritual, aesthetic, and communal vitality. Where the Negro-American elite of ball players, musicians, politicians, actors, writers, dancers, and so on once made its streets promenades of champions, Harlem now boasts few significant figures and remains under siege by the young criminals and the slicksters who provide the addictive poisons of one kind or another. Now and again, it seems to be rising from the muck bred by the corrupt, but the clubs can't stay open and the streets are never thought safe enough to draw the kinds of people who went to Harlem when it was in vogue precisely because so much of what came into vogue rose from the bittersweet urban blues of its throat. The extended family that provided such a remarkable alternative to the alienation of the city has fallen under the weight of teenage pregnancy and the fear of reprimanding adolescents who might be armed and dangerous or, at least, prefer to act and dress that way. Harlem is now a slum, pushed into decay during the second half of this century, when the six elements that have defined our times are the popular arts, atomic energy, television, liberation movements, international competition for markets, and drugs.

Sugar Hill is the story of Roemello Skuggs, a drug dealer played by Wesley Snipes. It has a very meditative pace and is influenced by the spiritual concerns of Sergio Leone's *Once Upon a Time in America*. In contrast to almost any film with black main characters, its subject is largely foreign to contemporary American films—the burden of conscience. Because *Sugar Hill* is so much about the state of Roemello's soul, those who saw Snipes as the remorseless Nino Brown in *New Jack City* will be surprised by this performance. It is filled with subtlety and a range of feeling worthy of the long close-ups.

Unlike Nino Brown, Roemello suffers from nostalgia for the roads not taken and is increasingly disturbed by the paths he chose to success. He wants to leave the hell of Harlem and go down South, return to the old country, where he thinks civilized black life is still possible. Using his face and eyes for nuances that often go far beyond his lines, Snipes tells us of Roemello's loneliness, his confusion, his self-disgust, his guilt, his charm, his canniness, his violence, his sentimentality, his weariness, his longing. The chameleon intricacy that comes of Roemello's brooding allows us to see that Marlon Brando was the Picasso of American acting. Where the Spaniard enriched Western plastic art with African abstraction, Brando brought into our cinematic iconography the posings and simmerings of the Negro facial expressions that we associate with people like Miles Davis. Extending upon this source, Wesley Snipes gives us his most brilliant piece of work, proving himself a richly talented actor, not just a star.

The emotion that Roemello exudes is quite different from that of Priest, the main character in *Superfly*, which set the black drug dealer in the classic mode of the gangster who wants to get out of the game. Priest was obviously a hustler; his clothes and car told the tale. His long, straightened hair was a rejection of the Afro. He was garish and knew nothing of glamour other than a huge bathtub and the symbolic success of a white concubine to flop around with in the suds. Harlem was his home, and the gatherings he attended were in the rank night world where fashionably plaid, big-hatted, and platform-shoed pimps and other scum revealed their distance from mainstream achievement by the communal poverty of their taste. Priest sold cocaine and used a lot of it; his example made the coke spoon on a chain around the neck a fashion essential among blue-collar black teenagers of the early seventies. A cold and sentimental man, Priest had done the best he could, given his lack of training.

Twenty years later, the world is different and Roemello could easily have gone another way. A well-educated and progressively sensitive man, he had received a scholarship to Georgetown but ended up out on the block, where he hardened himself to make his way through the grave-digging business of the drug trade. Roemello controls heroin in Harlem. His home is filled with books, he listens to the best jazz, the clothes he wears and the car he drives give the

impression of a young black professional, one of those who benefited from the Civil Rights Movement and the affirmative action
openings in the business world. He can afford the tabs at expensive
downtown clubs, where stars ranging from the screen to the street
gather in sterile ritual with their indiscriminate bimbos. None of
these things means much to him now, for Roemello is overcome by
a feeling of culpability. He is rattled by what Harlem has suffered
so that men like him can live their versions of the good life. His conscience twists him on a spit of memory and recrimination.

Roemello is full of pain and guilt because he is part of a family
that has been destroyed and made rich by heroin. The film opens as
he lies awake in a plush apartment and recalls the day his mother
died from an overdose in front of her two young sons. As a teenager
returning home from school, Roemello sees his father, A. R., beaten
and shot by Mafia drug suppliers and crooked cops. A. R. is an
addict who sells drugs for them but has also lifted some of their
money. When Roemello receives his scholarship to Georgetown, he
stares at the two chairs where his parents should be. Perhaps that
same evening, in the blazer of his private school, Roemello kills the
man who shot his father, but later works for one of his partners. He
becomes another of the predators bloodying their teeth on the flesh
of Harlem.

While his sons swagger in their wealth, A. R. still lives in the same
apartment the family had. It, like the community, is in decay, the
walls greasy and peeling. He has survived the Mafia shooting and
remains a drug addict, given to nostalgic memories of his youth,
when he was a "church boy" and knew nothing of the black and
degrading hole so many have lived and died in, their stories abbre-
viated in syringe marks. When Roemello visits A. R., feeding him
or listening to him sing and play the piano, there is always the visible
pain of standing before a terminal condition of self-destruction.

Roemello is given some of his spiritual lumps by the impossibility
of bringing his father and brother together. Raynathan, Roemello's
older brother, is his partner in the business. Unlike Roemello, he is
satisfied with what he does, though his bitterness toward their father
reflects the double moral vision of his universe. While brimming
with the power that comes of drug money, Raynathan is haunted by
the death of his mother and blames A. R. for introducing her to the

debasing sedation she came to love. Raynathan avoids seeing A. R. and when he does, it is at the behest of Roemello. Gathered for a dinner of fast food in A. R.'s apartment, the three men sit down. Roemello tries to joke. Almost immediately, Raynathan berates A. R. mercilessly and leaves in a rage. A. R. tells Roemello to leave with his brother. Helpless, Roemello says, "You two are breaking my heart."

Moral double vision is central to the film. It connects *Sugar Hill* to the doubleness at the center of our most demanding social problem, which is whether we will discover ways to make those born in the mud rise to positions of civilized vitality or merely allow them the circumscribed freedom to use unlimited brutal means for criminal success, the greater society settling for whatever barbarian entertainment spills over into the mainstream, like gangster rap or Def Comedy Jam. This doubleness also plays itself out in the characters of Rocmello and Raynathan, who contrast each other in the way George Raft and Paul Muni did in *Scarface,* or as the tenor saxophones of Lester Young and Hershel Evans functioned in Count Basie's band, or Bing Crosby and Bob Hope in the "road" comedies, or Miles Davis and John Coltrane in the trumpeter's band—the suave and understated next to the frantic and explosive, the scalpel and the meat hook. As Raynathan, Michael Wright quite effectively creates the jiggling brute monkey of the criminal warpath. He is insecure, sadistic, isolated, grandiose, petty, childish, and terrified, a perfect recipe for mayhem and maudlin reflection.

But the film doesn't stop there, for it raises questions far beyond what we expect of tales set in the black crime world. *Sugar Hill* seeks to define the collapse of blue-collar black communities. The focus is there because the wonder of Afro-American culture was the way in which those at the bottom rose either to middle-class success or helped prepare the way for their children, all the while vibrantly sustaining the household and community values that give a humane sheen to civilization. Harlem was most vital when there were far fewer opportunities, and its decline resulted form the erosion of three things—the tragic optimism of religion; the high-minded commitment to education and quality performance; and the replication of the discipline, grace, and sportsmanship represented by great athletes. *Sugar Hill* makes clear how the environmental pollution of illegal, addictive drugs begat a concrete jungle rot that spread and spread, destroying far too much of our most precious natural resource—our humanity.

A. R. represents the fall from religious strength. Clarence Williams III makes the self-pity and the delusion, the humor and fatalism of A. R. palpable and full of complex passion. His demise from an overdose is one of the finest moments in all of cinema. Williams achieves tragedy following a monologue about the Sunday when A. R. ran from church in the middle of a sermon and joined the hard guys who handed him heroin and a syringe, telling the boy, "*Here* is your God." Through the remarkable control of this actor we see a pulpy soul leave this beaten man as the drug enters his body and moves to kill him. No viewer will ever forget the way his eyelids very slightly flutter and close in that sweat-slick face as the hissing rattle of death rises from his throat.

Sugar Hill also makes criticisms of the middle class, which is represented by Roemello. As an educated man without a moral base, he is the corruption of the Afro-American dream, the shining son, the college boy willing to roll his community into the snake pit, then watch its horrible death from his penthouse. His success opposes the goal of civilization under capitalism, which is to fuse morality, ethics, and the profit motive. Roemello's corruption is mirrored by that of Lolly, the ex-fighter who sells crack, owns a gym, and with a cynical sigh, confesses to having awakened a rich man after throwing a major fight because "life is too short." Not stopping at the boxer who has repudiated the legacy of Joe Louis and Sugar Ray Robinson, the film is perhaps most shocking when it enters the vast apartment of a black basketball star who guzzles Dom Pérignon from the bottle and, his charm down, turns out to be a sexual sadist.

This is a cold picture of the criminal world and of the rot at the top, regardless of occupation. It also does away with the explanatory clichés that blame the white man and the devil machine of capitalism, while longing for the reiteration of some mythical African—or Third World—humanism. *Sugar Hill* shows that amoral greed is a worldwide phenomenon, transcending race and religion. In one superb club scene, Raynathan points out some well-dressed Nigerians to Roemello, observing that they get their heroin from Pakistan (a Muslim country), take it through Lagos, and make big money in the Bronx. Roemello comments, "We used to look to them for our history and our culture," to which his brother replies, "If you want history and culture, look in *National Geographic.*" Raynathan wants to do business with the Nigerians in order to get free of the Italian suppliers, whom he sees as "wop" colonizers. So the rhetoric of Pan-Africanism has sunk from basement politics to the sewer of the drug trade. But the Africans tell them that they can't do business with "black Americans, cotton pickers." The Harlem drug kings then pummel the Africans and disrupt the club, raising their true gangster colors. And since the slave trade of today is the drug business, the kinds of Nigerians who sell heroin are the same kinds who sold Africans centuries ago. The blue steel fact is that the cooperation of black people was and is essential to both.

One of the best moments is given to Abe Vigoda's Gus, the drug supplier who operates out of a neighborhood grocery and deli-catessen in Harlem. In a stunning moment of rationalization, he tells Roemello of how he came to Harlem thirty years ago at the command of his Mafia family. He says things were slow then but that Harlem was a beautiful place, its 125th Street bright and won-derful like 34th Street downtown during the Christmas holidays. Gus then talks about how the people went crazy and destroyed Harlem after King was killed, making it dangerous for "honest col-ored people" to walk the streets. He smiles as he remembers when it was "raining money" after the Vietnam junkies returned home. Rarely has the criminal distance from responsibility been better depicted.

The ethnic themes and the actors lift the film out of the familiar-ity of the tale—the criminal who wants to get out of the game and is sure that he can when he meets that certain woman. Theresa Ran-dle as Melissa is the certain one and she does much with a thinly written part. She brings spark, tenderness, pain, and terror to Melissa, who is essentially a would-be actress and party girl looking for a well-to-do guy. Her first scene with Roemello has an authentic quality of hard-boiled Negroid flirtation we rarely see done well. Leslie Uggams is wasted as her mother, a part even flimsier than Randle's. The white characters, with the exception of Gus, are car-toons. But the look of *Sugar Hill* is especially rich, taking advantage of the varied skin tones of Afro-Americans and reaching for the kind of emotion-deepening color Leone brought to *Once Upon a Time in America*. Still, the film is episodic and sometimes moves too slowly, much the result of an obtrusive score by Terence Blanchard that lays down one loud, loud fly-paper dirge after another, none particularly striking.

Though not nearly the artistic success of *Menace II Society*, *Sugar Hill* is important because it tries for so much more and brings a contemplative quality to its main character that is still fresh for the Afro-American context. We so rarely see black characters who have minds and souls, whether their writers are black or white, that this film is exciting in its ambition. It is also important because it understands the hollow glamour so many of our newly privileged mistake for the resonance of grace and sophistication. There is a troubling irony to the fact that a man like Roemello, who has done so much to destroy Harlem, would want to begin his life away from crime in the South. Perhaps that is the commentary on how badly we have handled the potential of our cities. The first migration was from the South to the North; the second from the cities to the suburbs; the third a return to the South. But is there, in a time when everything touches everything else, a place where we can escape the spreading erosion that begins in former cultural wonderlands like Harlem?

EGGPLANT BLUES:
THE MISCEGENATED CINEMA
OF QUENTIN TARANTINO

The recent opening of writer-director Quentin Tarantino's *Pulp Fiction* is a high point in a low age. Already slobbered over at Cannes and genuflected before by the New York press, it is, perhaps more than anything else, a continuation of Tarantino themes thus far missed and another startling aesthetic victory for a small, undeclared American film movement. By looking full face into the ethnic quirks and racial complexities of our identity, *Pulp Fiction* addresses issues most effectively pushed into the ambiguity, humor, and tragedy of art by such different works as *City of Hope, Mississippi Masala, One False Move, Driving Miss Daisy, A Bronx Tale,* and *Six Degrees of Separation.* In that respect, no matter his present focus on the underworld milieu, Tarantino is bringing a large and subtle talent to subjects that have eluded even the most consistently celebrated and publicized American directors of the last few decades.

Tarantino is deeply intrigued by the artistic challenges of the many miscegenations that shape the goulash of American culture and by how powerfully the influence of the Negro helps define even those whites who freely assert their racism. *Pulp Fiction* presents his most recent variations on Carl Jung's observation that white Americans walked, talked, and laughed like Negroes and that the black American was one of the two figures appearing most often in their dreams.

Drawing deftly imposing performances from an ensemble featuring John Travolta, Samuel L. Jackson, Uma Thurman, and Bruce Willis, Tarantino brilliantly twists his Jungian themes through the vehicles of clichéd crime novel plots until they achieve revelations sometimes so stinging that new life is shocked onto the screen. The human nuances and surprises in the writing provide fresh alterations of meaning as they render a grittier and more relaxed integration than we almost ever experience in American film. Those alterations reach far beyond the customary racial clichés that thud upon us frame by frame and the hostile or maudlin soap box oratory that washes all possible eloquence out of dialogue. The viewing experience is familiar and foreign: we feel we've seen it and not seen it before.

The virtuosity of *Pulp Fiction* is the culmination of the self-taught, thirty-one-year-old Tarantino's only previous works, *True Romance* and *Reservoir Dogs*. In those first Tarantino screenplays, black people exist the way they do in the films of Martin Scorsese. They are at the edge of things, briefly stepping into view, sometimes important but most often all-purpose inspiration for obsessive racist comments.

Directed quite effectively by Tony Scott in the swiftly cut style, color, and lighting of television commercials, *True Romance* clocks the adventures of Clarence and Alabama, a rock-and-roll outlaw couple played with superior perception by Christian Slater and Patricia Arquette. It is at once an ingenious variation on *Hamlet* and a chase film that reaches for the energy of anarchic destruction that defined one aspect of the American films made between the chaotic comedies of Mack Sennett and the patriotic slaughter of World War II Hollywood. That bloody disorder within the dramatic American tale was stretched out even further with *Bonnie and Clyde*, *The Wild Bunch*, *Godfather I* and *II*, and *Taxi Driver*.

True Romance is informed by all of that but goes its own way. The twice quoted "something is rotten in Denmark" means the dope world of casual sadism and murder. We see how the mistaken grabbing of a suitcase of drugs sets in motion a negative democracy of white "trash," black street criminals, Italian gangsters, aspirant actors, potheads, Jewish film producers, and law enforcement. That social sweep might have been introduced in the drug-dealing montage of stills *Superfly* used, but it has never reached the condition of art this film has. One essential reason Tarantino succeeds where others bit the dust of exploitation is that he truly understands his crime world within the larger context of our culture. Besides cocaine, there are also the deadening mass opiates of rock and roll, junk food, the amoral cartoonish gore of imported martial arts movies, and a set of comic book conceptions of romance, valor, and steadfastness that inspires the harsh violence of Clarence and Alabama, who are either trying for nobility or loyally responding to danger with hysterical, self-defensive rage.

In Detroit, Clarence spends one night with the novice prostitute Alabama and marries her the next day. The film's central icon is Elvis Presley, the white man who most successfully and joyously "went native" by bringing black pop rhythms into adolescent mass America. Presley is Clarence's spiritual father. The ghost of "The King" appears and orders Clarence to avenge his new bride's honor by killing Drexl, her murdering white pimp. A venomous minstrel, Drexl "thinks he is" black, sort of a Motor City Mr. Kurtz, a contemporary version of "going native" the worst way.

In his dreadlocks, with his gold teeth, his scarred face, his strained, contemptuous black speech rhythms and falsetto punctuations, Gary Oldman's Drexl is much more frightening than his Dracula and inhabits an integrated world of criminality we won't enter again until *Pulp Fiction*. At their showdown, Clarence tells Drexl before he kills him that his black street mannerisms aren't frightening because they don't include anything that he hasn't already seen in *The Mack*, a blaxploitation film with Max Julian and Richard Pryor. When told by Clarence of his deed, Alabama weeps with pulp emotion, because she considers the murder "so romantic." This Shakespearean idea that all the world's a stage is perhaps Tarantino's favorite theme. His people are executing roles drawn from mass media or personal contact, most of them miscegenations of style.

This theme is extended when a Sicilian-American Mafia don uses torture in an attempt to find out where the newlyweds have run with the dope Clarence unintentionally took from Drexl, thinking the suitcase contained Alabama's clothes. Christopher Walken is the don, and Dennis Hopper is Clarence's father, a retired cop. The don explains that lies won't work because Sicilians are "great liars—the best," and that they can read untrue faces better than anybody.

Hopper is then given lines that turn things around through one of the most startling monologues in cinematic history. It is perhaps his finest moment in film. Knowing that he can't withstand the torture, his character decides to make the don angry enough to kill him. He attempts this through the shrewd use of racial invective, informing the don that "Sicilians were spawned by niggers." The supposedly startled don smugly demures.

The father, a former alcoholic and security guard who spends time reading history, then speaks of the Moorish invasion and the sexual pillaging of Sicily, which is why Sicilians don't have blond hair and blue eyes like Northern "wops." He asserts that, obviously, the dark-haired and dark-eyed don's grandmother many generations back had "a half-nigger kid." In short, Sicilians are "part eggplant." The upshot is that in America, where neither national nor world history is well known, Sicilians who embrace traditional racism are also acting; they are "passing" for white. Absolutely manipulated, the don shoots him through the head.

Clarence and Alabama flee to Los Angeles in his purple Cadillac, where he arranges to sell the suitcase of cocaine. The remainder of the film pivots back and forth between scenes of either sadistic or chaotic violence and a telling send-up of self-absorbed Hollywood decadence, from the filthy homes of aspiring actors to the cellular phones and sports cars of drug-dealing producers. Almost everyone is doing some sort of an impersonation or seeking public recognition, even the cops, who demand credit for "the collar," the drug bust that will give them their media moment. An actor who is caught with some of the coke and made to wear a wire by the police says to himself as he prepares to betray his boss, "Eliot, your motivation is to not go to jail." It is as hilarious as it is harrowing.

Reservoir Dogs put Tarantino behind the camera, where he again showed off his gift for writing the sustained monologue and simultaneously revealed his unique command of narrative time. Tarantino uses a collage of recollected events and establishing flashbacks to move free of linear storytelling as we see a Los Angeles jewelry heist foiled by an undercover cop. Like the Scorsese characters of *Mean Streets* and *Goodfellas*, Tarantino's thugs talk about black people as repulsive inferiors, but they also accuse one another of verbally imitating their talk and express sexual attraction to Pam Grier types in the middle of a riotous discussion of domestic differences between white and black women.

The racial complexity is furthered by the fact that the undercover cop's instructor is black and teaches him how to "pass" for the kind of white criminal necessary to fool the robbers. In order to give his character authenticity, the undercover cop even tells a story that the black mentor scripted and rehearsed with him. The audience of racist crooks swallows it whole. This is another variation on the tradition of Negro composers and arrangers successfully writing for white bands that performed almost exclusively for white audiences. It is also a version of the black choreographer Lester Johnson tutoring John Travolta for *Saturday Night Fever*, where his character danced in an essentially all-white world and made Travolta into the disco Fred Astaire of the period. Such events raise the essential question of what we mean by "white" if, as in America, it's long gone from any kind of European "purity." Though one instance of torture in *Reservoir Dogs* goes too far for this writer's taste, the control of form, the ethnic complexity, and the understanding of criminal psychology are outstanding.

The evolution from *True Romance* and *Reservoir Dogs* to *Pulp Fiction* is expressive of a nearly astonishing talent. Tarantino's dark world of overlapping stories is itself an emblematic development of the filmmaker's sense of intricate racial counterpoint. Regardless of our color, the coarse and overstated pulp vision is what anchors so many of us and, ultimately, allows common frames of reference. Our opinionated conversations are full of commitment to the failures of feeling that shape the sentimentality and false moxy of popular culture. Tarantino knows that while those elements are either comical or obnoxiously pretentious in the straight world, they become sinister in a criminal context. He supplies us with a key to how evil works in our time of arrested moral comprehension. Every wrong is justified with an offhanded, narcissistic cynicism, a reflection of the flippant anarchy that gives counterfeit vitality to the mass-market rebellion of our rock and rap world. Even so, the unpredictable nature of chance and of human personality periodically arrives to produce a dissonant, gallows wit.

All of the central characters in *Pulp Fiction* course through a thickening smog of amorality. Their Los Angeles stories lead one into the other, usually focusing on couples—boy and girl robbers asserting their love through petty heists; a pair of seasoned hit men "getting into character" before performing the blood sport of their brutal work; the trusted thug given the job of entertaining Mr. Big's hot wife; a fighter who agrees to throw a bout but doublecrosses the crime boss central to all of the stories, then the fighter and the outraged boss murderously battling their way into a store, where they become sudden captives of two redneck sadists and are gleefully taken beneath their own underworld into a homemade hell. As prisoners, these two men discover that, for all their knowledge of hard knocks, murder, and corruption, there are arenas of evil where they are equal in virginity to the world's biggest squares.

So realities tumble one into the other—race into race, class into class—and make us realize, once more, how little separates us in our urban Wild West of contraband, drugs, bribery, and professional destruction. In this cosmos of unforced integration, there is a fundamental, hard-bitten morality: the sole taboos are the callous, unintentional, and indifferent crimes committed against the guilty as well as the innocent. Redemption is possible only through the rigors and dangers of compassion, the essence of a loyalty that reaches down as well as up, to those who don't understand and to those who do. We also realize that capturing the actual wackiness of American life frees our most insightful artists from the contrivances of surrealism.

Black and white form the central motif. John Travolta and Samuel L. Jackson, wearing black ties, black suits, and white shirts—like the robbers in *Reservoir Dogs*—are the killers working for black Ving Rhames, the millionaire criminal whose white wife, Uma Thurman, wears her hair black and has matching nails. As Bruce Willis flees the boxing arena in a cab, the Technicolor interior is backdropped by black-and-white street scenes from what looks like an old film. The rednecks take their prisoners into a basement of silver chains and black leather. Tarantino himself plays a middle-class friend of Jackson's whose home he and Travolta come to when they have the fierce problem of cleaning up and getting rid of a black corpse after a messy, accidental killing in their car. Tarantino's character, not wanting to risk his marriage, pushes them to do it fast and be gone before his black wife returns home from work. Harvey Keitel, a Jewish fixer in black evening clothes and white shirt, speeds to their aid. The Joycean sense of "here comes everybody" is basic.

What makes the film such an accomplishment is the clarity of the characters. None of them, even the cameos, are cartoons. They all have specific visions of the world, and most love to talk. Tarantino is one of those bent on bringing back to American film the combination of strong dialogue and open physical dimension that gave Hollywood its greatest moments, those points at which the verbal essence and the stage craft of spoken theater were extended by the camera's freedom of position and range of scale. Tarantino's words push the drama and the comedy, reveal the characters, and give the violence a power it never has in the periodic disruptions of formula action films, where spectacle gore replaces the dramatic intensification of feeling and adolescent smirks pose as antiestablishment irony. Even when Tarantino's people are posturing, they say things that unveil their psychological roots. A real-sounding but expansively rewritten biblical quotation, for instance, prepares the way for a murderer's totally unexpected spiritual revelation.

Possibly an ensemble masterpiece, the film contains the finest performances we've yet seen from Samuel L. Jackson and John Travolta. Each of them brings nuances of remarkable subtlety and rhythm to speech, gesture, and facial expressions, forming superb contrasts of sensibility that collaborate for murder, detail a friendship, and range into areas as widely removed as theological disputes and discussions of international hamburger quality. Uma Thurman gives a prickly magnetism to her spiritually mildewed sex kitten, a coke-snorting, failed television star who is bored and taken by the upper-class privilege resulting from her marriage to a widely feared and wealthy criminal. During her evening out with Travolta, Tarantino sends up both Planet Hollywood and our self-congratulatory faux nostalgia for pop trash. At Jack Rabbit Slim's, the pop museum and restaurant, black and white slides up again—the vanilla milk shakes are called "Martin and Lewis," the chocolate ones, "Amos and Andy." Later, the pampered gun moll's mistaking one kind of dope for another allows Tarantino to do a stunning reversal of the stake in the heart of the vampire—this time to save a life.

The lumbering crime boss whose girth and heavy voice are metaphoric of his power is done to a sullen fare-thee-well by Ving Rhames (his character's name—Marsellus—obviously connects him to the Roman references made in *Godfather II* and to the Greco-

Roman appropriations of American slavery, when such names were given to chattel). Effortlessly brilliant, Christopher Walken has a hilarious monologue about patriotism, family heirlooms, and the honoring of friendship that sparks a moral decision in Bruce Willis's fighter. Tarantino then bends a cliché over by making the dialogue's early homoerotic references to one character literal. The avuncular corruption of Harvey Keitel's Winston Wolf is another in what is an almost endless line of high points in varied styles of contemporary film acting, which includes the work of Tim Roth, Amanda Plummer, Eric Stoltz, Rosanna Arquette, and Maria De Medeiros.

One cannot be too impressed by what Quentin Tarantino has just accomplished in this time of shrill emptiness and our submission to what has become the sanctimonious profession of ethnic alienation. As they say in the South, Tarantino seems to have been "born knowing." His *Pulp Fiction* brings a detailed, visceral craft to our culture and makes it clear that he means to join those in our most invincible pantheon. Even at this point of development we can see what he wants—the epic sense of racial conflict and synthesis John Ford brought to his best westerns, the *His Girl Friday* snap of Howard Hawks, the inventive social satire of Preston Sturges, and the deglamorizing grunge of Scorsese's finest criminal portraits. But, finally, the lyrical cynicism and wit of *Pulp Fiction* recall the moral dilemmas of Orson Welles and Billy Wilder. The work of both identified the American tension created by what always opposes the high democratic vitality of empathetic individualism. Our perpetual nemesis is the protean and sentimental mob, instructed by the worst of our commercial culture, our greed, our cannibalizing of lacquered celebrity, and our narcissistic varieties of xenophobia.

Part Five

DIMINUENDO AND CRESCENDO: OUT-CHORUS ON A LONG, LONG LINE

MELTING DOWN
THE IRON SUITS
OF HISTORY

This was originally prepared for a conference held in Annapolis, Maryland, by the United States Information Agency. We gathered in November of 1994 to exchange our views, spending the first evening with Vice President Gore in Washington, D.C. The mix was varied as were the perspectives, which was the result of the organizers having invited a sweep from academics to politicians, theorists to poets. The title of the conference was "A New Moment In The Americas," and the subject was the political and cultural meaning of the spread of democracy throughout the hemisphere. I have since reworked what was intended, on my part, to sum up the meanings of the many conflicts in this hemisphere and examine some of the things that threaten democratic morale, perhaps our most important emotional resource in a time such as this one. In its symphonic ambitions—theme, variation, and recapitulation—this essay serves as a high style out-chorus for the collection.

In the Western Hemisphere, in the Americas—from the top to the bottom, from the bottom to the top—ours is too often a condition of mutual resentment. This condition determines some of the most sour themes of our dialogue, themes rife with the sentimentality and the self-righteous bitchery so basic to our time. Those who suffer from one form or another of underdevelopment speak of an ever-stinging exploitation that has pulsated since the conquistadors. They talk about having been systematically abused and excluded, continually held down in the wretched mud of injustice. The better off perceive this as bellyaching and are sure, no matter the apparent accuracy of the statistics, that it all breaks down to wanting the opportunity to get even with the descendants of those who smacked cold the civilizations of the indigenous peoples and slowly built a truly New World, one far beyond what anyone on the globe could have imagined.

I term these themes of mutual resentment "the iron suits of history," a term inspired by *The Man in the Iron Mask*. In that French novel by the mulatto Alexander Dumas, we are told the story of one identical twin imprisoning the other in a hard, metal disguise in order to make impossible the recognition of their brotherhood, their mutual origin. Fear of losing power or being replaced by the other was the motive. The mask was a symbol of battle, and he who ended up with his features hidden from view had lost.

In our time, we prefer to hide the whole form of the opposition, not just the face. The twin is so heavily closed in from head to foot that mobility is impossible. We then walk around this stationary figure and point out all of the things we don't like. Assuming the pompous moral superiority that comes with the mantle of the victim, we accuse the man in the iron suit of disrupting our innocence, shooting trouble upward or showering it down. We bitterly assert that pastoral societies at one with nature were destroyed by the collision with superior technology. Or we counter by claiming how endangered sophisticated societies are by the onrush of former barbarians who respect neither our highly evolved codes of hierarchy nor the well-worn paths of preparation. What we are all trying to do when we stoop down into that sort of resentful rhetoric is make a getaway. We are trying to slip past the unwieldy demands of modern life, that life in which we have extended our imaginations, our highmindedness, our needs, our shortsightedness, our fears, and our ruthlessness through machines that speak for us and against us. In effect, as we try to duck the democratic invention called for by our wacky world, we are hustling iron suits.

The mutual trouble with iron suits is that they keep us, as they say in the blues, sinking down. What we need now is an elevating but unsentimental vision. It has to be high-minded and tough enough to match the endless miscegenations so responsible for giving the New World such a marvelous and messy gathering of styles and societies. If we speak only from positions of resentment and paranoia, we resist the facts of an era in which satellite dishes and international trade continue to make all of us part of an enormous, counterpointing narrative. Through the power of electronic mass media, we now routinely see each other in celebration, protest, wealth, destitution, plague, war, corruption, scandal, athletic competition, beauty pageants, decadence, and so on and on. Our economies swell or contract on the basis of how well we now meet the various obstacles to international competition for the appetites of consumers worldwide. It matters little at this point what any national leader says when attacking the external competitors: if they make better tools or creature comforts, the people of his country will ignore him whenever their purchasing power allows and whenever those products are made available. The better mouse trap now seeks not to kill the mouse but to keep him buying.

So loyalty to quality and innovation, or to the shifting mysteries of mass tastes, now transcends any feeling of obligation to domestic products. The car manufacturers of Detroit, Michigan, learned that a long time ago, as did the makers of electronic consumer products in the United States. Their laughing first at the Volkswagen bug and later dismissing Sony didn't matter much to the car drivers and the buyers of stereo equipment. One car manufacturing executive in Detroit observed—gee whiz!—that they were all surprised when the opportunity to buy at a bargain fell down before the opportunity to get a better-made car. No one could remain in business by assuming the locals would forever be yokels incapable of determining what brands of goods gave the most utilitarian pleasure. That fact constitutes, ultimately, an economic extension of the miscegenations that now define the modern world. Mixtures of technological innovations and refinements course into the cultural bloodstreams of human society at large, just as they have for centuries in the Western Hemisphere, where European, African, Hispanic, and Asian factors have been boiling an increasingly thick gumbo, a gumbo made differently in many places, but a gumbo none the less. It is the continual motion away from any restrictive sense of "purity" that gives us our various identities, creates our dilemmas, and enriches our sense of human variety and human folly.

It is quite easy to say such things and be mistaken for one who would deny the tragedy so elemental to the very creation of the New

World. Though the Vikings made a short run into North America, it
was the arrival of Christopher Columbus and Hernando Cortés that
began the making of what we now know as the Americas. Those
arrivals let loose the demons of conquest, mass killing, and destruction. As Tzvetan Todorov discusses in his *The Conquest of America*,
the scale of exploitation and casual slaughter suffered by the Indians at the hands of the Spaniards seems to predict what we saw
enacted again with such might and rapacious certitude during
World War II. An international tribunal at Nuremberg coined the
term "crimes against humanity" to describe the unbridled barbarism
of the Third Reich. Our looking back to the point at which our
hemisphere began its travail into the modern world on the pikes of
conquest means something quite different from what we might have
liked to think at some other time. The repulsive blood sports of the
conquistadors are made far less distant by our familiarity with either
totalitarian purges or the genocidal wars of Bosnia and Africa that
presently break and chill the world heart. The historical boomerang
returns not only with yellowed and grim statistics but also with fresh
blood.

Yet the founding of a Spanish colonial extension with the edge
of a sword wasn't novel, even if it did take place in the New World.
The midnight darkness of history is filled with mass graves or corpses
left to bloody the teeth of scavengers. Most societies begin, as Saul
Bellow observes, with injustice—forcing others away from desired
land or into submission under an order asserted through the tools
and brutalities of war. However terrible, there is a logic to it all: once
murder during hand-to-hand combat or surprise attack is established
as basic, many kinds of violence and sadism seem inevitable. Pillaging, rape, torture, mass executions, slaughters of the innocent, and
the reckless orders of arrogant commanders resulting in the unnec-
essary loss of great numbers of their own men are documented, to
greater or lesser degrees, on both sides in almost any bitter struggle.

Todorov writes of the Spanish wars of conquest in the Western
Hemisphere, "Unlike sacrifices, massacres are generally not
acknowledged or proclaimed, their very existence is kept secret and
denied. This is because their social function is not recognized, and
we have the impression that such action finds its justification in
itself: one wields the saber for the pleasure of wielding the saber,

one cuts off the Indian's nose, tongue, and penis without this having any ritual meaning for the amputator." It is also of the first order of importance to acknowledge that the civilizations laid low by the Spaniards were themselves no Sunday afternoon strolls through the park. Though, for instance, the manners in the court of the Aztecs were recognized by the conquistadors as more refined than any they had seen in Europe, the Aztecs were also colonizers and equally at ease with bloodletting. They knew no innocence that stopped short of the stone, sacrificial knife, and the huge pits filled with the bodies of virgins.

Moreover, Todorov makes the point that there is a distinction between the often arbitrary, even playful, bloodlust of the Spaniards and the severe rituals in which many thousands of their own were sacrificed by the Indians in order to maintain good relations with the local gods. In the actions of the conquistadors, Todorov sees the suspension of Western morality, the kinds of brutal acts allowed "in some remote place where the law is only vaguely acknowledged . . . Massacre is thus intimately linked to colonial wars waged far from the metropolitan country." But Todorov helps us see that we can move beyond the historical sentimentality of iron suit building only when the critical sword of evaluation cuts both ways. In that respect, he raises a question that encapsulates the stern and simultaneously empathetic quality of modern assessment at its finest. Todorov asks, "But what if we do not want to have to choose between a civilization of sacrifice and a civilization of massacre?"

We understand the enormous price paid by the indigenous peoples of the Western Hemisphere only—I repeat: *only*—because we now live in a world where the idea of a transcendent humanity rose into visions of national and international social policy as a result of the Enlightenment. At our very best we do not believe that there is any justification for random and sadistic violence by representatives of the state, even conquering soldiers, because ours is now a world of complete human identification. Differences of language, religion, color, culture, and so on—no matter how initially strange to us—have ceased to justify the brute methods of immoral conduct. This is the moral conscience of democracy. It is what fires our evangelical concerns with world starvation and world health—the feeding of starving children, inoculation, water purification, rescue missions, and all that is done by professionals and volunteers in the interest of lessening the burdens of degradation. That is why the rights of animals and the environment itself are argued in our time with the same intensity heard throughout the entire gaggle of human complaint about the relationship of individuals and groups to the halls of power, definition, and policy.

It is our miscegenated indentity as Americans that brings all of those things together and allows us to understand where we fit in the whirlwind of modern life. We have been inside each other's bloodstreams, pockets, libraries, kitchens, schools, theaters, sports arenas, dance halls, and national boundaries for so long that our mixed-up and multiethnic identity extends from European colonial expansion and builds upon immigration. That identity now seems a prediction of what tomorrow's Europe may resemble, given the arrival of so many Africans, Asians, and Arabs into its nations. As each mother country presently lies down with the former colonials, the guest workers, and the refugees, we see complex contemporary variations on the serfs who left the feudal manors and began living the independent lives that provided fresh labor and gave shape to Europe's cities centuries ago. In short, big gumbo pots on the other side of the Atlantic are now boiling again. Of course, there are those hysterics in Europe who see this mix as a murderous, blinding, and suicidal curse of Oedipal import, an opening of the boudoir to crippled barbarians once rightfully left to die on the hills of underdevelopment. When they lament a loss of "indentity" or cry out for "authenticity," they are are perhaps suggesting that the Sphinx of colonial detention should never have gone down in flames. We in the Americas should know better. We have already been there.

On this side of the world, we are still arguing over immigration, trade, race relations, gender politics, sexual preferences, the environment, and national debt, but we have a common identity and a common set of conflicts resulting from relationships so intertwined we couldn't recognize ourselves if we were to somehow awake from sleep in a "pure" state. It is because of our miscegenated presence in the Americas that the ideas of the Enlightenment were so thoroughly enriched, so inclusively stretched beyond the idea that all Europeans had a human commonality precluding language, religion, and national boundaries. The indigenous Indian, the Spanish and Indian mixture that became the Hispanic, the African who became the Negro-American slave and also added another strain to the Hispanic, the Asians who arrived to help build the continental railroad of the United States, and every other variant of human ancestry pushed the democratic ideal further and further away from provincialism. In the Western Hemisphere, the nations of the world are present in the bloodstreams of people who supplied—through their countless achievements in every arena of endeavor—all necessary proof of infinite human possibility. That proof became the debating mortar of definition which holds together the increasingly different mixtures of bricks that form the entire cultural edifice of the Americas.

None of this has come about without the wounds so deeply scraped inside the iron suits of history and the blood that softens the earth on which we stand, suggesting to some that apocalyptic quicksand is our only future. However much such a dreary forecast might soothe those who love to lie in mudbaths of gloom, I don't think that is the case. Our task, as always in human affairs, just happens to be a rough one. We need now to temper our dialogue with the stern and empathetic assessment grounded in the sophistication and toughness of the democratic vision at its least sentimental. The job is to melt down the iron suits we are forced to wear by those who see history as no more than a melodramatic duel between the good guys and the bad guys. Some want to imprison the Western world and capitalism in an imperial iron suit by using the lock and key Edward Said calls "a politics of blame." Others have their own line of iron suits. They believe that those descended from innately less sophisticated oral societies are doomed by their genes or their class limitations and will never do more than impose burdens, ineptitude, and disorder on the civilized world.

Those are the two most dangerous tendencies in our contemporary world because they are religions of bad faith. The listing of either the atrocities of the powerful or the scurrilous crimes of the slum dwellers doesn't prove anything automatic about the limitations of specific groups—or classes—within the democratic struggle; it only distinguishes the challenges that lay before our humanity and our social structures. I am specifically talking about democracy because the actual iron suit that sank into the red mud made by its infliction of lies and ever larger wounds was Marxism. The toppling from nation to nation of the statues of Lenin expressed the outrage against closed societies in which human beings were no more than aspects of mathematics, figures who could casually be put behind the minus signs of murder in order to prove out the correctness of political theory.

Let us, though, maintain that double-edged sword of assessment and face up to the economic religion of commerce that deifies the market as an invincible god of production and consumption, a world spirit that hovers over goods and finance, perpetually moving to realize itself in mysterious expansions and contractions. Well, it is and it isn't. There are captains *and* pirates of industry, each group including individuals sometimes too interchangeable to make us comfortable. We in the United States, which is the most successful commercial culture in the history of the world, maintain a running battle with the most corrupt manifestations of capitalism. American citizens are familiar with scandals involving government contracts, price-fixing, insider trading, the willful sale of dangerously shoddy products, money laundering, hell-for-leather pollution, and the rest of it.

Yet that battle doesn't so much prove the fundamental evil of capitalism as it actually reveals a more fundamental aspect of the human struggle against folly, corruption, and mediocrity, the age-less demons that transcend all social and economic structures. After all, didn't it become international public knowledge that, even behind the barbed wire curtains of the totalitarian Marxist regimes, the fires of theft, selective privilege, favoritism, greed, abuses of power, and corruption rose as high in their stench as they ever have any place else in the world? The central virtue of democracy, how-ever, is that it is equally founded in individual liberty under the rule of law and the vigilant suspicion of power. Realizing that can-takerous virtue demands both continuous scrutiny and the eternal struggle to purify the relationships between the people and the law, the people and the business sector, the people and the elected gov-ernment.

We who accept the demands of democracy must maintain alle-giance to that struggle in order to stand tall in the face of our many dilemmas, one of which is the position secret espionage orders have had in our political lives. It is not news to us that the strategies created within smoke-filled rooms have led to the propping up of one dictator after another, the financing of death squads, deals with totalitarians involved in the international drug trade, disruptions of economies to speed the fall of political adversaries, assassinations, and a long list of known and as yet unknown deals that could so slimily wet the feet of democracy they would become the soft clay prefiguring the fall of the whole structure—were it not for the institutionalized freedom of that all important scrutiny as well as the right of critical redress through protest, investigative journalism, voting, and governmental response.

Those key elements prove and expand upon Thomas Jefferson's observation that the tree of liberty must be periodically watered with blood. Now we should understand that observation to mean not always the blood of domestic patriots, but just as significantly the blood of those in other countries whose suffering reveals the culpability of irresponsible people publicly or secretly functioning within the power structure of democracy itself. Scrutiny and redress allow us to pull the covers of false patriotism off those who would use thug methods while pretending to protect us and hold dear our highest ideals. Such fundamental democratic freedoms make it possible for us to redeem ourselves through new policies and bring about vast change short of violent revolution.

In this kind of ongoing democratic struggle, revolution always takes place in terms of policy, for democracy is an experimental and improvising form in which serious data supplies us with proof of our successes, our partial successes, and our failures. Our ideas must meet the measure of our accomplishments. Our actions must stand up to our accessments. But, by our very nature as human beings, we are destined to the periodic descents that all great religions, literature, and philosophy define as our frailty in the face of our ideals.

Democracy is the myth of Sisyphus extended to that exciting and terrifying creation of the amusement park, the roller coaster, that ride in which the rising and falling illusion of imminent destruction is checked and balanced by the precision of the engineering. The ultimate philosophical grandeur of democratic precision is found in its foreseeing and accepting the fact that we must always be prepared to slowly and painfully chug up out of the inevitable valleys created by our least attractive human drives. That is not a defeatist cynicism; it is a cynicism of engagement. Democracy is a vision, as I have written before, which is undaunted by the chronic imperfectability of humankind.

This does not mean that the misdeeds stretching from the top to the bottom, from the bottom to the top, can be washed away with a mighty river of high-minded eloquence, but it does mean that we can seek to avoid repeating or sustaining the failures of an arrogant or sentimental past. In order to do this we must reassert a confidence in the development of a democratic maturity that recognizes the rigors and subtleties of sophistication as the most refined manifestations of vitality. At present, the way that the iron suits of bad faith function within the United States can serve as concluding examples of the strange, colliding events that shake us out of all forms of innocence but also create some of the weirdest alliances—balling together protest, education, commerce, fads, and criminality. While their arrivals might superficially seem to mirror the finest processes of democratic redress and acculturation, they actually obscure and threaten democratic clarity.

Let us first step down into the valley. Rising from below has come a now-established disdain for the complexities of our democratic tasks. That disdain began with an increasingly detailed criticism of the many instances in which the highest ideals extending out from the Enlightenment were ignored through the institutionalized and greedily enforced variations on xenophobia—the fear and exploitation of others along the lines of race, class, politics, and natural resources. In the United States, this disdain has evolved into the profession of alienation and complaint that is joined at the hip to youth rebellion and has dissonantly hammered out the shape of its iron suit on the anvil formed of antiestablishment social movements and the disillusionment they express.

Those hammerings ring out from the destruction of the Civil Rights Movement by black power, from the international protests against the Vietnam War, from the romance of Third World Marxist revolution, from the Woodstock Nation's celebration of sex, drugs, and rock and roll as the expression of a contemptuous, even desperate, rejection of racism, of bourgeois suffocation, of imperial world politics. All of those dissonant hammerings were given their sour harmonic resolution by the Watergate scandal, which was interpreted as unarguable proof of every extreme and defeatist political criticism. Watergate supposedly made obvious the fact that the system was so rotted by its varieties of almost religiously devote corruption that only fools could ever believe in it again. The U.S. government was forever incapable of serving the democratic needs of the people.

Nope. The Watergate scandal actually proved the reverse of every charge founded in the belief that the ruthless men hiding behind the ideals of U.S.A. democracy were above the reproach of getting the bum's rush, the hand in the collar and the boot in the backside. Many were the arrogant who fell and even Richard Nixon had to resign and take a helicopter out of town, whirling away in humiliation. No matter, the very existence of the Watergate revelations was enough to help institutionalize what was then the growing profession of alienation, which presently spreads itself out from our academies to the world of popular culture and back. These professional complainers profit from the fact that protest has become a commodity and they move to manipulate us through our own reservations about power and our democratic willingness to listen to the other side, whether that other side is a composite of political, racial, and sexual criticism, or is no more than the expression of the anxieties and insecurities of youth.

In all, it amounts to the corruption of protest, which we who study history know is no less vulnerable than anything else. As Octavio Paz observed in *One Earth, Four or Five Worlds*, "Previous generations had seen the cult of the terrible father, adored and feared: Stalin, Hitler, Churchill, De Gaulle. In the decade of the sixties, an ambiguous image, alternately angry and orgiastic—the Sons—displaced the saturnine Father. We went from the glorification of the solitary old man to the exaltation of the juvenile tribe."

In U.S. popular culture, we now see "the adored and feared terrible father" replaced within "the exalted tribe" by the naively admired black sociopath, the "alternately angry and orgiastic" gangster whose "street knowledge" supposedly expresses the truest, least miscegenated, version of black culture—"the real deal." This is the ultimate extension of the romantic love of the outlaw, the bad boy, the nihilist, he who lives at the fantasy center of rock-and-roll anger.

Upshot? Snarling racial alienation is just one more item on the adolescent shopping list. The suburban white kid in search of savages noble or ignoble doesn't have to apply for a passport, put on a pith helmet, get inoculations, purchase expensive plane tickets, hire a guide, buy mosquito netting, and the rest of it. All he or she has to do is go to the record shop or turn on cable television. The alienated white adolescent then symbolically reaches down to pat the cap turned backwards on the head of the black commodity that has expressed "rock-and-roll anarchy" to a fare-thee-well. Ivory and ebony, ebony and ivory. They have worked it out.

The grand irony of this latest misinterpretation of street criminality as outlaw radicalism is that the growing power of international organized crime, ever an amoral threat to democratic freedom anywhere, is what makes possible the illegal drugs that determine the vicious gun battles and set the tone for so much of the street crime that gives a bloody image of the United States to the world. That anarchic reign of terror has unarguably removed individual freedom from the most beleaguered communities. In essence, the cable television executives and the record producers are no different than the South American drug lords who reside in palaces and on grounds that are paens to overstatement while supplying the powders that increase the desperation and speed the decay of the slums. These developments are as harrowing as the biracial cooperation that was essential to the slave trade. We observe the white captains of media industry profiting from the marketing of the ethos of the black pirates of the streets.

Because gangster rap so haughtily claims to express an "authenticity" unblemished by so-called white society, it also plays into the hands of those already convinced of Afro-American inferiority, those who would push Negroes into an iron suit of specious genetic theories and class-oriented ideas about the inevitability of lower-class failure. In the world of gangster rap, the boneheaded Malcolm X's popularization of the rhetorical phrase "by any means necessary" has been removed from the world of saber-rattling racial politics and pushed into the arena of crime. It is the ruling philosophy of those for whom the accumulation of money and power is defined as an end that validates the murderous emulation of the Mafia strategies we see flowering the world over, even ominously rising like a blood-encrusted phoenix from the ashes of the gangster politics that once ruled Soviet Russia. Gangster rap videos celebrate oversized gold and diamond jewelry, the endless guzzling of beer, the constant smoking of reefers, a bragging, impersonal and promiscuous sexuality that refuses to go beyond the glands. Thug rappers chant out the most trivial reasons imaginable for committing acts of violence in order to "get some respect." The racist stereotypes that such a popular fad reiterates with a pervasive constancy never present even in minstrelsy are not to be ignored. Those guardians who are so exasperated by the failures of social programs in the United States can now stand at the gates and assert, one way or another, "We didn't have to say that you were incorrigibly outside the fundamental morality and the methods of honest upward mobility in our democracy. We didn't have to say that your actions express an unrelenting hatred of the civilization that drives and sustains the United States. You did."

Quite obviously, what has taken a rather bizarre racial turn in the arena of rebellion as commodity has a distinctly clear set of precedents. It appeals to the conventional expression of adolescent anxiety through the language, clothing, and rituals of the outsider. This began building in the middle fifties with the arrival of the leather-jacketed biker who wore his hair greasy and was an urban outlaw development of the young, antisocial cowboy. The roar of his motorcycle was a technological extension of the horse galloping away from the impositions of civilization. That was the period when the U.S. obsession with youth institutionalized adolescence as a golden period doomed by the looming iron suit of adulthood. We should also be familiar with this from the strain of homosexual writing in which being a boy is all.

During the sixties, the intellectual pretensions of writers and musicians like Allen Ginsberg and Bob Dylan gave a hard and bittersweet glaze to the candied apples of an Eden young people were told they could return to by boldly embracing their primitive urges and throwing off every corruption and repression foisted on them by the sterile, greedy, and racist adult world. At one point, there was a rejection of money and an attempt to make everything communal and free of charge. That didn't last very long at all, but the possibilities of huge profit through the sale of alienation made louder and louder by rock-and-roll electricity grew beyond what anyone could ever have predicted. That mass commercial element sustained itself.

The most hostile form of commercialized youth rebellion is inextricably connected to the very world of middle-aged executive power it pretends to hate. This video theater of anger for sale, as proselytized through the mass media of radio and cable television, doesn't challenge the quality of big business; it submits to its most irresponsible tendency—the worship of the market god of profit, no matter the quality or the effect of the product. Because such increasingly minor talents are able to become such big stars, the horizons of democratic success within the arena of musical entertainment are reduced to the large salaries that come of promoting an urban version of a yowling Peter Pan backed up by a din of electrified clichés. This combination of anger, aggressive bad taste, nihilism, orgiastic frenzy, and the cults of the foul-mouthed hard rocker, as well as the equally vulgar but even more antisocial gangster rapper, tumble forward most consistently through the scourge of MTV, which broadcasts twenty-four hours a day into more and more world markets.

These trends do not supply sufficient responses to the disorder of our times; they help intensify that disorder. This is not a criticism of the essentially meaningless—and expected—bad taste and sentimentality of the adolescent fads that dominate pop music. Those dominant pop tunes provide the maudlin soundtracks and anthems for young love, express through their nose-thumbing the difficulties of developing an identity, and supply the ground beats for the hard partying we should know is no more than momentary refuge from the demands of an approaching adult life in the world of work. In the commodity of antisocial pop, however, what might once have been given its direction by the enthralling gallantry, earthiness, human insights, and tragic, communal lyricism of the very best blues has been reduced, at its furthest extreme, to combative squawking.

The insubstantial but popularized ideas of rebellion are also hooted into the air of American campuses by supposedly radical teachers who butter their bread with rants against the Western world and Western history. Their sloppy rhetoric of blame is posed as a reinvigoration of democratic discourse. These teachers pretend to have appropriated the criticism of bourgeois education that is essential to the broadening and the refining of basic information and its interpretation, which we expect of the academically sophisticated. Instead, these so often inferior scholars play upon the guilt of those in authority and the insecurity of their students. So-called minorities, women, and homosexuals are told that they will always be oppressed and that they run the danger of either being indoctrinated in self-hatred or remade into instruments of oppression—those denying their membership in the exalted tribe.

It is important to remember how this form of intimidation once worked for the so easily corrupted Black Panthers, a sixties' group of thugs with Marxist revolutionary pretensions who successfully cowed middle-class, well-educated North American Negroes like Angela Davis, who were caught up in the romance of Third World revolution and terrified of being prejudiced against their own kind. Rings of guilt were run through their noses and they were pulled along in their iron suits by lawbreakers who told them that they were incapable of speaking for the people or exhibiting the courage necessary to overthrow the racist, capitalist structure of the United States.

In a perfect example of ambition realized, Black Panther founder and leader Huey Newton turned the radical political front of his group into a screen for the sort of organized extortion and murder he so admired in Mario Puzo's *The Godfather*, which he emphatically ordered his closest followers to read. Addicted to cocaine long before his racket fell apart, Newton's death outside a crack house at the hands of a dealer working for a cocaine crew called The Black Guerilla Family was more than fitting.

Angela Davis worked for many years as a professor of alienation in the academy, where most of her loudest former colleagues are combinations of parlor pinks and colonial chieftains. As homemade parlor pinks, they have no interest in the real complexities of the world. As campus colonial chieftains, they don't truly engage in the highest levels of intellectual exchange. Instead, they accept the trinkets of tenure and segregated departments while supplying the goods and rituals of cardboard "identity" that keep the provincials of the exalted tribe quiet. Their bringing together of incompetence, half-truths, poor scholarship, and opportunism makes it much easier than it ever should be to dismiss the most insightful criticisms of the ways in

which we have conducted our affairs and have imposed the stereo-
typic categories that lessen the range of democratic engagement.

We also see perverse and parallel variations on the ideas of the
alternately angry and orgiastic in the arena of feminism, which, even
so, has been one of the most important movements toward our realizing the full potential of our society. The rhetoric of contemporary
feminism has been vulnerable to cynical appropriation at least since
a succession of famous women began posing nude in men's magazines and writing texts in which they described their layouts as ways
of asserting themselves beyond the dictates of sexist exploitation! We
now see the specter of Madonna, who represents yet another vul-
garizing corruption. She floozily sits atop a trend in which one
female singer or group after another confuses pornography with liberation. In such work, sluttishness purports to be the expression of a
manifesto. Young women are given the impression that their freedom comes not from achieving recognition as three-dimensional
individuals but from brazenly submitting to a set of bimbo images in
which the freelance prostitute who defiantly refuses to work for a
pimp is made a symbol of freedom. It is another commodity of false
rebellion, one whose fans fail to realize that even the most scum-
mish pornographers have always presented themselves as defenders
of free expression, when in fact they have done nothing but shrink
the complexities of romance and eroticism to a narrow set of
mechanical clichés. The rights of a Madonna or a Larry Flynt are
not abridged by our realizing who and what they are. They are not
rebels; they are actually hard-core conformists.

Those who look at all of these things from the command tower
erected in defense against what they see as the building threat of
barbarism have become obsessed with the reassertion of a United
States that never quite existed. Theirs is a vision that lacks the tragic
understanding basic to the very founding fathers they so frequently
allude to and quote. They have come to believe that the less government the society has the better. Washington, D.C., is perceived
as the enemy of the people, of the honest citizen and the hard working businessman. Their sense is that things went off the deep end
in the middle sixties when the Lyndon Johnson-led federal government attempted a Roosevelt redux with the legislation and social
programs that came forward under the banner of building "The

Great Society," a thrust intent on righting racial wrongs, lifting those stuck in the mud of the lower class, and battling with prejudicial hiring policies. They fail to realize that the distrust of government, large or small, has been building on the other side of the fence since the fall of Joe McCarthy; that distrust has rocked with steady disdain throughout the myriad scandals of local government and the revelations of the Civil Rights Movement, the Vietnam War, Watergate, and, most recently, Irangate, starring Oliver North as a contemporary Mr. Kurtz with amoral ambition and a paper shredder. Far too often, those residing in the command tower take on the stiffness of ideologues rather than the feeling of high-minded improvisers who realize that the United States is an extemporizing democracy that continually reinvents policy in order to come closer to resolving its difficulties in the face of folly, corruption, and mediocrity.

All of these muddling democratic phenomena in the United States make it very clear why we in the Americas cannot be intimidated by resentment from the bottom to the top, the top to the bottom. The corruptions of protest shouldn't make it impossible for us to assert the sophistication necessary to utilize the double-edged sword of accurate assessment. Nor should we be bullied by those who claim that we can only protect our civilization by excluding those at the bottom. History teaches us—over and over and over—that no community, young or old, is immune to the hopped-up irrationalities of scapegoating. We can never forget that almost all totalitarian orders begin as youth movements disgusted by nearly everything in the established order and impatient with the slow, difficult processes of actual human development within the context of individual liberty under the rule of law. It can never be said too often that the "temples of light," the pageantry, and the mindless incantation of Adolf Hitler made him the first rock star and perhaps the first gangster rapper as well. Appeals to resentment, alienation, separatist "authenticity," and tribal paranoia always seek to manipulate the anti-intellectual adolescent within all of us, regardless of our ages. We must also remember that the expedient reassertion of tradition—the return to former glory that has been betrayed by the decadent and perverse among us—is also one of the promises made by those who may have little interest in the exhausting processes of democracy. Such appeals and promises, one and all, produce old and rusty or new and polished lines of iron suits, whether they come from the top or the bottom, the bottom or the top.

We can most effectively move in the direction of melting down the iron suits of history by celebrating the fundamental vitality and policy implications of one charismatic fact: our multiple miscegenations don't imprison us in any of the many varieties of resentment and paranoia if we truly understand them. They supply our democratic liberation through the enrichments of identity. We can no longer afford to traffic in simple-minded and culturally inaccurate terms like "black" and "white" if they are meant to tell us anything more than loose descriptions of skin tone. We are the results of every human possibility that has touched us, no matter its point of origin. As people of the Americas, we rise up from a gumbo in which, after a certain time, it is sometimes very difficult to tell one ingredient from another. All of those ingredients, however, give a more delectable taste to the brew.

Here are but a few of the many luminous examples. Unlike the mutations and unintentional alliances of bad faith, they provide us with democratic clarity. No amount of anti-Hispanic propaganda stopped the emergence of the Latin lover as a symbol of magnetism and elegance; no amount of hostility toward the United States halted the influence of North American dance bands on South American music nor the appeal of Afro-Hispanic rhythms to North American musicians and dancers; none of the wars with Mexico limited the effect of Mexican vaqueros on the American cowboy. Anti-Semitism was no more than a sieve through which the Jewish stream of contributions to film, comedy, music, politics, science, law, and literature gushed; the rough and tumble chicanery of United States companies in Latin countries didn't keep American movies and writers from having significant impact on Latin American literature and film; Gabriel Marquez's friendship with Castro put no limits on the way in which his appropriation and personalizing of William Faulkner into "magic realism" came North and touched writers from the Atlantic to the Pacific coasts; the hysteria over the threat of Asian immigration was overwhelmed by the love of Chinese food, sushi, Asian philosophy, and martial arts; and neither racism nor segregation checked the boundless influence of Negroes throughout the Americas.

The richest music of the United States is jazz, itself a miscegenated mixture of elements African, European, and Hispanic. Jazz improvisation brought together a sensitivity to mutual invention within a form that fused Western harmony and thematic variation with the shifting, incantatory rhythms derived from Africa. Jazz achieves its power not through anarchy but through that creative cooperation in which the responsible quality of individual improvisation elevates the communicative power and the order of the whole. It calls for a gathering, not a scattering.

Jelly Roll Morton, himself a New Orleans Creole, the first great jazz composer and its first theorist, said that jazz music wasn't complete without "the Spanish tinge." Lous Armstrong, who was also born in New Orleans and appears as a giant of international cultural innovation in a number of novels and short stories written south of the border of the United States, spoke through his horn most eloquently of our rich mutations of indentity and culture in the Americas when he played the introduction to "The St. Louis Blues" in its tango rhythm. Lifting his trumpet to a scarred embouchure, he rose from the boiling gumbo pot of the Western Hemisphere like a brown Poseidon of melody. Armstrong was then calling up the heroic, Afro-American lyricism of hope swelling out beyond deep recognition of tragedy, and was also enriching our ambivalent sense of adult romance through the beat of that matchless dance in which all of the complexities of courtship and romantic failure seem to have located themselves in the Argentinian steps of endless ballroom couples so expressive of passionate nuance they seem forever mythic. The transcending power of such combinations is symbolic of the affirmative, miscegenated heat necessary to melt down the iron suits of history.

VICTORY IS ASSURED

INDEX

Ellison, Ralph, x, xi–xii, 21, 49, 76,
    82–92, 110, 121, 137
  Forrest compared with, 116, 117
  on rudeness of musicians, 173–74
Elmer Snowden's Washingtonians, 159
Enlightenment, 26, 35, 39, 56, 97, 243,
    244, 248
Ethiopia, 51–52
ethnic mask, 7, 149
Eugénie Grandet (Balzac), 102
Eurocentric conception of culture, 24,
    35–38, 43, 44
Evans, Bill, 175–78
Evans, Gil, 156, 175, 176
Evans, Hershel, 225

Farmer, Karen, 191
Farrakhan, Louis, 9, 61, 62, 70–71, 74, 148
Faulkner, William, 256
Feather, Leonard, 183
feminism, 14, 23, 254
Filles de Kilimanjaro (album), 171, 178–79
film, xv–xvi, 62, 64, 83, 207–36
Fitzgerald, F. Scott, 57, 120, 121–22, 147
Flaubert, Gustave, 120
Flood, Curt, 77
Florida A & M University, 27, 31
flying, history of, 27
"Flying Home" (Ellison), 117
Foley, Tom, 74
Ford, Henry, 8
Ford, John, 62, 211, 236
Fordham, Signithia, 27–28
Forrest, Leon, 82, 113–18
Fountain, Pearl, 194
France, German conflicts with, 40–41
Frederick the Great, 40
freedom, 17, 254
  democracy and, 49, 250
  of press, 11–12
Fuhrman, Mark, 79
fusion (jazz rock), 179

Galileo, 26
Garcetti, Gil, 79–80
Garcia Marquez, Gabriel, 256

Garland, Red, 172
gender antagonism, 22–23
General Electric (GE), 109
genocide, 63, 103
Germany:
  French conflicts with, 40–41
  nationalism of, 48, 207
  see also Nazis, Nazism
Germond, Jack, 31
Gershwin, George, 65
Getz, Stan, 163, 183
Gillespie, Dizzy, 36, 156, 167–68, 175,
    182, 186–89
Ginsberg, Allen, 251
Godfather, The (film), 219, 230, 235–36
Godfather, The (Puzo), 253
Going to the Territory (Ellison), xii, 85
Goodfellas (film), 215, 216, 219, 232
Gordon, Wycliffe, 194
Gore, Bob, 239
Gotti, John, 32
government:
  blues of, 10–11
  intellectual shadow, 37
Grant, Henry, 158
Gray, Kimi, 32
Great Gatsby, The (Fitzgerald), 120,
    121–22, 133, 147
Greco-Roman civilization, 38
Greeks, ancient, 18
Greeley, Horace, 59

Hamill, Pete, 61–62
Hamlet (Shakespeare), 230
Hammond, John, 151, 156–57, 163
Hammond, Ray, 28
Hancock, Herbie, 177, 178, 179
Handy, W. C., 51, 121, 147–48
Harlem Renaissance, 152
Harris, Bill, 163
Harvard Law School, 23, 75–76
Hawkins, Coleman, 163, 170
Hays, Kevin, 191
Heath, Jimmy, 171, 179, 182
Heath, Percy, 171, 172

mass media:
  black role models in, 29–30
  Unity '94 and, 66–69
Mean Streets (film), 232
Menace II Society (film), 211, 214–22, 228
Mencken, H. L., 57
Miles (Davis with Troupe), 167, 180–85
Milestones (album), 174–75
Milestones (Chambers), 181, 184
Miley, Bubber, 162
Miller, Mulgrew, 190–91
Mingus, Charles, 156, 164, 175, 177, 180
Mingus, Sue, 164
miscegenation, xii, xiii, 51, 57, 88–89, 148, 183, 229, 232, 244–45
  Simpson case and, 77–80
Miss Saigon, 76
Mobley, Sybil C., 27, 31, 32
Monk, Thelonious, 145, 156, 167, 170, 171–72, 174, 177, 181, 186
Moody, James, 177
Morrison, Toni, 79, 137
Morton, Jelly Roll, 51, 198, 257
Mr. Sammler's Planet (Bellow), 93–108
  Balzac's work compared with, 102, 105, 108
  moon in, 99
  rats in, 101–2
  sexuality in, 97, 98, 101
Muhammad, Elijah, 38, 148
Muhammad, Khalid, 62
Muni, Paul, 225
Murphy, Eddie, 180, 185
Murray, Albert, x–xi, 15, 21, 25–26, 57, 110, 137, 197
Murray, Charles, 146–49
music, 249–52
  Du Bois's view of, 50
  in *Hole In Our Soul*, 136–38
  making vs. rendering of, 15, 19
  rap, 8, 9, 30, 31, 250, 252
  rock, 8–9, 166, 167, 249
  see also blues; jazz

Music Is My Mistress (Ellington), 154, 155

NAACP, 70–71, 73, 163
Nance, Ray, 168
Nanton, Sam, 157
Napoleon I, 96–97
National Association of Black Journalists, 66
National Association of Hispanic Journalists, 66
nationalism, 7
  black, 39, 40, 42, 44, 73, 87, 116–17
  ethnic, 22–23, 57
  German, 48, 207
Nation of Islam, 23, 39, 40, 62–63, 70–71
Native American Journalists Association, 66
Navarro, Fats, 167, 168, 182
Nazis, Nazism, 7, 41, 242
  in *Mr. Sammler's Planet*, 93–94, 95, 99, 101, 103, 104, 108
New Jack City (film), 214, 218, 222
New Moment In The Americas, A" (conference), 239
New Republic, 28, 119, 146
Newton, Huey, 180, 253
Newton, Isaac, 26
Newton, James, 169
New York:
  in film, 221–28
  in literature, 93–108, 119, 121–23, 127–29, 131–34
New York Daily News, 146
New York Times, 27–28, 137–38, 202
Nietzsche, Friedrich Wilhelm, 166
Nixon, Richard, 11–12, 53, 249
North, Oliver, 255

Oakley, Annie, 135
Oakley, Helen, 157
Obote, Milton, 52
O'Connor, Sandra Day, 8, 23
Ogbu, John U., 27–28
Oldman, Gary, 231